Language Attrition

'Language attrition' describes the loss of, or changes to, grammatical and other features of a language as a result of declining use by speakers who have changed their linguistic environment and language habits. In such a situation there may, for example, be simplification in the tense system or in certain properties of subordinate clauses; some vocabulary items might fall into disuse and phonetic features may be restructured. These changes can be affected by factors in the speaker's environment, and also by his or her attitudes, and processes of identification. This book provides a detailed and up-to-date introduction to the way in which language attrition can affect language, as well as to the extra- and sociolinguistic features involved. It also familiarizes the reader with experimental approaches to attrition and data analysis techniques and provides hands-on guidelines on how to apply them.

MONIKA S. SCHMID is Professor of English Language and Linguistics and Rosalind Franklin Fellow at the Rijksuniversiteit Groningen.

KEY TOPICS IN SOCIOLINGUISTICS

Series editor:
Rajend Mesthrie

This new series focuses on the main topics of study in sociolinguistics today. It consists of accessible yet challenging accounts of the most important issues to consider when examining the relationship between language and society. Some topics have been the subject of sociolinguistics study for many years, and are here re-examined in the light of new developments in the field; others are issues of growing importance that have not so far been given a sustained treatment. Written by leading experts, the books in the series are designed to be used on courses and in seminars, and include useful suggestions for further reading and a helpful glossary.

Already published in the series:

Politeness by Richard J. Watts

Language Policy by Bernard Spolsky

Discourse by Jan Blommaert

Analyzing Sociolinguistic Variation by Sali A. Tagliamonte

Language and Ethnicity by Carmen Fought

Style by Nikolas Coupland

World Englishes by Rajend Mesthrie and Rakesh Bhatt

Language and Identity by John Edwards

Attitudes to Language by Peter Garrett

Forthcoming titles:

Bilingual Talk by Peter Auer

Sociolinguistics by Nikolas Coupland

Sociolinguistic Fieldwork by Natalie Schilling-Estes

Languages in Contact by Umberto Ansaldo and Lisa Lim

Writing and Society by Florian Coulmas

Language Attrition

MONIKA S. SCHMID

CAMBRIDGE
UNIVERSITY PRESS

CAMBRIDGE
UNIVERSITY PRESS

University Printing House, Cambridge CB2 8BS, United Kingdom

One Liberty Plaza, 20th Floor, New York, NY 10006, USA

477 Williamstown Road, Port Melbourne, VIC 3207, Australia

4843/24, 2nd Floor, Ansari Road, Daryaganj, Delhi - 110002, India

79 Anson Road, #06-04/06, Singapore 079906

Cambridge University Press is part of the University of Cambridge.

It furthers the University's mission by disseminating knowledge in the pursuit of education, learning and research at the highest international levels of excellence.

www.cambridge.org
Information on this title: www.cambridge.org/9780521759939

© Monika S. Schmid 2011

First published 2011

A catalogue record for this publication is available from the British Library

Library of Congress Cataloging in Publication data
Schmid, Monika S.
   Language attrition / Monika S. Schmid.
      p.   cm.
   Includes bibliographical references and index.
   ISBN 978-0-521-76040-9 (Hardback) – ISBN 978-0-521-75993-9 (pbk.)
   1. Language attrition.   2. Code switching (Linguistics).   3. Languages
in contact.   4. Sociolinguistics.   5. Bilingualism.   I. Title.
   P40.5.L28S365 2011
   306.44´6-dc22

                                                                      2010050537

ISBN   978-0-521-76040-9   Hardback
ISBN   978-0-521-75993-9   Paperback

In memory of Peter Dacher (14 November 1936–15 August 2008)

Contents

Figures

Tables

Preface

When I graduated from the University of Düsseldorf, Germany, in 1996, I had a topic for my Ph.D. dissertation all worked out. Fifteen years later, I can hardly remember what it was (something to do with a corpus investigation of different sentence types). However, around the same time, I got involved through personal connections in the transcription of a corpus of Oral History interviews with former citizens of Düsseldorf: German Jews, who had had to flee from Germany during the Nazi regime around sixty years earlier, and had lived in English-speaking countries ever since. Their testimonies were being collected for documentation purposes by a Holocaust museum. I was asked to help with the transcriptions, since I had some experience in working with spoken data.

Living with these narratives was a fascinating and moving experience in many ways, and I encountered many stories – about loss, pain and terror, about ignorance, intolerance and cruelty, but also about courage and generosity. Among the diversity of voices, characters and personalities that I came to meet through my headphones, however, one thing began to stand out to me: the astonishing range in the degree of confidence and proficiency which people had retained in their mother tongue. In some cases, if I hadn't known better, I would have sworn that they had never lived outside Germany for a day. In others, I would have been equally certain that they had learned German as a foreign language late in life.

At first, this preoccupation with linguistic issues seemed callous to me. After all, many of the narrators had lost close family, had been exposed to horribly traumatic situations, had been humiliated and robbed of everything short of their own lives. Then it began to dawn on me that the language was so important for precisely that reason: one would have thought that *knowledge* was the one inalienable possession, the one thing that the Nazis could not have taken away from those who escaped. For many, their native language was literally the only thing they retained which their parents had given them. On the other hand, it was also the language of the persecutors, and had therefore become tainted and despicable. As soon as World War II had broken out, being an expatriate speaker of German was furthermore something highly suspicious – people who had barely escaped from Germany with their lives were now being regarded as potential enemies and spies. For many, there was therefore no choice but to renounce any trace of their German identity, and to become English or American instead. One of the interviewees put it succinctly: 'When the war broke out, six months after my arrival in England, I vowed that I would never speak, write nor read German ever again.'

It also intrigued me that I was, at first, unable to discern any pattern as to who spoke German perfectly and who didn't. There seemed to be no clear relationship with immediately obvious factors, such as how old a person had been at the moment of emigration, the amount of use they made of German in their daily lives, whether they had migrated with their families or on their own, and so on. I therefore spoke to the professor who had previously agreed to supervise my Ph.D., Dieter Stein, and told him that I would like to change topics and investigate these interviews instead. He allowed me to go ahead.

My own experience in becoming an attrition researcher is typical in a number of ways. The original interest was sparked by personal involvement, although I may be somewhat atypical in that I got interested *before* I became an attriter myself (that did not happen until after I had finished my Ph.D. and moved to the Netherlands). This is something which often happens: someone encounters what they perceive to be symptoms of attrition, either in themselves or in someone close to them, and becomes intrigued. In many ways this can be a good thing, as a personal interest can help sustain the enthusiasm for the topic through the long years of research and all the bumps and setbacks one will invariably encounter in such a project (particularly if it is a Ph.D.). On the other hand, it also means that one has to be cautious: emotional investment is no substitute for dispassionate research, but it can have a habit of getting in its way. I remember all too well how torn I felt when I came across passages of text which told of homes being demolished, parents being brutalized, relatives being murdered – and had to count how many subordinate clauses they contained.

Secondly, while I was probably atypically lucky in having a Ph.D. supervisor who was kind, generous and supportive in every way one can imagine, my experience was similar to that of many other Ph.D. students who work or have worked on language attrition, in that he had no experience with attrition research. I therefore had to work out the methodology of my investigation more or less on my own, at least initially. About halfway through my project, I had another stroke of extraordinary good luck: a visiting scholar at my department, Richard F. Young, introduced me to two of the foremost figures in attrition research: Bert Weltens and Kees de Bot – who, at the time, both happened to be working at the University of Nijmegen, no more than an hour's drive from Düsseldorf.

Both these scientists, in particular Kees de Bot, helped me enormously over the coming years. I had regular meetings with them, where I could discuss my progress and my problems. Kees read my work, gave me advice, and even lent me his books (and greater generosity hath no man). I remember one particular incident, where I finished a chapter around 10 p.m. the day before an early morning meeting. I emailed him the chapter, so he would have the latest version – and by the time I got there, he had read it! Both Bert and Kees became, I think, my first true role models, and I am endlessly grateful to both of them – not least for the amount of laughter and teasing that went on during all this (which this particular over-committed and over-serious German Ph.D. student needed more urgently than anything else). There is no doubt that they were an instrumental factor not only in helping me finish at all, but also in remaining at least relatively sane throughout.

Many people, however, are not as lucky in finding a mentor, which is why young attrition researchers are so often in the position where they do not know better than to re-invent the wheel. This has had rather dramatic consequences for the methodology of our evolving field: while there is an increasing number of studies out there, it is hardly ever possible to compare findings. Everyone thinks up their own method of eliciting data and asking questions. They therefore often run the risk of repeating mistakes that have been made before or omitting things that have been shown to be important. If, in addition to that, they are relatively young and inexperienced researchers, basic errors with respect to the research design may also creep in. These will eventually find you out: either at the point at which you are trying to get your degree or when you attempt to get your findings published.

The good news is that things have changed to some extent over the past ten years. Those of us who work on attrition have come to know each other. In particular, a network of young researchers and Ph.D. students has come into existence. During the meetings of this group a number of issues has been discussed, ranging from questions of how to define attrition in the first place to problems relating to the collection and interpretation of data. In particular, we have tried to find experimental approaches which are suitable for investigations of language attrition. Our goal has been to develop a common test battery, which can be adapted for investigations of other languages and in other settings. The intent of this book is to try and make the result of these debates and deliberations available to a larger audience, and to help you in designing and carrying out your own research. Parts I and II of the book present the theoretical and background issues, questions such as what attrition is and how it can manifest itself, but also what the impact of social and personal background factors is on its development. Parts III–V contain a description of the test battery that has been developed. They suggest different instruments and experiments which have previously been applied to language attrition research, and familiarize you with how to develop, use, analyse and interpret them.

Throughout the book, I will try to provide as much hands-on information as possible. Some of the tips I can give may seem self-evident. If so, I apologize – but it is a truth universally acknowledged that if you try to make something idiot-proof, someone will immediately invent a better idiot (or turn themselves into one). The first and most important tip that I can give you is: organize a support structure for yourself. If, for whatever reason, you cannot get the necessary advice and help at the institution where you work, seek it elsewhere. Write to the people who have done similar studies. Go up to people at conferences and introduce yourself; or email them in advance and ask to meet them. Ask their advice. Nine times out of ten, the response will be positive, and you will find that even (or particularly) senior and very well-known researchers are kind, approachable and happy to help.

My own deep thanks go mainly to colleagues with whom I have had this exact experience: Kees de Bot and Bert Weltens, who were mentioned above; and Richard F. Young, who introduced me to them. Barbara Köpke, whom I met at a conference when we were both in the last year of our Ph.D. – and discovered that our posters were not only next to each other, but virtually identical in their gist (although hers was far better executed). This could have been a disaster leading to feuds and blood warfare, but instead turned into the most productive and enjoyable collaboration I have ever known. Aneta Pavlenko, who approached me after a talk at the 3rd International Symposium on Bilingualism (which she had attended by mistake, having got the room numbers wrong, for which temporary bout of anumeria I am deeply grateful), and whose support and encouragement were vital to me over the subsequent years, in particular while I was writing this book. I owe much of it to her critical reading and excellent advice, and Part I is based almost entirely on the framework she developed. Marjolijn

Verspoor, who was also kind enough to read and criticize the manuscript for this book, chaired the very first talk I ever gave at an international conference – and ten years later, I was not only working in the same department as she, but in an office a few doors down from hers. (I think I am beginning to sound like some rather creepy stalker...)

I'd also like to thank my present and former Ph.D. students Merel Keijzer, Hanneke Loerts, Tedi Mehotcheva, Farah van der Kooi and Gülsen Yılmaz for 'test-driving' large parts of this text (and Gülsen specifically for helping me with the endless tedium of checking the references and making sure I got the diacritics in the Turkish examples right), as well as the members of the Language Attrition Graduate Network. I have learned at least as much from those that I have attempted to teach as I have from those who taught me. Amber Nota, Bregtje Seton and Christopher Bergmann were invaluable in their help with the proofs.

When you are conducting research on language attrition, you furthermore depend crucially on the kindness of strangers – migrants who fall into your target population, and who are willing to donate their time and knowledge for research that is often tedious. More than anything else, I have often been surprised and overwhelmed by the generosity and helpfulness of the people that I was privileged to meet. I would like to name one person here specifically, Peter Dacher (formerly Dächer) of Vancouver, Canada. His kind help, and his quirky Rhenanian humour, were very important to me during my fieldwork there in 2004. Sadly, he died of cancer on 15 August 2008. I dedicate this book to his memory, in recognition of the help I have received from him and others in the expatriate community of Vancouver and elsewhere.

The work presented here would not have been possible without the financial support from the Dutch National Science Foundation NWO.[1]

Lastly, I would like to thank my husband, Chris McCully – whom, incidentally, I also met at a conference ... But that is another story, to be told another time.

Abbreviations

ANCOVA	analysis of covariance
ANOVA	analysis of variance
ATH	Activation Threshold Hypothesis
CAF	complexity, accuracy and fluency
CHILDES	Child Language Data Exchange System
CLI	cross-linguistic influence
ERP	event-related potential
EVT	Ethnolinguistic Vitality Theory
FiCA	Fluency in Controlled Association task (Verbal Fluency Task)
GJT	grammaticality judgment task
L1	first language
L2	second language
LOR	length of residence
ME	magnitude estimation
NP	noun phrase
PNT	Picture Naming Task
PWMT	Picture Word Matching Task
RSVP	rapid serial visual presentation
RT	reaction time
SLA	second language acquisition
SQ	sociolinguistic questionnaire
SRB	Serial Response Box
TTR	type-token ratio
UG	Universal Grammar
VFT	Verbal Fluency Task
VOT	Voice Onset Time
VP	verb phrase

1 Introduction

Mma Ramotswe had once come across somebody who had forgotten his Setswana, and she had been astonished, and shocked. This person had gone to live in Mozambique as a young man and had spoken Tsonga there, and learned Portuguese too. When he came back to Botswana, thirty years later, it seemed as if he were a foreigner, and she had seen him look puzzled when people used quite simple, everyday Setswana words. To lose your own language was like forgetting your mother, and as sad, in a way. We must not lose Setswana, she thought, even if we speak a great deal of English these days, because that would be like losing part of one's soul.

(Alexander McCall Smith, *The Full Cupboard of Life*[1])

Gertrud U. and Albert L. were born in Düsseldorf in the 1920s to families of German-Jewish descent. At the age of 13, they both fled to England to escape the Nazi atrocities. Gertrud U. subsequently settled in the United States, and Albert L. in England. In 1996, they were interviewed as part of an Oral History project by the Holocaust Memorial Museum of their native city, the *Mahn- und Gedenkstätte Düsseldorf*.

Their narratives constitute a rich and moving source of data, which is not only of historical but also of linguistic interest. After nearly six decades of life in an English-speaking environment, it is hardly surprising that both speakers sometimes use German in ways which are different from how native speakers who had never lived abroad would probably express themselves. However, there is a marked difference between the two speakers: Gertrud U. talks hesitatingly and slowly, her speech is marked by many pauses, filled pauses ('ahem', 'ah'), repetitions of words as well as self-corrections, and she frequently asks the interviewer to help her with particular German words which she has difficulty remembering. Most of the words she uses are fairly unspecific high-frequency items, and she avoids complex constructions such as subordinate or embedded clauses.[2] In addition, her narrative contains a high number of what native speakers of German would probably consider lexical or grammatical mistakes as well as code-switches into English, and she also has a marked American accent. An example of her use of German is presented in (1) (items which are underlined are instances of code-switches into English, the symbol # represents a pause).

(1)

G.U.:	wir hatten einen ähm # äh äh <u>refrigerator</u> äh
I:	Kühlschrank
G.U.:	Kühlschrank, elektrischen, und das war ziemlich neu in äh # dann äh at der Zeit und gra- grade wie die Nazis ah ma- in die Küche gehen um das zu zerstören der äh Kühlschrank # ähm machte einen wie wie wie die machten in mit gehen an
I:	der Motor
G.U.:	und de- de- da hatten sie Angst und da sind wollten sie nicht in die Küche gehen, und da s- sind so so die Küche war nicht zerstreut[3]

Translation:

G.U.:	*we had an ahm # ah ah <u>refrigerator</u> ah*
I:	Kühlschrank [= refrigerator]
G.U.:	Kühlschrank, *electric, and that was something quite new in ah # then ah at that time, and ju- just when the Nazis ah ma- go into the kitchen to destroy that, the refrigerator # ah made an what what what they did in with they start up*
I:	*the motor*
G.U.:	*and the- the- then they were afraid and they were didn't want to go into the kitchen, and then s- were so so the kitchen wasn't destroyed*

Albert L. also code-switches occasionally and makes some mistakes, and his speech, too, contains some pauses, filled pauses and repetitions. The overall impression, however, is that he uses German fluently and confidently and the only accent he has is a perfectly preserved instance of his native Rhenanian dialect. An excerpt from his narrative is presented in (2).

(2)

A.L.:	ich war dann auf einer sogenannten <u>preparatory school</u>, einer Vorbereitungsschule in Bournemouth, wo ich todunglücklich war # ich konnte kein- ich konnte kein äh Englisch, es waren einige andere deutsche <u>boys</u> da, die sind alle durch dieselbe Verbindung nach England gekommen

Translation:

A.L.:	*then I was at a so-called <u>preparatory school</u>, a* Vorbereitungsschule *in Bournemouth, where I was dreadfully*

> *unhappy # I didn't know any I didn't know any ah English, there*
> *were a few other German boys there, they all came to England*
> *through the same connection*

Most native speakers, when confronted with 'deviant' language use by
emigrants, share some of Mma Ramotswe's feelings described in the
quotation at the beginning of this chapter: they are intrigued, surprised and sometimes even shocked. To forget your native language is
perceived as something unnatural and sad – 'like forgetting your
mother' and 'like losing part of your soul' – to the extent that the term
given to this phenomenon is usually not even 'forgetting' but 'losing'.
This terminology is interesting, since the term 'loss' often implies a
discrete, all-or-nothing process: you do not lose a little bit of your
purse, you either have it or it is gone. Speaking of 'language loss', then,
implies that once the system is compromised, you are no longer 'a
native speaker'. You have, in effect, become a foreigner in the culture
that you were born to. We shall see in the course of this book that this
perception is probably not entirely accurate.

The term 'loss' is problematic in another way; particularly when used
within the context of linguistic research: *language loss* may be an accurate term for the phenomenon of change or reduction of linguistic
knowledge by emigrants. It is, however, somewhat unspecific, as the
same term can also refer to the *shift* from one language to another in a
community over several generations, or to the overall extinction or
death of a particular language. A more accurate and specific term for
the loss of a language by a healthy individual (that is, loss which is not
caused by brain injury or some pathological condition, such as aphasia
or dementia) is *language attrition* (see Figure 1.1) – and this term does
allow for a more flexible and gradual interpretation of the forgetting
process than the starkly dichotomous *language loss*.

The term *language attrition*,[4] then, refers to the (total or partial) forgetting of a language by a healthy speaker. This process of forgetting takes

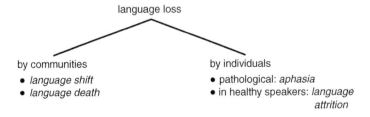

Figure 1.1 The terminology of language loss

place in a setting where that language is used only rarely, e.g. by immigrants such as Gertrud U. and Albert L. for whom the language of the country where they live has become the predominant medium of communication in everyday life. In such situations we may witness a kind of reversal of what we often observe in bilingualism: second language (L2) learners typically do not use the L2 in exactly the way native speakers of the same language do. For example, they often have a foreign accent, they may not apply all grammatical rules consistently, and their vocabulary knowledge may be less extensive than that of the native speaker. Many (but probably not all) of these phenomena are the outcome of the fact that the first or native language (L1) exerts some degree of influence on the L2 (a phenomenon known as *cross-linguistic influence* or CLI). This is schematically represented in Figure 1.2.

If a second language speaker is integrated into society and uses the language on a daily basis, the L2 system may be extended, CLI may become less and less, and eventually the L2 system may become *native-like* or *near-native*. There is a large body of research on CLI and second language acquisition, and I will not go into these processes

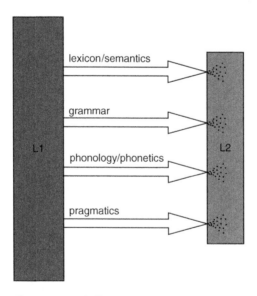

Figure 1.2 L1 influence on L2 in second language acquisition (from Schmid and Köpke, 2007: 2, their Figure 1, used by kind permission by John Benjamins Publishing Company, Amsterdam/Philadelphia. www.benjamins.com)

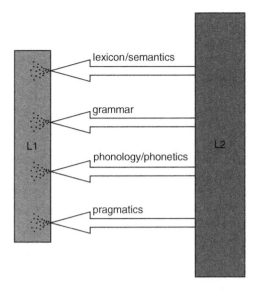

Figure 1.3 L2 influence on L1 in L1 attrition (from Schmid and Köpke 2007: 2, their Figure 2, used by kind permission of John Benjamins Publishing Company, Amsterdam/Philadelphia. www.benjamins.com)

any further here. However, a consequence of this change in the overall circumstances and in language use often appears to be that the L1 system is restructured and shrunk to some degree, and that it will show evidence of traffic from L2 on many linguistic levels (see Figure 1.3).

The examples of spoken German given in (1) and (2) above illustrate that even speakers who emigrated at more or less the same age, have lived in emigration for roughly the same time span, and have equal opportunities to use their L1 can vary dramatically as to the skill which they retain in their first language. Could we say that both speakers are attriters? Or would we suggest that, while Gertrud U. probably has experienced considerable attrition, we are not so sure about Albert L.?

As this example illustrates, it is often difficult to distinguish an *attriter* from a *non-attriter*. The onset of L2 influence on L1 is gradual and probably happens far earlier than one might suspect. There is also a great variety of ways in which CLI can assert itself, not all of which may be what we might call 'attrition proper'. In the course of this book, various approaches to the concept of language attrition will be introduced. We will look at ways in which the second language can influence the first and try to establish which of them may be indications of attrition, and which may indicate other phenomena linked with bilingual language use. Later on, we will explore experimental and quantitative ways in which attrition may be detected and investigated.

THE STRUCTURE OF THIS BOOK

The aim of this book is to give you an overview of what attrition is, how it manifests itself, and how we can investigate it. Gertrud U. and Albert L. will remain our companions through the coming chapters, but we will also encounter other attriters and other examples.

Part I will provide a more detailed overview of attrition phenomena on different levels of the linguistic repertoire. The chapters in Part I will look at more extensive samples of text and at other types of data, and show you what you may expect to find in the language of attriters. Perhaps even more importantly, they will point out what you can probably expect *not* to find in such data. Different linguistic levels – the lexicon, phonetics and phonology, morphology and syntax – will be considered.

I pointed out above that, although Albert L. and Gertrud U. appear highly comparable in many ways – the age at which they emigrated, the length of their emigration span – their current level of proficiency seems to be quite dramatically different. Part II will look at personal background factors which may influence the degree of language attrition in the linguistic system of the individual, such as age at the time of emigration, age at the time of investigation, or length of time since emigration. We will also look at how habits, attitudes and linguistic behaviour of the speaker can influence the degree to which attrition phenomena will manifest themselves.

Parts III to V are concerned with the methodological and practical aspects of conducting research. The chapters in these parts will provide you with a number of tools that you can use to set up your own study, and demonstrate how you can convert your raw data into meaningful results.

NOTE

Throughout this book, I shall try to provide as many examples as I can in order to illustrate the process of attrition, its investigation and its analysis. Many of these come from my own research, and are therefore either German or Dutch, but I will use other languages and other researchers' examples as well. Where my own work is concerned, the examples will largely come from two studies. The first is an investigation of thirty-five autobiographical interviews with

German Jews – that is the corpus which comprises the two speakers you encountered above, Gertrud U. and Albert L. This study was published in 2002, and I shall refer to it as 'Schmid, 2002'. A second study is a larger and methodologically more diverse investigation which I conducted with German attriters in Canada and the Netherlands. This study is described in an article I published in 2007, and many of the examples I use throughout the book originate from this corpus referred to as 'Schmid, 2007'.

ATTRITION VS INCOMPLETE ACQUISITION

There is one important terminological distinction which needs to be made at the outset: studies on language attrition have not always agreed on whether and how to draw the line between *incomplete L1 acquisition* on the one hand and *L1 attrition* on the other. There are definitions of attrition which subsume the former under the latter (e.g. Polinsky, 1994: 257). On such a view, speakers who were very young at emigration as well as speakers who were born to migrant parents (second-generation immigrants) are regarded as attriters. However, recent investigations suggest that there is a difference between the types of change which set in before the linguistic system has stabilized (i.e. before puberty) and attrition among mature speakers (I discuss these issues in more detail in chapter 6 below). On the current view, therefore, incomplete acquisition and language attrition are qualitatively different phenomena which should not be subsumed under one heading or confused in investigations. For this reason, the discussion in this book will be confined to speakers for whom the onset of attrition (i.e. the moment of migration) took place after the onset of puberty, unless indicated otherwise.

PART I
Linguistic aspects of language attrition

2   What is attrition?

What is attrition? What is it that attriters do in their first language which is different from what monolingual speakers do? What kinds of code-switching and code-mixing phenomena do they use? What kinds of 'errors' do they make? And – perhaps even more importantly – what kinds of errors do they *not* make?

This chapter will acquaint you with the phenomena you can expect to find when you listen to attriters using their first language spontaneously and naturally.

In chapter 1 I introduced two native speakers of German who had both grown up using their first language exclusively in their daily lives until age 13, when they moved to an English-speaking environment. Nearly six decades later, one of them – Albert L. – retained a fairly fluent command of German, while the other – Gertrud U. – had great difficulties expressing herself in that language.

This discrepancy raises the question of what attrition is and where it begins. Is there a clear and perceptible boundary in linguistic skills which marks the distinction between an attriter and a non-attriter? Can we define it in terms of time – can we, for example, say that it sets in after ten years? Obviously not, or not exclusively: Gertrud U. and Albert L. had both been living in an English-speaking environment for approximately the same length of time. Can we, then, define *linguistic* criteria, and say that a person who makes more than a certain number of errors, or who has a foreign accent, is an attriter, and someone who is below that threshold is not?

In a way, that question is reminiscent of the debate of what constitutes 'bilingualism'. The non-technical, everyday use of this term covers only what linguists call 'balanced bilinguals' – individuals who can speak and use two languages equally well, in all situations (it is highly doubtful whether such speakers exist at all; if they do, they constitute a tiny minority of those who are able to use more than one language: see

11

Cook, 1991; Grosjean, 1989). In present-day linguistic research, the term 'bilingual' is usually extended to cover *all* levels of proficiency. This includes 'minimal bilinguals' who have only a very rudimentary knowledge of a second language, as long as they have progressed beyond the 'tourist' knowledge of a number of rote-learned phrases and are able to apply some of the rules of grammar productively (Cook, 2003).

A similar case can be made for language attrition. Again, for a long time it was assumed that attrition will only begin to manifest itself in individuals who are highly advanced L2 speakers and have not used their first language for a very long time (Seliger and Vago, 1991). There is, however, reason to believe that, as soon as a speaker becomes bilingual, there will be some degree of traffic from L2 to L1. That is, the words, sounds and grammatical structures of your school-learned French will very subtly influence your native language many years later, even if you have not used the language much in the interim.[1]

It is therefore conceivable that part of the phenomenon which we refer to as 'language attrition', and which often provokes shocked, pitying or even outraged reactions from 'non-attrited' native speakers, may only be the somewhat more visible tip of the iceberg of L2 influence on L1 – something which all bilingual speakers experience, but which has become noticeably pronounced in the speech of some.

NOTE

In my own work on language attrition, I use the label 'attriters' when I speak about migrants living in an L2 environment, and 'controls' to designate those speakers who are still living in the country where they grew up and are surrounded by their L1 in their daily lives. Others sometimes object to this classification: in their opinion, I have to establish conclusively (that is, empirically) that the bilingual-migrant population has, in fact, undergone attrition before I can call them attriters.

It is understandable that we want clarity of classification. We want to be able to look at a group of migrants, and be able to draw a clear line through it, separating the attriters from the non-attriters. However, in my experience, this does not work. A migrant who performs worse than a non-migrant on one task may be just as good or even better on another, or half an hour later, or on a different day. For me, therefore, 'attrition' is not so much a *linguistic phenomenon* as a *linguistic circumstance*, and an attriter is someone for whom the language of the environment is different from the language she or he grew up with.

It is a pervasive assumption that bilingual speakers normally have one linguistic system in which they are indistinguishable from monolingual native speakers – the L1 in the case of second language learners, and the L2 in the case of language attriters – and that CLI only or predominantly takes place in one direction: from the dominant language to the weaker. An example of such a model is the one developed by Weinreich (1953) and taken up again in the context of attrition by Seliger and Vago (1991). On this view, second language learners start out with what is called *compound bilingualism*: knowledge of L2 is still patchy, so the L1 is used to 'fill in the gaps', and that is the source of CLI. In this stage, the L2 system is merged with that of the L1. In stage 2, *co-ordinate bilingualism* develops, the two linguistic systems are differentiated and can develop independently of each other. The last stage in bilingual development, according to Seliger and Vago, can be called *compound II bilingualism* – according to them, this is the phase at which language attrition can set in. At this stage it is assumed that, due to the highly advanced proficiency levels in L2, the two grammars become intermingled again, and traffic is reversed. This model is schematically illustrated in Figure 2.1.[2]

As I pointed out above, this neatly compartmentalized representation of bilingual development is probably too simple. A fully independent existence of the two linguistic systems, as the model proposes for the intermediate stage of co-ordinate bilingualism, is not supported by insights from psycholinguistics and neurolinguistics. Rather, it has been proposed that, since both (or all) of a bilingual's languages exist in the same mind, 'they must form a language super-system at some level, rather than be completely isolated systems' (Cook, 2003: 2). In this super-system, which Cook has dubbed *multicompetence*, bilingual users have the ability to switch and merge their languages, but also to differentiate them and use them separately and selectively. However, since both languages co-exist in the same space, rather than as completely separate, encapsulated entities, we can expect them to interact with each other to some degree – and this interaction can go both ways.

NOTE

When you begin to learn a new language, you cannot 're-initialize' your brain: the language(s) you already know will affect the way you learn and use the new one. That is why you may have a foreign accent or use the grammar of the language in a way that marks you as a non-native. However, the new knowledge which you are acquiring may also impact back on the language(s) that you already know, and affect

Monolingual proficiency:

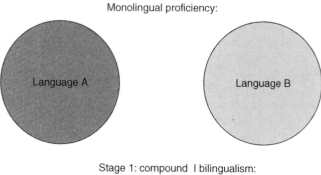

Stage 1: compound I bilingualism:

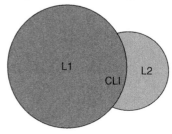

Stage 2: co-ordinate bilingualism:

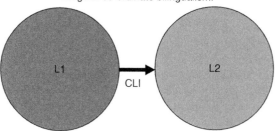

Stage 3: compound II bilingualism:

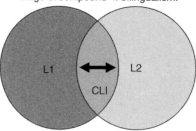

Figure 2.1 A schematic representation of compound and co-ordinate bilingualism

the way in which you use them – including your native language. For example, monolingual speakers of Korean use the word *paran sekj* ('blue') to mean a colour which is greener and less purple than the one referred to with the same term by native Koreans who also know English (Caskey-Sirmons and Hickerson, 1977). Similarly, American-French and French-American bilinguals pronounce the speech sound /t/ in both their languages differently than monolingual speakers of either American English or French (Flege, 1987).

In the introduction to this book, I gave two schematic representations (Figures 1.2 and 1.3 above) of CLI in second language learning and first language attrition. If we approach the issue from a *multicompetence* point of view, these figures become merged into one interactive system (see Figure 2.2).

There is, however, a second important factor in the process of L1 attrition which is *not* common to all situations of bilingualism. Attriters not only know a second language and use it on a highly frequent

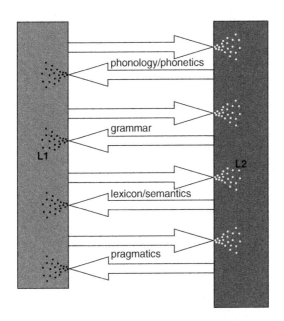

Figure 2.2 An integrated view of cross-linguistic influence in bilingualism (from Schmid and Köpke, 2007: 3, their Figure 3, used by kind permission of John Benjamins Publishing Company, Amsterdam/Philadelphia. www.benjamins.com)

or daily basis, they also experience a significant reduction in input and use of their L1: the move to a different linguistic environment often isolates them to some degree from other speakers of their native language. This lack of exposure may lead to changes which are not due to CLI, but to the fact that memories and knowledge become more difficult to access if they have not been used for a long time. The question then is whether there are differences between phenomena of L2 influence on L1 which are universal to the bilingual situation, and of L1 attrition which is exclusive to those speakers for whom exposure to the L1 has become significantly reduced.

NOTE

The neurolinguist Michel Paradis puts this point succinctly: 'attrition is the result of long-term lack of stimulation' (2007: 125). He has developed a framework called the *Activation Threshold Hypothesis* (ATH) which is very useful for language attrition research. The ATH is based on the fact that, while at some level our brain probably retains and preserves most things that we have once known, it is easier to retrieve some of them from memory than others. We all know the phenomenon that we simply cannot recall a name or a word, even though we know that we know it (this is referred to as the *tip-of-the-tongue* state). This is because accessing something that is stored in memory needs a certain amount of neural impulses. The more frequently the item has been used before, the less effort is needed to activate it again. However, if something is not accessed for a long time, the amount of energy that is necessary to access it again slowly goes up – that is, the Activation Threshold increases.

A bilingual who speaks his or her second language every day, but has not used the first for a long time, therefore has words and structures that belong to the L2 which are highly active and easy to access, but the corresponding bits of the L1 may have a very high Activation Threshold. This is why the L2 can often get in the way when a speaker attempts to use the L1.

The following chapters will describe phenomena that you can commonly observe in data from language attriters. In chapter 3 I give an account of the area of linguistic knowledge that is most quickly and most obviously affected by both CLI and L1 attrition: the mental lexicon. I will first give an account of how a bilingual's two languages can interact in this area, producing novel forms and novel uses of words. In chapter 4 I discuss how internal deterioration and reduction may manifest themselves in the mental lexicon. In chapter 5 I give an account of common phenomena of both CLI and L1 attrition in the more structural areas of the linguistic system – phonology, morphology and syntax.

TIP

Attrition is a diverse process which may affect virtually any part of the language. The following chapters are intended to demonstrate and illustrate the phenomena which you may expect to find when you study attrition, not to provide a comprehensive and complete account.

3 Cross-linguistic influence and the mental lexicon

> In what ways can the mental lexica of two languages interact with each other? What types of phenomena can we expect to see? This chapter will introduce a framework of cross-linguistic influence proposed by Pavlenko (2004) and show how it can be applied to attrition contexts.

Of all areas of linguistic knowledge which have been investigated in the process of L1 attrition, the *mental* lexicon is the one in which most change can be seen. This is hardly surprising: unlike grammatical and phonological systems, the mental lexicon is what has been called an *open-class* system. This means that it is relatively easy to add new items to the lexicon or to change the meaning of existing ones, even in predominantly monolingual contexts: the overall vocabulary of a linguistic community and the meaning of words can change quickly. Young speakers often use terms which older generations find strange (or offending); when new technological developments are introduced, terms are either borrowed or coined to describe them, and so on. In situations of intensive language contact (for example when a society is conquered by speakers of another language, or when there is massive immigration) this process can be speeded up.

There are many speakers who hold the impact of foreign vocabulary on their language to be a process of corruption and disfiguration, and who strongly oppose the use of words of foreign origin. In some countries this has even led to the establishment of official bodies, such as the *Académie française*, whose task it is to ensure that as few foreign terms as possible are allowed to 'contaminate' the 'pure' native tongue. Among linguists, a different perspective is usually taken: mere borrowings from other languages are not seen to pose a threat to the language which receives them, in particular if they are integrated into the phonological and morphological system (pronounced and inflected according to the rules of the recipient language). They are generally viewed as a means for the expression of new or different concepts, and thus constitute an enrichment – and not a corruption – of the language (for further discussion see Aitchison, 1991).

Among speakers who are bilingual, lexical traffic from one language to the other is a common phenomenon, for example the use of an item from one language in a stretch of speech predominantly framed in the other, a phenomenon known as *code-switching* (see e.g. Isurin, Winford and de Bot, 2009). Bilingual speakers have to co-ordinate the lexicon of two languages. Among proficient speakers, both will consist of thousands of items.[1] There will often be substantial overlap in meaning, and sometimes in form, among these two vast repertoires of knowledge, so that it is almost inevitable that one will sometimes influence the other in various ways.

NOTE

The psycholinguist Judith F. Kroll (2005) has illustrated the problem of bilingual lexical access by means of a photograph of a mass of bicycles outside Amsterdam Central Station: this picture always reminds her of a bilingual's mental lexicon, since seeing these hundreds upon hundreds of bicycles just makes it seem so unlikely that anyone would actually be able to find their own ever again. Locating a particular word or a particular bike in such an environment is not so much like finding a needle in a haystack, but finding a particular needle in a large box of needles – all items are more or less the same, so how we ever select the one we wanted in the first place is a bit of a mystery.

Again, we can find a variety of attitudes: in some bilingual communities, and among some individual speakers, cross-linguistic traffic in the lexicon is accepted as a normal and natural phenomenon of living bilingually, and may even carry a certain *cachet*. Other speakers may frown upon it, condemn it, and claim in the strongest terms that they always keep their languages separate. Actual investigations of the language which these speakers produce, however, usually do not bear out these noble sentiments: for bilinguals who live in a context in which both languages are used on a regular basis it is close to impossible to entirely avoid code-switching.

The two lexical systems can also influence each other in more subtle ways, as anyone who is bilingual has probably experienced to their cost at some point. For example, Phillipson (2003: 140) mentions the rather unfortunate example of a recently appointed female Danish politician who attended her first meeting as chair of a European committee in Brussels and apologized (in English) for not fully being up to speed on things, as she had 'just started her period'. Apparently, this speaker was unaware that for native speakers of English the word *period* used in such a context would not refer to a term in office but to the menstrual cycle. As this example illustrates, when the languages of a bilingual contain items which appear very similar but have a slightly different meaning, it is often difficult for the speaker to keep them entirely separate.

The ways in which both the form and the meaning of items in both languages can influence each other are intricate and complex. A very useful framework to distinguish different types of CLI has been proposed by Pavlenko (2004), who identifies four processes in which the lexicon of one language can be influenced by that of the other: *borrowing, restructuring, convergence* and *shift*.[2]

BORROWING

We speak of 'borrowing' when elements from one language are integrated into another. Borrowing is the most overt type of CLI, as it is the entire lexical form which is adopted. Borrowings can be ad hoc occurrences in cases where a speaker uses an L2 form in her L1 on a one-time basis, or they can recur so that the L2 item is routinely used in otherwise L1 discourse. In other words, the borrowed elements do, in fact, become part of the L1 system, either momentarily in the context of a particular utterance or permanently if they are adopted by the overall speech community or a subgroup. Such words are typically integrated phonologically, i.e. pronounced according to the phonological rules and conventions of the recipient language. For example, many originally French words which have been borrowed into British English are pronounced with different stress patterns: *Beaujo'lais* becomes *'Beaujolais*. Morphologically, borrowings are adapted to L1 standards as well, so that the Latin word *museum* which was originally pluralized as *musea* acquires the English plural form *museums*.

Among immigrants L2 borrowing is a very common and frequent process. One of the reasons for this is that migrants often feel that words from their first language cannot adequately capture some of the phenomena they are confronted with in the new country. An example of this is given by Ben-Rafael (2004) in her description of what she calls *Franbreu* (a blend of *Français* and *Hébreu*): the mixed French–Hebrew code of Francophone Jews who emigrated to Israel to join a kibbutz.

The social structure of kibbutz life is quite different from the situation that these migrants came from, and so Hebrew terms are used frequently in otherwise French discourse to refer to institutions or practices related to this or to the immigration experience.

Two such borrowings occur in the example from Albert L.'s narrative given in chapter 1: he uses the English words *preparatory school* and *boys* in an otherwise German stretch of text. The former is relatively straightforward: upon his arrival in England, Albert L. was enrolled in a school form that was different from the school he had attended in Germany, and for which there is no corresponding German term. He thus uses the English word, and then literally translates it into German as *Vorbereitungsschule*, presumably for the benefit of the interviewer who may not be familiar with the English educational system.

The second borrowing is somewhat more complicated and also more interesting: when Albert L. mentions that there had been a few other German *boys* at the same school, he again uses the English word. Since he does not comment on this, e.g. by indicating that he cannot remember the German term or asking the interviewer to provide it as Gertrud U. does with the word *refrigerator*, any interpretation of this code-switch has to remain entirely speculative. It is possible of course that it is unintentional and/or the outcome of his having forgotten the German word *Jungen* or *Jungs* (which he also does not use elsewhere in the interview). However, given the range of Albert L.'s vocabulary, it seems rather unlikely that a word as frequent as this would have become inaccessible to him. On the other hand, *boy* was probably among the first words of English he acquired, given the setting that he found himself in (an all-male boarding school) upon his arrival in England. This word may therefore have acquired a more specific meaning for him than the corresponding German term, and feel like a more appropriate description of the pupils at this school – the context in which he probably first heard the word used.

Borrowings can also occur unintentionally, sometimes without the speaker even being aware that she is using an item which does not belong to the language she is currently speaking. For example, a German immigrant in Canada reports a telephone conversation he had with his sister back in Germany on the subject of his dog Benjamin, in which he used the English term *growl* instead of the German *knurren*:

(3)
vor kurzem hab ich sie angerufen und hab gesagt,
also hier der Benjamin der hat die Marilyn ange*growl*t,

da sagt sie mir was hat der?
ja der hat die ange*growl*t,
und dann sagt sie
du meinst doch sicher angeknurrt?
in dem Moment ange*growl*t war für mich ein deutsches Wort.
a while ago I called her and said,
imagine Benjamin *growled at Marilyn,
she said, he did what?
yes, he *growled at her,
and then she said,
you probably mean angeknurrt,
at that moment, angegrowlt *was a German word for me*

It is interesting to see that this speaker has integrated *to growl* both phonologically and morphologically into German: he uses the circumfix *ge*-verb-*t* to indicate the past participle and pronounces the diphthong /aʊ/ and the /l/ sound in accordance with German phonology.[3] He is, furthermore, unaware that he is using an English borrowing until his sister alerts him to this fact.

In other cases, speakers may borrow an L2 term since they cannot locate the corresponding L1 term at that moment, but be aware of this. There are, for example, several German speakers in Canada who appear to have a problem with finding an appropriate German equivalent for the English *involved*, as the following examples show:

(4)
ich hab hier eine Bekannte die war sehr sehr ## *involved.*
I have a friend here who was very very ## involved.

(5)
ja vor allen Dingen meine Frau ist auch bei Kolping sehr sehr *involved*
yes and particularly my wife is very very involved with Kolping.

(6)
so da ist man dann schon genug ah *involved* nicht mit Sachen.
so you are already sufficiently ah involved in things, right.

Drawing conclusions as to why a speaker would use a particular borrowing is a tricky matter, since we cannot read their minds. However, the fact that two of these speakers repeat the preceding adverb 'very', that the first speaker pauses before the word *involved* and that the last speaker precedes it with a filled pause might indicate that we are indeed dealing with an unsuccessful attempt to locate a particular German word. In such cases, disfluency markers (hesitations, filled pauses, repetitions or self-corrections) are often used as a stalling technique. In fact, the utterance following (4) given in (7) corroborates this impression, since the speaker actively requests a translation of this word from the interviewer:

(7)
ich hab hier eine Bekannte die war sehr sehr ## *involved*
was ist jetzt *involved* in Deutsch ähm?
I have a friend here who was very very ## involved
how do you say involved *in German uhm?*

The borrowings in the examples above appear to be ad hoc phenomena, which the speakers use at one particular point in time but probably not on other occasions and almost certainly not structurally. However, speakers often indicate that there are certain L2 terms which they have more or less integrated into their L1. These often concern items which are used and referred to frequently in daily life, such as household commodities. This is evident in the discourse from a married German couple in Canada:

(8)
WIFE: es gibt Worte die man in Deutsch überhaupt nicht mehr benutzt,
             nicht,
             wie zum Beispiel der Ofen oder der Kühlschrank oder der Abfall
             oder, alles alles solche Worte sind praktisch nur in Englisch da,
             nicht
HUSBAND: Sachen, die man vorher nicht gehabt hat, nicht,
             auch die meisten Sachen so beim beim Auto oder so,
             wo wir dann gewöhnlich die englischen Worte brauchen
WIFE: *there are terms which we don't use in German any more at all,*
             right,
             like for example the oven or the fridge or the garbage
             or, all all these words are almost always in English, right
HUSBAND: *things we didn't have before, right,*
             like most things to do with the with the car or something,
             where we usually use the English words

This little stretch of discourse suggests the interesting possibility that with respect to some everyday items which have been subject to a great deal of technological development and change through the past decades, such as modern conveniences or cars, the L1 term may to some extent remain frozen at the stage of development at which a speaker migrated. For this particular couple, that was in the 1950s – so while *fridge* denotes a twenty-first-century appliance, *Kühlschrank* may evoke the mental image of what such an item looked like half a century ago.

NOTE

Although these speakers indicate that they do not use the German
words for certain items in the normal run of things, they are perfectly
able to access these terms and use them in this particular instance.
Unlike Gertrud U. in (1) above, the speaker in (8) uses the German term
Kühlschrank, not *refrigerator*. One should therefore be extremely careful
not to interpret the use of an L2 word by an attriter as an indication
that she has lost the corresponding term, or is unable to access it. It is
very possible that the borrowing has merely become the more usual
synonym for the corresponding, yet still accessible, L1 item. Disfluency
phenomena such as the ones pointed out above may be indications
that access is momentarily not possible. This does not, however, mean
that the item is permanently forgotten, or that the speaker would not
be able to retrieve it, given sufficient time.

There is also the possibility that borrowings do indeed replace inaccessible L1 items, but that these are terms which have not so much been
lost by the speaker, as never been known in the first place. Such
borrowings occur particularly frequently in the context of work and
professional life: long-term migrants who have developed their career
in emigration will almost invariably have a large repertoire of terms
which they have encountered in the new country for the first time. The
following example illustrates such a case:

(9)
und dann hab ich eine Arbeit gekriegt als technische ah *technical librarian*
wie kann man das auf Deutsch sagen?
and then I got a job as a technical ah technical librarian
how do you say that in German?

Similar borrowings may occur for other phenomena which are specific
to the experience of emigration, such as particular elements of the
local flora and fauna (the L1 of many migrants to Canada has borrowed
items such as *moose, raccoon, maple* etc.), characteristics of the socio-
political system and so on.

A last area in which lexical borrowings are highly common is health.
Since studies on language attrition typically focus on speakers who
were adults when they emigrated and who have been living in the
migrant context for decades, the populations under investigation are
often comparatively old, which can sometimes imply a preoccupation
with health issues. Again, for many speakers, terms dealing with issues
such as hip replacements, heart attacks, strokes and so on may be

unfamiliar in the L1. The following stretch of discourse originates from the same couple we encountered in (8) above:

(10)
WIFE: das passiert uns schon
               daß wir oft überlegen müssen fürn deutsches Wort, für manche
               Sachen
HUSBAND: meinetwegen für einen *stroke* oder so,
               da wüßte ich jetzt auch nicht,
               was ist das deutsche Wort für
WIFE: Schlaganfall
HUSBAND: oh ja, okay, jetzt jetzt kommts bringst du mich drauf,
               aber im ersten Moment würd ich würd ich das jetzt nicht äh nicht
               wissen
WIFE: *oh yes, it happens to us sometimes*
               that we have to think about a German word, for some things
HUSBAND: *let's say for a stroke or something,*
               I wouldn't know that either now,
               what is the German word for
WIFE: Schlaganfall
HUSBAND: *oh right, now now it comes back to me now you mention it*
               I remember,
               but just like that I wouldn't I wouldn't ah know that now

Borrowings in areas such as health, which may be issues on which the speaker feels sensitive or vulnerable, should be interpreted with even more care than borrowings in general. The use of L2 items may be motivated by the same circumstances as were described regarding borrowings for household and everyday items above: if the speaker is talking about her own health or that of someone close to her, these terms are probably used quite frequently in her current situation. The L1 equivalents may have been unused for decades, so the L2 terms are familiar and easy to activate although the L1 ones are by no means forgotten. Furthermore, it is very possible that, because of the development of medical knowledge, the L2 equivalents the speaker knows may, for her, describe a conceptually very different condition than the L1 terms did at the time that she was exposed to them: their meaning might be frozen at the state of medical insight with which she has learned to associate them prior to emigration, in a similar way as was suggested with respect to technological developments above.

On the other hand, there may also be more personal and emotional reasons for code-switching associated with health issues. If a speaker encounters L2 terms on a highly frequent basis, both used by herself and others to describe her individual and very personal situation, they may acquire an intimate and emotional component. The more distant and therefore impersonal L1 words, which have only ever been used in reference to other people, lack this component. In other situations, the opposite may equally well be the case: depending on the emotional role that L1 and L2 play for our speaker, she may use L2 terms to keep an emotional distance from a threatening situation.

NOTE

It is impossible to determine which of these possible scenarios applies in any individual case, and the researcher should therefore keep an open mind when dealing with borrowings. Go ahead and speculate, ask your attriters how they feel about certain words – but *never* assume that you *know* what is going on.

L2 lexical borrowings are a highly frequent phenomenon in the L1 of migrants. They can occur either on an ad hoc or on a structural basis – in other words, they may be used on only one occasion, or be fully integrated as synonyms or replacements for their corresponding L1 terms. The reasons for such borrowings can vary – the L2 items may have acquired a slightly different and more accurate meaning for a particular speaker; they may refer to a phenomenon which is different in the country of emigration due to social or geographical circumstances; or the L1 term may have remained frozen at the level of development which had obtained at the moment of migration. In addition, lexical borrowings and code-switches may serve a large variety of functions – lexical, semantic, stylistic, emotive. They may be used to emphasize that the speaker is quoting someone else or adopting someone else's voice or point of view. In some cases, a speaker may resort to them since she cannot, at a particular moment in time, access an L1 equivalent.

There is only one thing which is certain with respect to lexical borrowings: they should never be interpreted as straightforward evidence that attrition has taken place.

To sum up, the process of borrowing involves items from the L2 being integrated in the L1. This constitutes a semantic enrichment of the recipient language, in that they are felt to have a meaning which is somewhat different from its translation equivalent. This process is represented schematically in Figure 3.1.

RESTRUCTURING

The process called *restructuring* refers to the re-analysis of L1 items on the basis of the rules or the scope of corresponding L2 items.

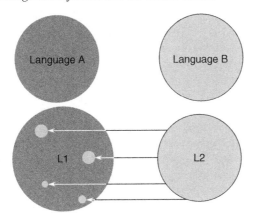

Figure 3.1 A schematic representation of borrowing

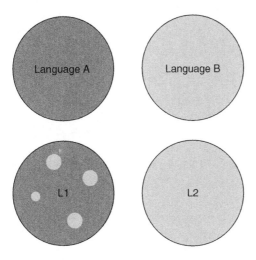

Figure 3.2 A schematic representation of restructuring

In contrast to borrowing, no new elements are integrated into the system, but existing ones gain different values (see Figure 3.2).

This process is often evident in the lexicon of bilinguals when the meaning of certain words is extended or narrowed to correspond with the scope of meaning in the other language. In American English, for example, the verb *to run* can be used in collocations such as *to run short of something* or *to run for office*, but such constructions cannot be used in, for example, German or Spanish. However, there are instances where bilinguals use constructions like *ich renne kurz an Briefpapier* ('I'm running short of writing paper', Hutz, 2004) or *correr para gobernador* ('to run for governor', Otheguy and Garcia, 1988). Pavlenko (2004) points out that this is a process which is particularly frequent in the area of abstract terms, such as the vocabulary used to denote emotions, which often differ greatly in how they are conceptualized across languages and cultures.

Lexical restructurings are less immediately obvious phenomena of CLI than borrowings. In such cases, the actual lexical item is not taken over from the donor language. Instead, the meaning, collocation, or use of an item in one language changes to match that of its equivalent in the other – as was the case in Phillipson's example of the word *period* quoted above. This implies that restructuring occurs where relatively similar items exist in L1 and L2, while borrowings often affect L2 items which have no close equivalent in the L1. Furthermore, borrowings typically involve words which are not frequently used in the L1, and for that reason have become less accessible to the speaker. Conversely, restructurings often affect those items which are of high frequency but of relatively unspecific meaning.

This is particularly true for lexical verbs which, due to their frequency, have acquired the flexibility to enter into various collocations where often the original, literal meaning of the verb is no longer apparent, as was the case for *to run* in the examples listed above (a phenomenon referred to as *semantic bleaching*, see Hopper and Traugott, 1993). Other verbs which are very frequently affected by such interlanguage effects are *take, make, know, do, be* and so on. Consider the following example:

(11)
und hab ich mir nie die Mühe genommen den Akzent zu verlieren
es gibt viele Leute die haben sich die Mühe genommen
das kann man, diesen Akzent zu verlieren
ich hab mir nie die Mühe genommen
ich war da nicht so fleissig.
I have never taken myself the trouble to lose my accent
there are a lot of people who have taken themselves the trouble
you can do that, to lose the accent
I have never taken myself the trouble,
I wasn't that keen

Here, the speaker bases her utterance on the English collocation 'take the trouble to do something', which in Standard German is not expressed with *nehmen* 'take' but with *machen* 'make', so that a non-attrited German speaker would probably say 'ich habe mir nie die Mühe <u>gemacht</u>' (interestingly, the Standard German grammatical frame of the collocation, which uses a reflexive, is preserved in the restructured version above, making the overall expression sound decidedly odd).

The extension of English 'take' to German *nehmen* is very common among German attriters in English-speaking contexts, and is often used in contexts which involve educational settings ('taking a class', 'taking an exam', where again the appropriate German word is *machen*). Similarly, in the following example, the meaning of English 'know' in the sense of 'know the rules, be able to do something' is transferred to German *wissen* 'know', where the appropriate item would be *können* 'be able to':

(12)
ich habe die Grammatik # wohl <u>gewusst,</u>
aber ich konnte nicht sprechen
wie das so mit Sprachen ist
wenn man sie auf der Schule lernt
I did <u>know</u> the grammar
but I <u>couldn't</u> talk
the way it is with languages
when you have learned them in school

In these examples what is affected is the supporting verb in a construction where the verb itself does not contribute much to the overall meaning. The German expressions may seem slightly weird to L1 speakers with no knowledge of the attriter's L2, but remain under-standable. This is different in cases where the verb is a more essential component of the collocation, as in the following examples:

(13)
da war er mal ganz <u>schlecht</u>
and one time he was <u>very bad</u> [i.e. he was very ill]
[Standard German interpretation: he did/behaved very badly, the target expression is 'es ging ihm sehr schlecht']

(14)
leider das geht nicht,
weil die Frau von meinem Sohn die ist ja Kanadierin
und wissen Sie <u>das würde nicht arbeiten</u>
die sprechen nur Englisch.
unfortunately that is not possible,

> *since my son's wife is a Canadian*
> *and you know that wouldn't work*
> *they only speak English*
> [*arbeiten* 'work' can only be used in the sense of 'to carry out a job, to work professionally' in Standard German, the target expression is 'das würde nicht gehen']

(15)
da will ich nicht mehr durchgehen
I don't want to go through that any more
[*durchgehen*, 'go through', can only be used in the literal sense, 'to walk through something' in Standard German, the target expression is 'das will ich nicht noch einmal durchmachen']

Such utterances might merely lead to confusion in a monolingual L1 context, but there are, of course, also the possibilities for fairly serious misunderstandings. Maria Volynsky of Temple University, Philadelphia, reports an occasion where a bilingual Russian–English speaker used the Russian verb *иметь* /imet'/ 'have' in the following context:

(16)
moya mama imela menya v 17 let
my mother had me at seventeen

English, of course, allows several readings of 'having someone', one of which includes the meaning of sexual intercourse. In (16), the context sufficiently disambiguates the utterance towards the interpretation 'give birth to'. In Russian, however, this is not the case, and Volynsky remembers being rather shocked by this utterance until the misunderstanding was cleared up.

It was pointed out above that restructurings often concern verbs which have undergone a relatively high degree of what has been called *semantic bleaching* (the literal meaning of 'to run' is not preserved in expressions such as 'to run short of something'). They can also affect items which are not so much of a lexical but of a functional nature, such as modal auxiliaries or prepositions. Prepositions are often used to express a literal, spatial relationship ('the book is *on* the table'), but if a more abstract relationship is referred to, the literal one can be metaphorically extended ('Let us meet *on* Monday'). The prepositions used in such expressions vary across languages, of course – for example, German uses the preposition *at* for temporal relationships ('Wir treffen uns *am* Montag' = 'Let us meet *at the* Monday'), and while in English, you would congratulate someone *on* their birthday, in Dutch you congratulate them *with* it and in German *to* it. Again, it is very common both for L2 learners and for L1 attriters to transfer such collocations from their stronger to their weaker language.

The fact that restructurings often affect items that are more towards the functional/grammatical and less towards the lexical/semantic end of the spectrum also suggests that restructurings are a more subconscious and unintentional phenomenon than borrowings. As we saw above, by borrowing a word bilinguals often create expressions which feel more appropriate, more exact, or stylistically more apt than the corresponding L1 term. However, the alternation of verbs such as *take* and *make* or *know* and *can*, or of prepositions such as *on*, *with* and *to*, does not provide a better or more precise meaning. We can therefore assume that the stylistic, semantic, emotive or cognitive functions which were suggested for borrowings in the speech of bilinguals above probably do not apply to restructurings, and that these are then most likely involuntary processes that the speaker is not conscious of in the majority of cases.

CONVERGENCE

The process of convergence involves items from both systems, merging or integrating them to create something new that is distinct from both original languages (see Figure 3.3).

While in lexical restructurings, an existing item in the L1 gains a meaning which it would not necessarily have for native speakers, in the case of convergence, the actual form of the item is also affected to some extent. Again, in order for convergence to occur, it is necessary for a similar item to be present in both languages. The difference between convergence and restructuring is that in convergence the items are similar in form, but there is a substantial difference in their content, whereas for restructuring to occur the content must be similar to some extent, while the form can be totally different – as in the case of English *take* and German *nehmen*. In other words, lexical convergence often affects items which have been termed *faux amis*, 'false friends': words which look similar in two languages but have a different meaning.

Recall (3) above, where a speaker transferred the English *growl* to German, coming up with *growlen* or *graulen* instead of the translation equivalent *knurren*. This transfer was probably aided by the fact that German does indeed have the verb *graulen*. However, both its meaning and its argument structure are different from the intransitive *knurren* which may take a prepositional object (*jemanden anknurren* 'to growl at someone'). *Graulen*, meaning 'to dread something, to be frightened by something' can only occur in the passive with an expletive pronoun or

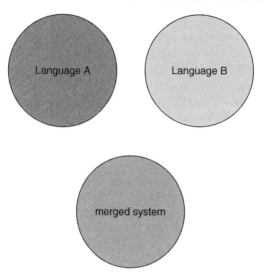

Figure 3.3 A schematic representation of convergence

the oblique object pronoun in the pre-verbal position, or as a reflexive with a prepositional object:

(17)

$es_{\text{EMPTY SUBJECT}}$	*grault*	$mir_{\text{PASS. AGENT}}$	*vor ihm*$_{\text{PREP. OBJECT}}$
it	dreads	me	of him

   or

(18)

ich_{SUBJ}	*graule*	$mich_{\text{REFLEXIVE}}$	*vor ihm*$_{\text{PREP. OBJECT}}$
I	dread	myself	of him
'I dread him'			

In (3) above, the speaker mapped both the meaning and the argument structure of 'to growl' onto this existing verb, creating a blended form.

Another interesting example of convergence in attrition is provided by Sharwood Smith (1983: 225), who quotes a speaker referred to as J., an Englishman who has been living in a Dutch environment for many years. In this example, J. is talking to an L1 speaker of Polish, who is also fluent in Dutch and English (referred to as E.):

(19)

J.:   ... of course it's easy to overdrive.
E.:   oh, can you say 'overdrive' in English! I thought it was only 'exaggerate'!
J.:   no no, 'overdrive' is okay, you can say both

The CLI process at work in this particular example hinges on the fact that *exaggerate* is 'overdrijven' in Dutch. For J., these two items have apparently become merged to the extent that he is not even post hoc open to E.'s doubt as to the meaning (N.B.: an interesting speculation is whether the reaction would have been any different had the interlocutor been a native speaker of English). The phonological similarity with the L2 item probably contributes to this merger: the German word for *exaggerate* is morphologically identical to the Dutch, but phonologically different, *übertreiben*, and it is difficult to imagine an L2 speaker of German experiencing this particular instance of restructuring.

Phonological similarity leads to a similar instance of restructuring in the stretch of discourse from Gertrud U. regarding the word *zerstreut*. The literal meaning of German *zerstreut* is 'scattered', it can also be used to mean 'scatterbrained' or 'absent-minded'. However, Gertrud U. clearly uses the word as an equivalent of the similar-sounding English *destroyed*:

(20)
und da hatten sie Angst
und da sind wollten sie nicht in die Küche gehen,
und so die Küche war nicht zerstreut
and then they were afraid
and they didn't want to go in the kitchen
and so the kitchen wasn't scattered (=> destroyed)

Interestingly, this is not the only occurrence of *zerstreut* from this speaker, or indeed in the overall corpus. Earlier in the interview, talking about the same traumatic event (the pogrom of 9 November 1938) Gertrud U. uses the same word repeatedly:

(21)
es war schon vielleicht zwei Uhr am Morgen wenn jemand kam
und haben unser Haus zerstreut
und meine Mutter hat mich in ihr Schlafzimmer ins Bett getan
und dann haben sie nicht das Schlafzimmer zerstreut
sie haben gesagt, wo ein Kind ist zerstreuen wir nicht
und aber das ganze Haus war zerstreut
alles Glas und die Porzellan und Silber und alles war zerstreut.
it was probably around two a.m. when someone came
and scattered our house
my mother put me to bed in her bedroom
and then they didn't scatter the bedroom
they said, we won't scatter where there is a child
but the whole house was scattered
all the glass and the china and silver and everything was scattered

Nor is she the only person to use this particular instance of convergence: another interview with a former resident of Düsseldorf contains a stretch of discourse relating to the same event, and describing a similarly traumatic occurrence:

(22)
die kamen in die Wohnung #
und haben alles alles <u>zerstreut</u>
ich *I mean* meine Großvater machte die Tür auf
und dann haben die gesagt,
geh weg *you know* zurück ins Bett mit dir
und dann hat der im Bett gewartet #
und hörte das natürlich alles ähm
wie ähm *dishes* äh sil- äh alle diese- ähm Kristall, Geschirr alles ist <u>zerstreut</u> worden
they came into the apartment #
and <u>scattered</u> everything
I I mean my grandfather opened the door
and they said
go away you know go back to bed
and so he waited in bed #
and of course he heard everything ah
how ah dishes ah sil- ah all those ah crystal, dishes, everything was <u>scattered</u>

NOTE

In cases where there are such similar forms, particularly in similar contexts, one should always ask whether it is possible that one speaker has adopted a non-targetlike form heard from the other. The two speakers who are interviewed here live in different parts of the United States (Florida and California) and are, to the best of my knowledge, not acquainted with each other. Since both indicate that they have not used German in years, a transmission of this blended term from one speaker to the other would be highly unlikely even if they did know each other: had they talked about their experiences with each other, they would almost certainly have done so in English.

Instances of lexical convergence are less common than borrowings or restructurings, but they do occur. Fairly frequent examples of convergence between English and German include English *eventually* and German *eventuell* ('conceivably', 'perhaps'), English *fast* ('quick') and German *fest* ('firm') or English *hard* ('I tried very hard') and German *hart* (as in 'a hard surface').

Since convergence necessitates the presence of *faux amis*, it is more common between languages which are typologically closely related, as in the case of German and Dutch. Among bilingual speakers of these languages, convergence is a fairly frequent occurrence, for example between Dutch *lastig* ('difficult') and German *lästig* ('annoying', 'cumbersome') or Dutch *eerlijk* ('fair') and German *ehrlich* ('honest'). This suggests that languages which have few cognate forms may be less susceptible to convergence than closely related languages.

SHIFT

In the process of shift, the L1 system partly or wholly shifts towards structures, boundaries or values specified by the L2 (see Figure 3.4).

One area where bilingual speakers often experience this phenomenon relates to expressions of politeness. Paradis (2007) mentions the example of compliments in French and American culture: a French speaker who had recently arrived in the US would typically over-interpret a routine compliment such as 'I like your dress'. While in American culture, such a statement is a relatively empty politeness marker, in France it would suggest genuine appreciation. Modesty would then dictate that the French speaker reacts by downplaying the value of the item ('It was very cheap, I bought it at a flea market . . .' etc.). With continued exposure to US culture, the French speaker might become familiar with the way that compliments are used there, and learn that the appropriate response is an equally automatic 'Thanks'. After a prolonged stay, she might eventually react in the same way to a genuine compliment from a French speaker.

Similarly, bilinguals in general and emigrants in particular frequently express their frustration at intricate systems of politeness, pronouns of address, apologies etc., which are highly culture-specific and very difficult both to learn in the process of second language acquisition and to maintain in the process of attrition (e.g. Pavlenko, 2004: 53).

In the area of the lexicon, shift is more difficult to detect than the processes described above, since this phenomenon does not affect *one* lexical item only but entire lexical fields. Because we can probably never gain a full picture of an individual's linguistic knowledge, and usually have only a very small segment available, it can be tricky to determine to what degree wholesale processes of change have taken place here.

An attempt to identify a process of shift was made by Pavlenko (2002, 2004) in her analysis of the Russian emotion vocabulary. Pavlenko argues that where there are cultural differences in the

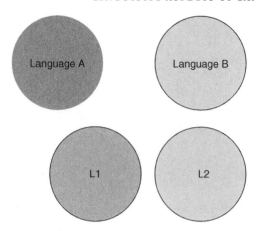

Figure 3.4 A schematic representation of shift

conceptualization of emotions and in the ways in which these emotions tend to be framed in the discourse, bilinguals may experience a conceptual restructuring of emotion categories. Her argument draws on Wierzbicka's (1992) analysis of the conceptualization of emotions in Russian and English, where it is suggested that Russian speakers conceptualize emotions as inner activities engaged in more or less voluntarily, while in English, they are conceptualized as passive states with external causes. Linguistically, this is manifested by the fact that Russian speakers often express emotion by means of verbs, while English speakers tend to use adjectives.

Pavlenko (2002, 2004) investigated the conceptualization of emotions by Russian and English monolinguals and Russian–English bilinguals by means of film-retellings. She concludes that there is no wholesale shift among the bilinguals: overall, they pattern with the monolinguals in each of their languages, in preferring adjectives to denote emotions in English, and verbs in Russian. They are also not fully native-like in either of their languages, however. Both in their L2 English and in their L1 Russian, they show some instances of deviations from the native norm. Pavlenko concludes that 'the view of emotions as an active process' appears to have started to disappear in the Russian bilinguals' L1:

> While the bilinguals still favour verbs ... some also attempt to substitute verbs for adjectives, and some ... shift between the two conceptualizations. As a result, the bilinguals' Russian narratives contain instances of semantic and morphosyntactic transfer in which narrators incorporate perception copulas and change-of-state verbs in their texts, thus exhibiting the influence of English on their Russian (2002: 67).

CONCLUSION

In the bilingual mind, the form, the meaning and the distribution of lexical items from both languages can interact, leading to expressions which may, on occasion, be different from how a monolingual speaker would use them. In some cases, traffic from L2 to L1 may be intentional, in others the speaker may be unaware of the divergence from the native norm. When confronted with instances of CLI from their own discourse, such as the speaker who used *graulen* instead of *knurren* ((3) above) or the speaker who used *overdrive* instead of *exaggerate* ((19) above), they may sometimes realize the mistake, and in other cases accept it as a perfectly normal way of using the L1.

4 Attrition in the mental lexicon

What are the different processes of change due to cross-linguistic influence and to attrition? How do the latter manifest themselves in the mental lexicon? This chapter will demonstrate how a wholesale reduction of lexical diversity can be detected in the speech of attriters.

All of the processes described in the previous section have one thing in common: while the L1 lexical system may be changed or restructured to some extent due to L2 influence on L1, this change does not actually imply a *reduction* of vocabulary for the speaker. In Figs. 3.1–3.4, this is captured by the fact that the circle representing the L1 does not become smaller (in one case – borrowing (Figure 3.1) – it actually grows, symbolizing semantic enrichment as new elements are integrated into the system, enlarging the vocabulary and making it more precise).

However, the mental lexicon of an attriter can also be affected by a process that is not so much due to L2 and L1 interacting, but to L1 items becoming inaccessible: a speaker may forget certain words, or experience difficulties in retrieving them from memory. The crucial difference between this process and the ones illustrated above is that we assume that the latter are all *externally induced*, that is, caused in some way by interference from the L2. Bilinguals have to store and manipulate a great deal of information that is very similar, e.g. words that mean (nearly) the same or sound (nearly) the same in both their language systems. When the speaker wants to retrieve a word from memory, similar items will compete with each other, and sometimes an item from the non-selected language is stronger (perhaps because it has been used more often, or more recently). This item may then interfere with the access to the corresponding item in the target language, leading to one or the other of the interference processes described above.

However, in the process of language attrition there may also be changes which do not originate in the second language. This is linked to the fact that information which we have stored in memory can

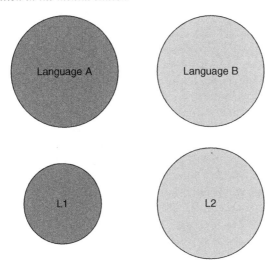

Figure 4.1 A schematic representation of attrition

'degrade' if it is not called upon from time to time (see above). When lexical items of the L1 have not been used for a long time, their Activation Threshold can raise to the point where they become temporarily or permanently inaccessible. In these cases, the change to the mental lexicon is due to *internal* simplification. This process is schematically represented in Figure 4.1.

Let us have another look at the excerpt from the interview with Gertrud U.:

(23)

G.U.:   wir hatten einen ähm # äh äh <u>refrigerator</u> äh

I: Kühlschrank

G.U.:   Kühlschrank, elektrischen, und das war ziemlich neu in äh # dann äh at der Zeit und gra- grade wie die Nazis ah ma- in die Küche gehen um d<u>a</u>s zu zerstören der äh Kühlschrank # ähm machte einen wie wie wie die machten in mit gehen an

I: der Motor

G.U.:   und de- de- da hatten sie Angst und da sind wollten sie nicht in die Küche gehen, und da s- sind so so die Küche war nicht zerstreut

G.U.:   *we had an ahm # ah ah <u>refrigerator</u> ah*

I: Kühlschrank

G.U.:   Kühlschrank, *electric, and that was something quite new in ah then ah at that time, and ju- just when the Nazis ah ma- went into the kitchen to destroy that, the refrigerator # ah made an what what what they did in with they start up*

I: *the motor*
G.U.: *and the- the- then they were afraid and they were didn't want to go into the kitchen, and then s- were so so the kitchen wasn't destroyed*

The first problem the speaker encounters is that she cannot recall the word *Kühlschrank* ('refrigerator') and asks the interviewer to provide it (it is clear from her intonation that the word 'refrigerator' is a request for the appropriate German word). To what degree such difficulties of access are permanent we cannot determine. It is entirely possible that even without the help of the interviewer, Gertrud U. might have remembered the word *Kühlschrank* seconds, minutes, hours or maybe even days later. This, however, would not repair the communicative breakdown that occurred at the moment that she needed to use the item – had the interviewer not been familiar with the L2 term, communicating the event would have become very difficult.

Investigating impaired lexical access, particularly in spontaneous speech, is a fairly difficult endeavour. In examples such as this one, where a speaker fails to retrieve an item, there are always a number of different possible explanations:

(a) Gertrud U. has never known the word *Kühlschrank* and therefore has not forgotten it either
(b) she knows the word *Kühlschrank*, but the word *refrigerator* is so highly active that she cannot bypass it to access the German term
(c) she did at some point know the word *Kühlschrank*, but has not used it for so long that she cannot remember it

In this particular case, explanation (a) is highly unlikely. It is evident from the quote that the fact that the U. family had such a commodity was something quite unusual at that time, so the child must have been familiar with the term. It is impossible to say whether (b) or (c) apply in this case, and claims that a speaker's overall mental lexicon has suffered from attrition should therefore never be based exclusively on such individual indications of problems of lexical access.

On the other hand, a look at the overall quote suggests that, whether or not Gertrud U. has (permanently) forgotten this particular word, her overall vocabulary appears to be quite reduced in comparison with that of more fluent speakers: she appears to use a relatively small range of words, and virtually all of these are rather high-frequency items. This may be an indication that her overall vocabulary knowledge has degraded to some degree beyond what can be ascribed to competition from the L2.

Lexical attrition, in the sense of an internally conditioned wholesale reduction of the range of words that are accessible for active use, is more difficult to observe, analyse, and establish than any of the processes of cross-linguistic influence described above. As was pointed out, these processes all result in observable changes of particular lexical items, where their form, their meaning or collocation (or all of these) are changed under the influence of L2. This results in structures which are more or less immediately obviously 'odd'. If a speaker's overall vocabulary, or the accessibility of a large number of lexical items, has diminished due to language attrition, this is something which may not be as readily apparent. In other words, we can detect CLI by investigating *what is there*, but to detect attrition, we have to investigate *what is not there*. It is therefore necessary to apply different diagnostic tools or experimental methods.

LEXICAL DIVERSITY (TYPE–TOKEN RATIO)

The most straightforward way to measure whether there is a decrease in lexical diversity in the naturalistic speech of an attriter is by investigating the type–token ratio (TTR). TTRs are based on a stretch of discourse, measuring (a) how many *total* words it contains (tokens), (b) how many *different* words it contains (types), and (c) what the ratio is between the two (types divided by tokens). In Gertrud U.'s case, once all hesitation markers, false starts and repetitions are eliminated there remains a total of sixty-four words, but only thirty-five different ones. This corresponds to a TTR of 0.55 (35 : 64 = 0.55). The overall stretch of discourse quoted from Albert L.'s interview is somewhat shorter, it contains thirty-seven words, of which twenty-eight are different lexical items,[1] so that his TTR is considerably higher at 0.76, indicating a more diverse vocabulary.

Of course, TTRs which are based on such very short stretches of discourse are unreliable. I therefore analysed a longer stretch of data of 1,000 words from thirty-five similar interviews for TTRs (Schmid, 2002). The findings from this analysis are graphically represented in Figure 4.2, and show that the TTR from Gertrud U. is one of the two lowest ones in the entire corpus. In other words, the vocabulary of these two speakers is the least diverse: they use the lowest proportion of different lexical items.

You may have noted that the analysis presented here was based on a stretch of discourse of equal length from each interview (1,000 words). When calculating TTRs, this is important, since language contains a large number of very high frequency function words (such as articles, conjunctions and prepositions). TTRs therefore decrease in longer texts, as these items inevitably begin

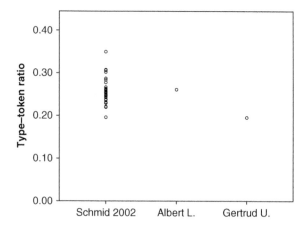

Figure 4.2 Type–token ratios in the corpus analysed by Schmid (2002), in comparison with Albert L. and Gertrud U.

to recur. There are, however, ways to compensate for this other than making sure the samples have equal length. One way is to calculate a measure which has been termed 'D'. The formula for calculating this, based on random sampling of repeated stretches of text, was developed by Malvern and Richards (2002).[2] A different method of compensating for texts of varying length is Dugast's *Uber*-formula discussed by Dewaele and Pavlenko (2003: 129), or Guiraud's index which divides types not by tokens but by the square root of tokens (Vermeer, 2000).

LEXICAL SOPHISTICATION (LEXICAL FREQUENCY PROFILES)

There may be more to L1 attrition than a wholesale reduction of lexical diversity: it has often been suggested that attrition will mainly or particularly affect those lexical items which occur with relatively low frequency (e.g. Andersen, 1982). Consider the following two stretches of text (borrowed from Jarvis, 2006):

(4)
(a) There was a girl who was alone and hungry. She stole some bread from a bakery and tried to run away, but she ran into a man, and they both fell down. That gave the police enough time to find her and catch her.

(b) A destitute and lonely young female stole a loaf of bread from a bakery. She attempted to flee, but she collided with a man who was walking toward her, and both of them fell down. In the meantime, a policeman arrived and detained them.

As Jarvis points out, both utterances contain exactly the same number of tokens (44) as well as types (35), so that the TTR of both texts is identical. However, it is obvious that the second text uses lexical items which are less frequent to describe the same set of circumstances (e.g. 'tried to run away' vs 'attempted to flee'). Jarvis therefore suggests that, in addition to 'blind' measures of lexical diversity, such as TTRs and D, other factors, such as the rarity of the items used, should be considered. Such analyses can draw upon resources such as the British National Corpus (www.natcorp.ox.ac.uk), a collection of over 100 million words from a wide range of sources. Searching a word will tell you how frequently it appears in the overall corpus, and you can find out here that, for example, 'try' occurs about twice as often as 'attempt' (20,848 vs 11,237 times).

In Schmid (2002), I conducted an analysis of such lexical frequencies: I collected a list of all lexical items (nouns, verbs and adjectives) which had been used in a stretch of 1,000 words from each of my thirty-five interviews, totalling 2,047 tokens (15,983 types). For each of these words, the frequency in overall language use was established on the basis of two frequency dictionaries of German (Meier, 1967 and Ruoff, 1985).[3] On the basis of how many occurrences were noted for each word that a given speaker had used in these two corpora, the average frequency of all lexical items used by each speaker was then calculated. The result of this analysis is displayed in Figure 4.3.

You will notice that Figure 4.3 looks very similar to the one presented in Figure 4.2 above (if you were to turn that on its head). Again, Gertrud U. and one other speaker (the same one who shared the lowest TTR) show by far the strongest preference for highly frequent vocabulary. A Pearson Correlation (this test is discussed and explained below in chapter 17) of the two measurements confirms this impression: the correlation is highly significant ($p < 0.001$) and the *Pearson coefficient* is 0.885, suggesting that these two variables do, in fact, measure the same phenomenon. While very short stretches of text, such as the ones quoted from Jarvis (2006) above can have similar TTR ratios even though the sophistication of the vocabulary they use is very different, lexical diversity and lexical sophistication will probably become more and more strongly correlated the longer the text stretches under observation.

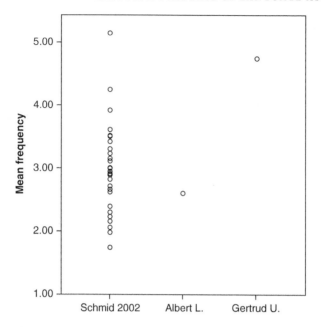

Figure 4.3 Mean frequency of lexical items in the corpus analysed by Schmid (2002), in comparison with Albert L. and Gertrud U.

Given how time-consuming frequency analyses are (particularly if no electronic tools and large published corpora are available in a given language), the costs and benefits of frequency analyses over TTR analyses should therefore be weighed carefully.

LEXICAL ACCESSIBILITY (DISFLUENCY PATTERNS)

A last way of determining attrition in the area of the lexicon lies in an analysis of hesitation patterns. Lexical access in free speech is a taxing endeavour at the best of times: given that at a normal rate, natural speech contains around four words per second (Hagoort and Brown, 2000), the speaker has around 250 milliseconds (ms) to retrieve each target word from a mental lexicon which contains several thousand productive items. The question whether or not lexical items affected by attrition are permanently deleted or have simply become too difficult to activate (but are still stored in memory) may therefore be interesting to linguists and psychologists but have relatively little practical relevance: if you cannot retrieve a word in this very short space of time, it is effectively gone, and communication becomes impeded.

One strategy for dealing with word-finding difficulties which *all* speakers employ is to resort to disfluency markers. It is common to pause when one cannot locate a particular word or when one experiences a tip-of-the-tongue phenomenon, or to use a filled pause ('ahem', 'ah'). We saw such strategies in (4) and (6) above, where the speakers preceded the code-switched word *involved* with an empty and a filled pause, respectively, and I speculated that they might have used the time this gave them to try and think of the German word. However, there is a great deal of research on such disfluency phenomena which suggests that they can also be used for other strategies, such as structuring the discourse, giving emphasis to particular parts of the message, and so on (for an overview see Schmid and Beers Fägersten, 2010). Moreover, hesitation phenomena are language-specific, and both their frequency in natural discourse and their distribution and form vary across languages (de Leeuw, 2004, 2007).

Analyses of the increase of disfluency phenomena in the process of language attrition therefore have to consider carefully whether an increase can indeed be attributed to attrition (that is, to the loss or reduced accessibility of lexical items), or whether a non-native-like pattern of hesitations may not be the result of discourse-pragmatic L2 influence on L1. For example, it has been shown that native Dutch has a higher proportion of filled pauses than either native English or native German (de Leeuw, 2004). Schmid and Beers Fägersten's (2010) investigation of L1 German attriters in an English-speaking and in a Dutch-speaking environment showed that both attriting groups had a higher incidence of empty pauses than a native control group, but only the L2 Dutch group also had more filled pauses. On the other hand, a group of L1 Dutch attriters in an English setting which was investigated in the same study, while also employing more empty pauses than the Dutch control group, used less filled pauses than the control group. Based on these findings, Schmid and Beers Fägersten hypothesized that, while the increase of empty pauses for all attriting groups was probably an indication of a reduction in lexical accessibility, the speakers were shifting towards the L2 norm in their employment of filled pauses.[4]

CONCLUSION

In summary, while a smaller or less readily accessible L1 lexicon is probably one of the first symptoms of language attrition, and one of the areas in which the attritional process manifests itself most mark-edly, there are substantial practical problems involved in detecting this in an experimental setting. To some degree, it may be possible to employ specific, controlled experiments, such as naming tasks (a number of such tasks will be discussed in more detail in Part IV below). However, if we want to gain an impression of attrition as a natural, everyday phenomenon, we may find such tasks questionable. In real life, people do not show you a picture of an aeroplane or an orange and require you to name it within as few milliseconds as possible, nor do they ask you to list as many animals as you can think of in the space of sixty seconds. What *does* happen in real life is that people ask you about your family, your job, your childhood, or your daily experiences and routines. If we think of attrition as a phenom-enon which affects what people actually and naturally do with their language, we should look for it in the kind of speech which people produce on a daily basis. This means using more painstaking, difficult and time-consuming methods of analysis, such as the calculation of type–token ratios, detailed lexical analysis of specific word classes, or in-depth investigations of hesitation phenomena.

5   Attrition and the structure of language

What is the difference between lexical and grammatical, or structural, attrition? Can attritional processes affect the phonological and grammatical repertoire of a language? This chapter will look at these phenomena and show to what extent we may expect to find them in language attrition.

In the previous chapters, I have discussed ways in which language attrition may affect the lexicon of a language. I have pointed out that the lexicon of the average speaker consists of thousands of items, changes quickly even in predominantly monolingual communities, and often overlaps a great deal between languages. It is therefore not surprising that we often find indications of change, both due to CLI and to attrition, in the lexicon of attriters.

The situation is quite different when it comes to those things that we normally consider part of linguistic *structure*: phonology and phonetics, morphology and syntax. Here, we are dealing with much smaller sets of items. For example, most languages have only a few dozen phonemes (phonemic inventories vary between as few as fifteen and as many as eighty items according to Crystal, 1980). Similarly, most languages have a rather limited number of inflectional endings, although there are some exceptional cases where this set is much larger (some notable examples are discussed by Mithun, 1998 and Senft, 1996). That means that while a speaker may only hear or use a certain word a few times over many years, and may even know words which he or she has never actually produced him- or herself, the sounds, grammatical morphemes and sentence patterns present in a language will usually all be heard (or read) and produced multiple times in any interaction. They are therefore reinforced much more often than even the most frequent lexical word.

Furthermore, small networks such as the phonological or inflectional system of a language are usually far more tightly interconnected than the large web of lexical items. This means that if the value of one item changes, this modification will have ramifications for all others. If the meaning potential of one individual word changes in one of the ways that I discussed above, this does not necessarily imply that other words have to be affected, too. However, if a functional element is affected by language attrition, other items in the same network will need to adjust as well.

NOTE

Many languages, among them English, have morphological ways of indicating whether an item that is being referred to is in the plural (*apple* – *apples*). If such a marker exists, it has to be provided every time several items are referred to, even if the context makes it perfectly clear that more than one are meant (*one apple* – *two apples*). This means that words which are not marked for plural imply a strong assumption of singularity, and the phrase *two apple* will be perceived to be odd, even if it is perfectly understandable. Some languages, however, distinguish more than just one vs many. Hebrew, for example, also has a *dual* inflectional marker used, for example, for periods of times: *shavu'a* 'one week' – *sh'vua'ajim* 'fortnight' – *shavu'ot* 'weeks (pl)'.

It is conceivable that a Hebrew speaker who had lived in an English-speaking setting for a long time, and therefore encountered multiple instances where a simple plural marker was used to refer to 'two weeks', might begin to lose the dual–plural distinction and use the numeral *two* with the plural *shavu'ot* to refer to the time period of a fortnight.[1] In such a case, it is not only the dual marker which is affected by language attrition but also the plural, which has to change in order to encompass the meaning 'two of something'.

Given that the items which make up the structural system of a language are typically limited in number, used (and therefore reinforced) very frequently, and exist in a close-knit network of interdependence relations, we may assume that they will be far more stable in native language than lexical words. Can they, then, still be vulnerable to attrition effects?

In order to answer this question, we first have to be clear about what we mean by 'vulnerable'. Are we referring to an occasional digression from underlyingly intact grammatical and phonological representations (for example a single case of a Hebrew speaker using *shavu'ot* to refer to a fortnight), or do we mean a full restructuring of the underlying system, by which Hebrew dual marking would be entirely deleted and replaced by the plural?

In the early years of attrition research, this question – which emerges from the Chomskyan distinction between *competence* (under-lying, rule-governed knowledge) and *performance* (actual utterances which can sometimes deviate from that knowledge) – was often dis-cussed. For example, Seliger and Vago (1991) point out that

> effects of performance (accessing, processing, control) need to be sorted out from those of competence (tacit knowledge): it is erosion that reaches the level of competence that allows for interesting claims about and meaningful insight into the attrition process (p. 7).

This assumption is taken up by Sharwood Smith and van Buren (1991), who find it

> important to know whether a given subject has lost *or is even able to* lose those kinds of underlying mental representations of his or her first language that may be referred to as L1 competence. (p. 17)

Sharwood Smith and van Buren further go on to identify ways to determine whether a given case of attrition is a matter of competence or performance – the latter would be the case, they say, 'if the subject occasionally still produced the standard forms/structures in question' (p. 18).

This chapter will address attrition in the structural system of a language, pointing out what changes and phenomena we may expect to find in different areas of linguistic structure among attriters. How-ever, the assumption that L1 attrition can ever affect underlying lin-guistic structures has not been validated for migrants who were older than twelve years when they left their country of upbringing. The situation is dramatically different where younger migrants are con-cerned (this is discussed in more detail in chapter 6 below), but once the grammatical and phonological L1 system has stabilized it appears to be astonishingly impervious to change or loss, even when it is not used for decades.

PHONETICS AND PHONOLOGY

Achieving a native-like pronunciation is the hardest component of second language acquisition (SLA) for most L2 learners. We probably all know speakers who, while they are impressively proficient in terms of the L2 lexicon and morphosyntax, retain a strong foreign accent even after many years of immersion. This accent is usually a combin-ation of articulation, intonation and stress and hesitation patterns, and it is immediately obvious and noticeable to a native speaker (according to Flege (1984), hearing someone for 30 milliseconds can be enough to determine whether or not they are native speakers). Nor is the ability to judge nativeness limited to our own L1, or to languages that we know very well: apparently, we can make fairly accurate judgments even in a language that we do not know at all (Major, 2007). In the introduction to this book, I claimed that Gertrud U. had a 'marked English accent', while Albert L. still sounded very much like a native speaker of Rhenanian German. You may have wondered (and I hope you did!) whether I merely based that claim on my own intuition. The answer to that question is that the assessment was based on an experiment in which I took short excerpts of about half a minute from each of the thirty-five interviews in my corpus, had a group of thirteen native speakers of German listen to them, and asked them to tell me whether they thought the speaker that they had just heard did have German as his or her L1. The findings from this experiment are represented in Figure 5.1 (there appear to be less than thirty-five circles in the chart because some of them are superimposed on each other, indicating that the average rating was the same for two speakers).

As you can see in Figure 5.1, the group data from the attriters covers a large range: some of them are perceived to be definitely native (they appear towards the bottom of the chart), while others are clearly identified as foreign language speakers. Albert L. is at the lower end of the continuum since most raters (eleven out of thirteen) identified him as a native, and only two of them were uncertain. Gertrud U., on the other hand, was judged not to be a native speaker by every single one of the raters.

The perception of global foreign accent by native raters is a very valuable way to identify changes which might have taken place in attriters' speech patterns. Other investigations have also found that attriters may come to be perceived to be less native-like (for example de Leeuw, Schmid and Mennen (2010) looked at German attriters in the Netherlands and Canada).

These studies address *global accent*, but it may also be interesting to ask more specifically how the actual pronunciation has changed in phonetic terms: what exactly is it that attriters and L2 learners pronounce differently from natives? It is known that speakers who are proficient in two languages 'merge' certain speech sounds if they are similar but not identical in their first and second languages (Flege, 1987; Major, 1992; Mennen, 2004). Again, it is helpful to look at these differences in terms of Pavlenko's framework of *borrowing, restructuring, convergence, shift* and *attrition* (Pavlenko, 2004), which was applied to effects of attrition and CLI in the lexicon in the previous chapters.

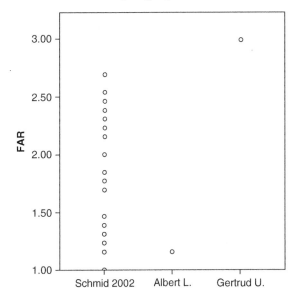

Figure 5.1 Foreign accent rating (FAR) by native speakers of speech excerpts from the corpus analysed by Schmid (2002), in comparison with Albert L. and Gertrud U.

Borrowing

Borrowing of sounds in the process of attrition is usually confined to lexical loanwords. For example, many language attrition studies have employed a film retelling task which involves showing the participant a ten-minute excerpt from a Charlie Chaplin movie, and asking them to narrate what they have seen (this task is described in more detail in chapter 4 below). During this retelling, German and Dutch speakers in Canada had the tendency to pronounce the name *Charlie Chaplin* the way an English speaker would, while the controls adapted it to the pronunciation of their own language. Phonemes or sounds alone are usually not borrowed and implemented into the L1.

Restructuring

Phonetic restructuring, on the other hand, can occur in the attritional process, as can be seen in the case of Gertrud U. (recall that she was very clearly perceived to be non-native). One case in point is her pronunciation of the phoneme /r/. In Standard German, /r/ is pronounced as a uvular fricative, [ʁ], while in her variety of American English it is realized as a retroflex approximant, [ɻ]. Furthermore, the

Table 5.1 *Restructuring in the pronunciation of /r/ in Gertrud U.'s L1 German*

Item	Standard pronunciation	Gertrud U.'s pronunciation
Kühlschrank ('refrigerator')	kyːlʃʁaŋk	targetlike
grade ('just')	gʁaːdə	targetlike
das war ('that was')	das vaː	das vaɹ
zerstreut ('distracted')	tsɛːʃtʁɔɪt	tsəɹʃtʁɔɪt

variety of German with which Gertrud U. grew up is non-rhotic (the r-sound is not pronounced unless it is followed by a vowel), while her L2 does have consistent rhoticity. There is quite a bit of variation in the way that Gertrud U. pronounces /r/. However, in the majority of cases, she uses [ʁ] in those positions where other speakers of her variety of German would use it, but [ɹ] where they would have zero, as illustrated by the examples in Table 5.1.

It therefore seems that the phoneme /r/ may have been slightly restructured in Gertrud U.'s variety of German: where the non-rhotic accent that she grew up with has the allophones [ʁ] and [Ø], she now has [ʁ] and [ɹ]. Some inconsistency notwithstanding, these are generally distributed in the same way that [ʁ] and [Ø] are in target-like versions of that variety.

Convergence

The most frequently and clearly observed process of phonetic change in attrition, however, is *convergence*. In those cases where the same underlying phoneme is pronounced differently in two languages, bilinguals often articulate an intermediate version in both languages. This has been demonstrated with respect to Voice Onset Time (VOT): when speakers pronounce voiceless plosives, such as the /t/ or /p/ sound, there is a short delay between the moment where air is released and the beginning of vibration of the vocal chords, and this time-lag varies between languages. For example, VOT is longer in monolingual American English than in monolingual French, but American speakers living in a French immersion environment produce English VOTs which are shorter, i.e. closer to the standard in their L2, than those of monolingual Americans. The opposite is true for French speakers living in the US: their L1 VOTs have become longer than the native norm. Both groups of speakers also diverge from the native norm in their L2, producing VOTs that are closer to the norm of their L1 than the monolingual standard. In other words, a merger of the two phonetic systems has taken place here (Flege, 1987). Similar findings have been reported for bilingual speakers of American English and Brazilian Portuguese (Major, 1992).

Shift

Like the other processes mentioned above, *shift* can also affect pronunciation. A good example is Gertrud U.'s pronunciation of the speech sound /l/. Standard German has alveolar [l], whereas American English has velarised [ɫ] Gertrud U. uses the latter quite consistently, e.g. in *Kühlschrank* ('refrigerator'), *elektrischen* ('electric'), *wollten* ('wanted') etc., so that we can conclude that for her, this speech sound has shifted to the American English value. The only large-scale investigation of L1 attrition in the domain of acoustic and articulatory phonetics to date, de Leeuw (2008), confirms that such a process of shift is common among L1 German attriters in an English-speaking setting for at least some aspects of the phoneme /l/.

Attrition

Lastly, the question is whether there could be actual *attrition* in the areas of phonetics or phonology. This would presumably mean that there are not merely slight changes to the way in which an underlying sound is articulated, but that some phoneme or phonemic contrast is lost entirely in terms of production or perception or both – for example, if a Chinese speaker were to lose the ability to discriminate tones in his or her native language or to produce them accurately. Among mature speakers, such cases have never been documented, and I think it is quite unlikely that they ever will be.

While it is therefore common for L1 attriters to experience some degree of adaptation in the way in which they pronounce their first language, this process will not usually affect the underlying phonemic system but be confined to slight drifts in articulation and intonation. Some attriters may not be perceived to be unambiguously native-like by other L1 speakers, but even after many decades of migration attriting populations, they will usually compare favourably with foreign language learners in terms of their perceived pronunciation (Hopp and Schmid, forthcoming). These changes are therefore due to cross-linguistic influence and speech habits, and do not constitute attrition of the underlying sound system.

GRAMMAR: MORPHEMES AND SYNTAX

Like the phonemic system of a language, the grammatical system is usually made up of a very limited number of items, namely *grammatical morphemes* and *rules*, and these constitute a *closed-class* system, as opposed to the *open-class* system of lexical words. It is rare for a language to add a new sound, a new inflectional ending, or a new word order variant to its productive repertoire. However, there is also an important difference between the grammatical and the phonemic system: while there are typically only a few dozen underlying phonemes in any language, each one of those will be pronounced slightly differently every time a speaker uses it. Grammatical elements such as inflectional endings or word order patterns, on the other hand, are *categorical*: words can appear in either one order or the other, inflectional endings can be either correctly present or not. There is therefore usually far less room for very subtle changes in the grammatical repertoire than in either the sound system or the lexicon of a language.

To some extent, this makes analyses of attrition in the grammatical system more straightforward than investigating changes in pronunciation or in the lexicon. Recall the example from Jarvis (2006) which was quoted earlier:

(25)
(a) There was a girl who was alone and hungry. She stole some bread from a bakery and tried to run away, but she ran into a man, and they both fell down. That gave the police enough time to find her and catch her.
(b) A destitute and lonely young female stole a loaf of bread from a bakery. She attempted to flee, but she collided with a man who was walking toward her, and both of them fell down. In the meantime, a policeman arrived and detained them.

These examples illustrate the range of lexical options available to describe the same referent or event – the expression *girl* in the first text and *destitute and lonely young female* in the second both describe the same character in a film, *tried to run away* and *attempted to flee* refer to the same action, and so forth. By contrast, the grammatical frame in both sequences determines a limited number of options for both texts. For example, all sentences have to contain a finite verb in a certain position (following the sentence subject), this verb has to be marked for tense (here they are almost all in the simple past, e.g. *ran into*, *collided*, *stole* and so on), once the character has been identified, it is referred to with the same anaphoric pronoun *she*, the same word order patterns apply, and so on.

If we want to determine grammatical accuracy and complexity, we have to keep in mind in what ways and to what degree these grammatical frames determine the use of certain features. It is not enough to look at how often they have occurred inaccurately over a certain stretch of text: some features are obligatory (for example, every finite verb in English has to carry a certain tense marking), and so we have to relate the number of mistakes to the total number of contexts. However, the value of these features is often optional – if you are uncertain about how to form the past tense of certain verbs, you can simply choose to stick to the present and avoid the problem. We should therefore try and assess whether the distribution of *grammatical variants* in attrited speech is the same as among monolinguals in order to see whether the overall picture has changed.

Let us have another look at the speech excerpt from Gertrud U., which for the present purpose I have 'cleaned up' a bit by eliminating hesitation markers and repetitions (this, of course, is something one should never do in practice, but here it makes the example more readable). There are many grammatical phenomena here which we might want to investigate, but I am going to confine the analysis to tense marking and word order for now. This might produce an annotated text looking like this:[2]

(26)

	wir hatten einen <u>refrigerator</u>
tense	simple past (correct)
word order	SVO
clause type	main clause (correct)
	we had a refrigerator
	und das war ziemlich neu at der Zeit
tense	simple past (correct)
word order	Conj SV AdvP PP
clause type	main clause (correct)
	and that was quite new at that time,
	und grade wie die Nazis in die Küche gehen
tense	present (incorrect)
word order	Conj Adv SubjConj(temp) S PP verb
clause type	subordinate clause (correct)
	and just when the Nazis go into the kitchen
	um das zu zerstören
tense	infinitive (correct)
word order	Conj Obj verb (infinitive)
clause type	non-finite

	to destroy that
	der Kühlschrank machte einen
tense	simple past
word order	SVO (incorrect)
clause type	main clause
	the refrigerator made an
	wie die machten
tense	simple past (incorrect)
word order	relative pronoun SV
clause type	subordinate clause (correct)
	what they did
	gehen an
tense	present
word order	verb
clause type	fragment
	they start up
	und da hatten sie Angst
tense	simple past
word order	CONJ Adv VSO
clause type	main clause (correct)
	and then they were afraid
	und da wollten sie nicht in die Küche gehen
tense	simple past
word order	CONJ Adv ModAux S NEG PP infinitive
clause type	main clause (correct)
	and they didn't want to go into the kitchen
	und so die Küche war nicht zerstreut
tense	simple past
word order	CONJ Adv S V NEG participle
clause type	main clause (correct)
	so the kitchen wasn't destroyed

For the speech sample from Albert L., the same analysis would produce the following result:

(27)

	ich war dann auf einer sogenannten preparatory school
tense	simple past (correct)
word order	SV Adv PP
clause type	main clause (correct)
	then I was at a so-called preparatory school
	wo ich todunglücklich war
tense	simple past (correct)
word order	Subor.Conj Subj ADJ verb
clause type	subordinate clause (correct)
	where I was dreadfully unhappy

	ich konnte kein Englisch
tense	simple past (correct)
word order	S V NEG O
clause type	main clause (correct)
	I didn't know any English
	es waren einige andere deutsche <u>boys</u> da
tense	simple past (correct)
word order	pro(empty) verb adv adv adj S prep
clause type	main clause (correct)
	there were a few other German <u>boys</u> there
	die sind alle durch dieselbe <u>Verbindung</u> nach England gekommen
tense	periphrastic past (correct)
word order	S AUX ADV PP PP participle
clause type	main clause (correct)
	they all came to England through the same connection

Based on such an analysis, we can then determine to what degree and with what frequency the speaker makes full use of the available range of tenses, word order patterns or clause types, applies them correctly, inflects them correctly (for example using the irregular past tense form *stole* instead of the regularized *stealed*) and so on. This then allows us to investigate changes in the grammatical system by comparing attriters and monolinguals. Again, the different types of phenomena that we can commonly find in such data can best be investigated within Pavlenko's framework of CLI and attrition (Pavlenko, 2004).

Borrowing

As was the case with phonology, grammatical *borrowing* is a very rare phenomenon. It is difficult to see how, for example, an English speaker who had lived in Russia or Finland for a long time might 'borrow' an inflectional ending into English to mark the instrumental case, instead of using a prepositional phrase such as 'I broke the window *with the hammer*'. Grammatical features are probably too much part of the fabric of a language to easily lend themselves to this kind of process except in cases of drastic change which affect entire speech communities, such as creolization.

Word order patterns, on the other hand, can sometimes be transposed to a bilingual's other language. I remember how an American colleague who had been living in Germany for a long time once told me about a disastrous journey rife with missed connections, cancelled flights, and arrogant and bored personnel at check-in desks. At some point, he said, he blew up at one of these service people and said 'What for a Mickey-Mouse airline are you running here?' In German, this sentence would be well-formed, but in English it is not, so the speaker was constructing a sentence for which he borrowed the grammatical frame from German. As it was the only time I ever heard him do that sort of thing, I think it was probably an ad hoc occurrence (and my impression was that he was not aware of its ungrammaticality at the time).

Restructuring

Restructuring can affect the grammatical system, and one example of this process can be found in the stretches of text analysed above in (26) and (27). If you compare the tense marking in the two excerpts, you will find that Gertrud U. consistently uses the simple past tense, while Albert L. alternates simple and periphrastic past (auxiliary + participle). These two tenses are structurally identical in English and German, but differ functionally. In English, they are associated with aspect: the simple past tense describes an action that was completed in the past: *we had a refrigerator* means that we no longer have it, and have not had it for a while, but *we have had a refrigerator* describes a situation where the item is still possessed or was so until very recently. In German, the two tenses make no aspectual distinction and are distributed mainly stylistically: the simple past is more appropriate to the written language in some contexts, and the periphrastic is then preferred in the spoken form (this is often a source of errors for German learners of English who overuse the periphrastic past even when it is aspectually inappropriate). We therefore have a case where two tenses are *formally equivalent* (they are constructed in the same way) but *functionally different*, and it may well be that for speakers who have lived in an English-speaking environment for a long time, the simple past may gain an aspectual meaning which it lacks in Standard German. They may then begin to use it in spoken contexts where a non-attrited speaker would prefer the periphrastic past.

If such a restructuring has taken place, we should be able to see it if we compare the *overall use* of tenses between attriters and non-attriters. I therefore counted all verb forms which occurred over a stretch of 1,000 words of spoken text from each of the interviews in the corpus analysed in Schmid (2002), as well as from a control group of ten monolingual speakers. Figure 5.2 shows the percentage of simple past tense verb forms among all past tense verbs occurring in this data for each speaker. These data do not suggest that any restructuring has taken place; the overall distribution of simple past tense forms across

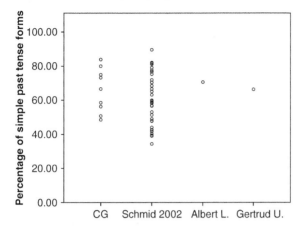

Figure 5.2 Percentage of simple past tense forms of all verbs framed in the past: comparison of monolingual control group (CG), attriters from Schmid (2002), Albert L. and Gertrud U. across a stretch of 1,000 words of spoken language

the groups looks very similar. Both Albert L. and Gertrud U., furthermore, appear to lie within the general trend.

Grammatical restructuring is therefore a process of CLI which can affect two structures that are formally very similar but differ functionally. In such cases, it is possible for attriters to transpose the function of this rule from L2 to L1. Similar processes can affect other areas of the grammatical system, for example the subtle differences in meaning associated with *modal auxiliaries*.

Modals, such as *can, may, must* etc., often begin life as lexical verbs but are affected by language change processes in ways that limit how they can be used. In English, for example, they cannot be used as an infinitive ('I am going *to do* this' but '*I am going *to can* this'), they have to take a lexical verb as a complement ('I *can read* this by tomorrow'), and they cannot co-occur ('*You *must can* do this.') These limitations vary across languages – in German, for example, there is no grammatical rule which prevents the co-occurrence of two or more modals.

On the other hand, modals also develop different meanings which are linked not so much to the actual event but to the way in which the speaker relates to it. Consider the sentence 'You must be very careful'. There are two possible interpretations: firstly, it might be considered a kind of imperative, where the speaker assumes the authority to instruct or oblige the addressee to do something. This type of meaning is called *deontic* modality. On the other hand, the sentence might also be used to express the fact that, according to the speaker's judgment, the addressee appears to be a very careful person (say, for example, if I saw five thick folders with insurance policies on your bookshelf and twenty fire extinguishers distributed across your house, I might say 'Well, you must be very careful!'). The type of modality that expresses speaker beliefs and speaker attitudes is called *epistemic*.

Modal auxiliaries are extremely variable in the extent to which they can encode such subtly different types of meanings across languages. Historically, in the change from full lexical verb to modal auxiliary, for example, deontic modality tends to precede epistemic modality (these diachronic processes are discussed by Traugott and Dasher, 2002). Again, this is a case where *formal equivalence* (which in typologically related languages often means cognates, such as English *must*, Dutch *moeten* and German *müssen*) coupled with very subtle, speaker-based differences in meaning might lead to some extent of restructuring of the grammatical subsystem of modal auxiliaries in the process of language attrition.

Convergence

Where *convergence* is concerned, two grammatical phenomena which have previously been investigated in the context of language attrition are case marking and pronominal reference. Languages which have morphological case marking usually have one *nominative* for the grammatical subject of a sentence and two or more *oblique* cases to refer to other constituents, such as the direct object, the indirect object, the patient, the instrument etc. As in the case of modality discussed above, there appear to be historical trends in language development: complex case systems often change over time by merging several cases to one larger category, as was the case in classical Latin where the locative and vocative cases were largely merged into the ablative and nominative, respectively. Such diachronic changes are common and have happened in many languages, but they can become especially productive in situations where there is a great deal of language contact.

Some evidence of such a process was found by Leppänen (2004) who conducted an investigation of second-generation Finnish speakers in the United States. Finnish has a mind-boggling fifteen cases, divided into 'grammatical', 'local' and 'other' cases, and Leppänen found that among her population 'grammatical' cases had remained quite intact, 'local' cases were affected somewhat, and 'other' cases had changed the most. Based on such studies of migrant communities, it has often been proposed that a complex case system might be one of the categories which could also be vulnerable in the process of language attrition, and that speakers might begin merging two or more oblique cases into some superordinate category.

Where our two speakers Gertrud U. and Albert L. are concerned, convergence in the case system would imply that the German system, which distinguishes four cases (nominative, genitive, dative and accusative), and the English system, in which case is not marked morphologically except on pronouns, would have merged into a system that had, for example, only the nominative and one oblique case (most probably the accusative). Cast your mind back to the stretch of text from Gertrud U. Even in this short piece of text, she correctly uses three of the four German cases:

(28)

nominative:	die$_{NOM}$ Nazis (the nazis), der$_{NOM}$ Kühlschrank (the refrigerator)
genitive:	not attested in this excerpt and rather uncommon in spoken German generally
dative:	*at* der$_{DAT}$ Zeit (at the time)
accusative:	in die$_{ACC}$ Küche (into the kitchen), um das$_{ACC}$ zu zerstören (to destroy that)

While errors in case marking are not uncommon among L1 German attriters, these few examples alone suggest that Gertrud U.'s overall case marking system has probably not converged with English, resulting in a wholesale reduction of cases. In order to establish this more thoroughly, I compared the number of noun phrases in the accusative (ACC) and dative (DAT) in 1,000 words of each of the interviews investigated in Schmid (2002), as well as in similar interviews from ten monolingual speakers of German (CG). As Figure 5.3 shows, there might be a very slight tendency to underuse the dative and overuse the accusative among the attriters, but it certainly is not the case that either of the two has disappeared for any of the attriters, including Gertrud U.

A somewhat more subtle case of a grammatical phenomenon that might be affected by convergence is the reference potential of anaphoric pronouns. Some languages (for example Italian or Turkish) allow the omission of the overt pronominal form in some contexts, and are therefore called *pro-drop* languages. For example, consider the English sentence in (29) (this example is borrowed from Sorace, 2006: 140):

(29)
Why did Lucia$_i$ not take her keys? – Because she$_i$ thought she'd find you at home.

Although it is perfectly clear from the context that the person indicated by the pronoun in the second of these sentences – that is, the so-called *antecedent* for the pronoun – can only be *Lucia* (I have indicated this by marking both items with the subscript letter i), the English sentence requires the subject pronoun *she* in order to be grammatical.

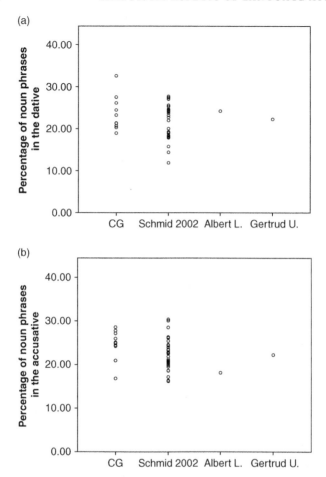

Figure 5.3 Case-marking of noun phrases: (a) percentage of NPs in
the dative, (b) percentage of NPs in the accusative, comparison of
monolingual control group (CG), attriters from Schmid (2002), Albert L.
and Gertrud U. across a stretch of 1,000 words of spoken language

However, pro-drop languages such as Italian allow the omission of
pronouns in cases where the reference is unambiguous:

(30)
Perchè Lucia$_i$ non ha preso le chiavi? – Perchè Ø$_i$ pensava di trovarti a casa.

The symbol Ø (zero) in this sentence indicates that this is where the
pronoun *lei* 'she' has been omitted. Since the overt pronoun is not

obligatory in these cases, and would usually be omitted by native speakers, the assumption is that when it is realized it marks *contrastive* reference: that is, it indicates someone who would not normally be expected at this point in the discourse. So, in the example above, 'Perchè lei pensava . . .' might lead to the confusing assumption that someone else had thought that the addressee would be at home.

This feature of the language can therefore be exploited to reduce ambiguity. For example, in English the sentence

(31)
The old woman$_i$ greets the girl$_j$ when she$_{i/j}$ crosses the street.

could either mean that it is the old woman who is crossing the street or the girl (again, the subscript letters after the nouns and the pronoun indicate which of the possible antecedents the pronoun can refer to). Native speakers of Italian, on the other hand, are strongly biased to interpret (32a), which does not contain an overt pronoun, as indicating that it is the old woman who crosses the street, while in (32b) it is the girl (or some other person).[3]

(32)
(a) L'anziana signora$_i$ saluta la ragazza$_j$ quando $\emptyset_i$ attraversa la strada.
(b) L'anziana signora$_i$ saluta la ragazza$_j$ quando lei$_{j/k}$ attraversa la strada.

Findings from L1 attriters of Italian and other pro-drop languages, such as Greek and Turkish, indicate that convergence can take place here: if an attriter's L1 has several possible pronouns (e.g. anaphoric pronoun vs zero pronoun) but the L2 has only one, the subtle differences expressed between the original options may not always be preserved in the attritional process. That is, attriters may not be able to correctly interpret sentences (32a) and (32b) above, and in natural speech, they may overuse anaphoric pronouns in those contexts where a monolingual would use a zero pronoun (a study investigating these phenomena is described by Tsimpli, Sorace, Heycock and Filiaci, 2004). The ensuing system is thus not exactly like the English one, which does not permit zero pronouns at all, but also differs from the monolingual unattrited L1 system in the overall distribution of the pronouns.

Shift

Wholesale *shift* might also to some extent affect grammatical options within the process of attrition. Such a process could, for example, take place with regard to L1 German word order in a contact situation with L2 English. The main difference between these two languages concerns verb placement: in English, regardless of clause type (main or subordinate clause), the finite verb follows the subject which can either appear at the beginning of the sentence or be preceded by preposed elements. This invariable word order, which is called SVO (subject-verb-object), is illustrated by (33a–c).

(33)
(a) I read the book last year.
(b) Last year I read the book.
(c) I would like to see the film because last year I read the book.

German, on the other hand, has a different word order in main and subordinate clauses. In main clauses, the verb always occupies the second position, a structure that is typical for Germanic languages and known as V2 (verb second). If the subject occupies the first position in the sentence, the word order is therefore also SVO, but if any other element (for example a temporal phrase) is topicalized and placed at the beginning of the sentence, the subject has to appear after the verb. This alternation is illustrated in (34a) and (34b).

(34)

(a)	Ich	las	das Buch	letztes Jahr.
	subj	verb	obj	temp.phrase
	I	read	the book	last year
(b)	Letztes Jahr	las	ich	das Buch
	temp.phrase	verb	subj	obj
	last year	read	I	the book

In subordinate clauses, on the other hand, the finite verb occupies the last position. This word order is illustrated in (34c) below:

(34)

(c)	Ich möchte den Film gern sehen	weil	ich	das Buch	letztes Jahr	las[4]
		conj	subj	obj	temp. phrase	verb
	I would like the film to see	because	I	the book	last year	read

I would like to see the film because last year I read the book.

As these examples show, sentences which have a word order that parallels English SVO are possible and perfectly grammatical in

German (see (34a) above). It is therefore conceivable that attriters might come to prefer these SVO structures, underusing topicalizations of elements other than the subject (see (34b)) or subordinate clauses (34c). Such a process would constitute a shift from German to English word order.

Again, a brief look at the examples above shows that both Gertrud U. and Albert L. avail themselves of all possible sentence patterns. Gertrud U. has a number of sentences where the subject precedes the verb (*wir hatten einen Kühlschrank* 'we had a refrigerator'), but she also uses structures where a different element is preposed (*da hatten sie Angst* 'then they were afraid') and a subordinate clause (*wie die Nazis in die Küche gehen* 'as the Nazis are going into the kitchen'), and Albert L. also uses all of these clause types.

In order to detect whether there has been a wholesale process of shift, however, we again have to consider a larger set of data and see whether what these attriters do is noticeably different from the speech patterns used by monolinguals. I conducted such a comparison on the corpus which by now you know very well (Schmid, 2002) and a control group of ten monolingual speakers. Figure 5.4 shows how many main clauses with a preposed element other than the subject (Figure 5.4a) and how many subordinate clauses (Figure 5.4b) these speakers used per 1,000 words.

The results which I have visualized here suggest that the word order patterns in the main clauses have not changed for the attriters. The range represented here is somewhat larger than in the control group (the little circles are distributed over a wider area), but we would expect that, since the group of attriters is larger ($n = 33$) than the control group ($n = 10$). However, in both cases the circles are grouped roughly around the same area (I will discuss ways to statistically assess whether such data are different or not in chapter 17 below). The picture is different with respect to the subordinate clauses: these are quite clearly less frequent in the attriters' speech than in that of the controls.

While the attriters represented here therefore appear to prefer simple main clauses over complex subordinate ones, this preference cannot really be interpreted as a case of shift towards an L2 word order, as the main clauses which they use also diverge from the English pattern. It may therefore simply be the case that the simplification which is evident in the lower proportion of subordinate clauses is linked to problems of cognitive control: for a speaker who has not used a language for a long time, lexical access, grammatical structure and pronunciation might take up more resources than are available, and this may lead to a preference for simpler constructions, regardless of the templates available in L1 and L2.

(a)

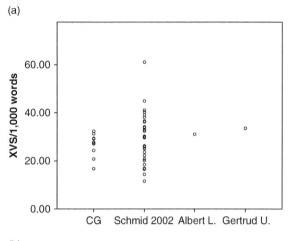

(b)

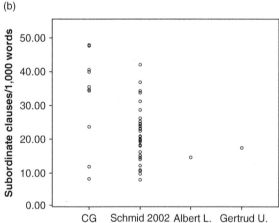

Figure 5.4 Word order patterns: (a) main clauses with element other than subject in pre-verbal position, (b) subordinate clauses per 1,000 words, comparison of monolingual control group (CG), attriters from Schmid (2002), Albert L. and Gertrud U.

Attrition

All of the types of cross-linguistic influence and examples mentioned above have one thing in common: they only occur occasionally in the data from attriters, particularly in natural speech, and are therefore probably indications of a temporary merger of the two language systems. Actual *grammatical attrition*, on the other hand, is probably the process which Seliger and Vago (1991) or Sharwood Smith and van Buren (1991) had in mind when they mentioned the term *competence*: can we determine, on the basis of what we have seen so far, whether an attriter 'has lost *or is even able to* lose those kinds of underlying mental representations of his or her first language that may be referred to as L1 competence' (Sharwood Smith and van Buren, 1991: 17, their emphasis)?

I think the data which I showed you above, both from my own previous work and that of others, suggest very strongly that we have not, so far, seen anyone who actually *has* lost this elusive thing that is meant here: the underlying, ingrained and automatized knowledge that allows native speakers to produce utterances which (usually) conform more or less to the rules and conventions of their language, and to understand such utterances. Which leaves us with the question: are attriters ever able to lose it?

NOTE

The speaker whom I refer to as Gertrud U. is the most strongly attrited migrant I have ever encountered. She left Germany at the age of thirteen, under extremely traumatic circumstances, and indicated that she had not used her L1 for almost sixty years at the time when she was interviewed. Gertrud U. does make more grammatical mistakes when she speaks German than any of the other attriters whose speech I have analysed. However, even in this particular case, the number of correct contexts far outweighs the incorrect ones. For example, her entire interview, comprising some 4,500 words, contains 10 mistaken assignments of grammatical case and 28 errors in the verb phrase. When I counted overall obligatory contexts for these two features in a stretch of 1,000 words from her interview, I found 274 case-marked elements and 150 verb phrases. This means that, overall, her errors affected less than 1 per cent of all case inflections, and less than 5 per cent of all verb phrases.

Loss of grammatical competence? I don't think so!

CONCLUSION

The present section has tried to give you an impression of what the linguistic process of language attrition can look like in real-life contexts. I have tried to show you some examples of processes of cross-linguistic influence which you might expect to see in areas such as the mental lexicon, the phonological and phonetic repertoire, and the grammatical system of speakers who have lived in an L2 setting for a long time. We have seen what the extent and limits are of the processes that might make a migrant 'seem like a foreigner' (as Mma Ramotswe put it) and I have tried to convince you that, on the whole, the extent of such changes is usually much smaller in practice than one might have thought.

The fact remains, however, that there *are* differences between attriters and monolinguals. Not only that: there are also differences – quite large ones – between the attriters themselves. Recall the graphs which you have seen over the last pages, and how widely distributed the circles were which indicated the score of an individual speaker on a certain feature.

So, what we would like to know next is what it is that makes one attriter perform at the top of his or her cohort, for example with respect to grammatical accuracy or perceived nativeness, while another is much less accurate and sounds like a foreigner. This is the question that I shall address in Part II.

PART II
Extralinguistic aspects of language attrition

Surely it all very much depends on personal circumstances
i.e. background, age, time of emigration amongst others.
(Letter from Sigmund W.)

In Part I you were introduced to some of the characteristics of attrited languages. I tried to address questions such as: how can two languages intermingle in the attritional process? To what extent can aspects of an attriting language become reduced or simplified? And, on the other hand: which parts of the linguistic system are relatively stable and less vulnerable to attrition?

When you are investigating a group of speakers who have experienced language attrition, you may expect to find some or all of these characteristics in the way in which they use their first language. What you may also expect, however, is that some speakers will have a far higher amount of attritional features than others. In Part II we will look at the reasons for this difference.

Let us again start with the two speakers to whom I introduced you at the beginning of this book, Gertrud U. and Albert L. You saw in the last chapters that there is a striking difference in the amount of attrition to be found in their speech: Gertrud U. was noticeably disfluent, used a simplified lexicon, and had a range of non-targetlike structures, including an English accent. Albert L., on the other hand, would probably only be perceptibly different from a non-attrited native speaker on much closer investigation.

Imagine, for the moment, that you had encountered these speakers without knowing anything about their life history, and that all that you had to go by was their use of their L1, and the degree of attrition that you can perceive from that. What would your intuitions be about their experiences – what reasons could you think of for the fact that one was more strongly attrited than the other? Take a moment to write down at least five factors which occur to you.

The list that you have come up with will probably contain factors that can be grouped into three larger sets. Firstly, there are background factors which are related to a person's overall development and not directly linked to language itself. For example, as in L2 learning, the *age* at which the development starts is a very important determining aspect of language attrition: younger migrants will attrite more strongly than older ones. Of course the *time* available for the development is also important – someone who has learned a language for ten years will, all other things being equal, be a better speaker than someone who has only spoken it for five years; and attrition also progresses over time. Other personal background factors, such as *education* or *gender*, may also play a role, as may the fact that some people simply seem to have a 'knack' for language learning, while others don't.

The second set of factors bears more directly on language itself, and has to do with frequency of *rehearsal, exposure* and *use*. This may sound obvious to the point of being trivial – which is probably the reason why it has, to date, so seldom actually been investigated in the context of language attrition. I will try to show below that the link between L1 use and L1 attrition is far less straightforward than you may think.

Lastly, we have to consider the possibility that attrition is also conditioned by internal and psychological factors such as *identity*, *attitudes* and *emotions*. Emigration is a disruptive event with far-reaching implications. In some cases it may be experienced as a positive occurrence which brings more prestige and a better standard of living, while in others it is an escape from persecution and violence, demanding huge personal and material sacrifices. These factors are very important for second language learning, and may also have consequences for the process of attrition.

6 Personal background factors

> To what extent do factors such as age at migration, length of time elapsed since emigration, or age at testing determine how far a speaker will attrite? This chapter will investigate the impact of such *personal background* variables for the attritional process.

THE AGE FACTOR

When the journal *Science* was 125 years old in 2005, the editors compiled a 'survey of scientific ignorance' entitled 'What don't we know?' for the anniversary edition: a research agenda consisting of 125 questions on matters such as extraterrestrial life, the cause of ice ages, how much of personality is genetic, how to cure cancer, and so on. Also on that list is the question that splits linguistics straight down the middle: why are children better at language learning than adults?

NOTE

The controversy about this issue goes back at least fifty years, and centres on a simple question: Is there a stage in human development (situated around the onset of puberty and often called the 'Critical Period') when a *language-specific maturational change* takes places in the brain, which makes language learning through the original, dedicated processes impossible and forces older learners to develop compensatory strategies? Or are older learners hampered by an *accumulation of factors* which are more *general*? These factors may include the fact that the higher level of cognitive development and analytical skills that older learners draw upon is more suitable for the acquisition of other types of knowledge, but can hamper language acquisition. Also, of course, our ability to learn and memorize things generally deteriorates as we get older.

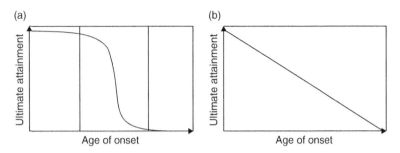

Figure 6.1 A schematic representation of the age–ultimate attainment
function, (a) with and (b) without a Critical Period

A great deal has been written both in favour and against the so-called
'Critical Period Hypothesis' (CPH). Large-scale investigations of second
language learners who started the acquisition process over a wide
range of ages have conflicting results where the age effect is concerned. The strong version of the CPH implies pre-puberty learners
should all reach a very high level of ultimate attainment, regardless
of their age when they first start learning the language. After puberty,
a sharp drop should occur, and then the curve should stabilize again.
This curve is schematically represented in Figure 6.1(a), and some
studies have indeed found such an effect. In other studies, however,
ultimate attainment decreases gradually and steadily over the entire
age span which was investigated, leading to a more linear curve
(a good overview of this debate can be found in Birdsong, 2006).

Furthermore, it has been shown that age does not determine
language skills quite as decisively as was originally thought: speakers
with high language aptitude (a 'talent' for languages) may manage to
attain native-like or near-native proficiency, even if they start learning
a new language later in life (Abrahamsson and Hyltenstam, 2008).

AGE AT ONSET OF ATTRITION

Whether, and to what degree, the age at which emigration takes
place is of importance for language attrition is a subject that has
received much less systematic attention than the impact of age at
onset for L2 learning. While there are a great number of studies
comparing success in (second) language acquisition across virtually
all age ranges and in a variety of different situations (see Birdsong,

2006), studies of first language attrition which investigate the age factor in both pre- and post-puberty attriters are extremely rare. Where the attrition of a first language among very young migrants is investigated at all, it is almost invariably through case studies with very limited numbers of subjects. The few quantitative investigations which count both pre- and post-puberty learners among their informants do not, as a general rule, use 'age of onset of attrition' as a predictor variable in their design (for an overview of such studies see Köpke and Schmid, 2004: 9f.). The only exceptions are the Ph.D. studies by Ton Ammerlaan (1996) and Linda Pelc (2001), and for both of them, the age factor emerges as the most important predictor of attrition. Furthermore, the amount of loss reported by studies which look at young children almost invariably appears far more drastic than anything that studies investigating subjects who were older at the time of emigration have ever found (for example, Elena Schmitt's (2001) Ph.D. on the attrition of Russian in two migrant children finds erosion of case marking on a completely different scale to the small effects I found in my investigations of post-puberty German migrants).

It is only very recently that an attempt has been made to specifically assess the role of age for L1 attrition. A study conducted by Emanuel Bylund (2008, 2009) investigates the L1 of Spanish speakers who emigrated to Sweden between the ages of 1 and 19 years and concludes that the native language does, indeed, stabilize around age 12. If migration occurs before that age, the L1 can deteriorate dramatically or even be lost completely. For speakers who are older than 12 at the time they emigrate, the knowledge of the language is impervious to attrition – and it does no longer matter how old someone was at the moment of migration. It therefore seems reasonable to assume that the effect of the Critical Period is reversed with respect to language attrition: if the onset of attrition takes place at a relatively early period in life, the deterioration of the linguistic system will be far more dramatic than in those cases where the change in linguistic environment occurs later.

NOTE

Given that the differences in ultimate proficiency between pre- and post-puberty migrants are so dramatic, a very careful distinction needs to be made in how we refer to them: second-generation bilinguals, who were born to families speaking a language different from that of the environment, are *heritage speakers*. Pre-puberty

migrants are referred to as *incomplete learners* or *incomplete acquirers* –
and only speakers who emigrated when they were older than 12 years
can be called 'L1 attriters'.

Language transmission and international adoption

An important factor with respect to attrition in general and attrition
among children in particular is whether the language learning situation of the potential attriter is one of *additive* or of *subtractive* bilingualism. Most investigations look at the linguistic development of
children whose emigration took place within the family context. While
in such cases a reversal of language dominance often occurs within a
relatively short period of time and the acquisition of the first language
may be slowed down considerably, the input in that language usually
does not cease abruptly and totally. On the contrary, parents often
report that they make a considerable conscious effort to transmit their
own first language to their children, sometimes by insisting on the use
of that language in the home and the family and sometimes by
following the *one parent, one language* method. The following example
is typical for the situation described by migrants:

(35)

M.S.S.:   How important was it for you that your children would learn to speak
          German?
INT.:   Oh, it was very important to me, always. For many years, for five or
          seven years, we sacrificed the free Saturdays and took them to the
          German school. And in most families the oldest children usually speak
          German quite well, but from the second one it kind of fizzles out . . .

The linguistic situations investigated in this respect are therefore, at
least to some extent, contexts of what Gardner and Lambert (1972) call
additive bilingualism: a speaker is exposed to a first language (from
birth), and then at some point in his or her linguistic development,
adds another linguistic system either through instructed acquisition
in school or through immersion.

Only in recent years has it been recognized that investigations of
subtractive bilingualism, the situation where the new linguistic system
completely replaces the old one, might provide additional insights. It is
relatively rare, of course, for such a radical break in linguistic input to
occur. One type of situation where exposure to the birth language of a
developing speaker ceases suddenly and totally, to be replaced by a
different system, is that of children who are adopted into a different
country. Such a development is investigated by Isurin (2000) in a case

study of a Russian child adopted into an American family. She reports a rapid breakdown of first language proficiency, which after a relatively short period (around one year) was followed by an unwillingness and refusal of the subject to interact in her first language at all with the investigator.

The most striking findings in this respect come from a quantitative psycho- and neurolinguistic investigation of adult speakers of French who were adopted from a Korean-speaking background at ages 3–10 (Pallier, 2007; Pallier et al., 2003; Ventureyra and Pallier, 2004). In one of the experiments in this study, the participants listened to the numbers from one to ten recorded in eleven different languages, and were asked to indicate whether the language they had just heard was Korean or not. The adoptees were no better than a French monolingual control group in identifying Korean. Furthermore, fMRI scans did not show more brain activity among the adoptees than among the controls when they listened to Korean. These and other findings suggest that, even though the adoptees had on average been between 6 and 7 years old when they came to France, their native language had been completely erased from their mind.

NOTE

While exposure to a foreign language before puberty may facilitate its acquisition, the deterioration of a first language may be quicker and more radical if the input is reduced or ceases during the same age span. How precisely this breakdown in linguistic competence happens, and what the relevant age limits are, remains to be investigated.

Adolescence, identification and acculturation

Studies of first language acquisition do not usually continue into the period of adolescence – the age from about 12 to 17 years old. It is assumed that the linguistic system, at least where its grammatical aspects are concerned, has stabilized by this age and that few findings of interest to L1 acquisition can be gathered from this age group. On the other hand, the period of adolescence is characterized by the search for social identity, 'that part of an individual's self-concept which derives from his knowledge of his membership of a social group (or groups) together with the value and emotional significance attached to that membership' (Tajfel, 1981: 255). In this period, it is therefore not the stabilization of a (linguistic) knowledge system, but of the sociocognitive factor of identity and identification that impacts most heavily on linguistic development.

Emigration is probably almost invariably an unsettling and to some degree difficult experience. However, it is arguably most difficult and traumatic for adolescents. On the one hand, these speakers have passed the age at which learning a new language through immersion may appear effortless, and they often have to work quite hard at achieving sufficient proficiency in the new language. More importantly, adolescence is the age where we cease to define ourselves exclusively or even predominantly within the context of our immediate family, and start the search for integration and identification in the wider society. At this stage, being 'different' can often be felt with devastating sharpness, and this feeling of deviance is enhanced by reactions from the surrounding society towards any perceived difference.

A former citizen of Düsseldorf recounts the constant bullying that she had to endure at the hands of an anti-Semitic teacher when she was around 14 years old (in 1934). At one point, she was singled out in front of the entire class and told that she had to realize that, as a Jew, she was merely a tolerated guest in Germany, and should behave accordingly. She says:

(36)
That was very very painful, although I knew her attitude towards us, but to say something like this, in front of the entire class – I mean, I was fourteen at that time, that is a difficult age in any case, even without this kind of bullying. I must say I was very hurt, it was almost like the end of a love affair, and that was the point where I realized that our love affair with Germany was over.

Typically, adolescent emigrants will attempt to integrate into the L2 community as quickly as possible, and make every effort not to be recognizable as a non-native speaker. This tendency is also borne out by reports from first generation emigrants who attempt to maintain their L1 as a home language and encourage their children to learn and speak it: almost invariably, they will report that this became difficult or even impossible at the time that the second child reached school age, encountering more and diverse L2 contexts and L2 role models. The siblings will find that they can communicate with each other in the L2 and form a 'united L2 front' within the family, and often become reluctant to use the L1 any further, or even refuse to do so altogether.

NOTE

Things are often different in cases where there is a very strong migrant community, as has been reported, for example, with respect to the Turkish and Moroccan immigrant communities in the Netherlands.

In such cases, demographic factors may help the heritage language to achieve sufficient prestige to make it appear desirable to maintain the home language for younger migrants and heritage speakers.

There is little research into how this tendency to assimilate completely into the host society influences the development of L1 attrition among adolescents. Again, empirical studies which investigate the impact of age at onset of attrition among this age group are scarce, but two quantitative analyses which do make a distinction between 'younger' and 'older' emigrants do not find any difference: Köpke (1999) compared attrition in a group of speakers who were between 14 and 25 years at the time of emigration to that among speakers who were between 26 and 36 years, and Schmid (2002) set the groups at 11–16 and 17–28. In neither study is age of onset a significant predictor for language attrition.

OLD AGE AND LANGUAGE REVERSION

The majority of studies on language attrition investigate speakers who are quite old – the average age is around sixty. This is mainly due to practical reasons: we usually want speakers who were adults when they emigrated, and who have lived in emigration a fairly long time, so our target group really starts with speakers who are middle-aged. Also, elderly speakers who are no longer professionally active often have more leisure to participate in investigations which can sometimes be time-intensive.

The fact that the majority of the volunteers for many attrition studies are in their sixties or older may also be related to more psychological reasons. In this phase of life, distant memories often resurface and people find themselves thinking about events and places which had lain half-forgotten. Among immigrants this quite commonly implies a kind of nostalgic preoccupation with the culture of origin, and often also a return to a language that had hardly been spoken for decades. Many older migrants as well as their families or their caregivers report a 'reversion' in language dominance: they feel that the second language, which they have used in their daily lives for decades, recedes or deteriorates and the first language becomes stronger again, allegedly sometimes to the point that they cannot even communicate with their own children if the latter are not fluent in their L1.

It is very difficult to separate fact from fiction in such reports and observations. While there are many references to a process of 'language reversion' among older migrants, they are usually vague and inconclusive; for example, 'It is common knowledge these days . . . that ageing is often accompanied by language reversion' (Haines, 1999: 12) or 'research . . . clearly shows that language reversion in later life is very common' (Fronditha Care Inc., 2005: 3). Often the conclusion that language reversion has occurred is not based on actual observations of linguistic behaviour (and comparisons to earlier behaviour) but on self-reports (de Bot and Clyne, 1989). The only large-scale investigation into the language skills of older migrants to date does not actually find any evidence for the deterioration of their L2 skills or a reversion to the L1 (Crezee, 2008).

All in all, while language attrition and language reversion in old age appear to be the situations that are surrounded by the most persistant myths, and which are potentially most confusing and disturbing to both the speaker and those closest to him or her, they are also the situations where there is least empirical research. It seems critical to investigate these claims in large-scale, quantitative and, wherever possible, longitudinal studies, in order to provide answers and advice to those who find themselves faced with such communicative difficulties.

LENGTH OF RESIDENCE

It is often confidently asserted that language attrition is a process that takes place gradually and over decades. The underlying assumption is a steady, probably more or less linear, process of loss or reduced accessibility. However, we are not even close to the ability to chart this attritional process, as the available evidence is (yet again) confusing and sometimes contradictory.

There are indications that the onset of language attrition can occur fairly quickly after emigration. For example, speakers may become faster on a picture-naming task in their L2 than in their L1 around seven years after migration (Mägiste, 1979). One study even found a stronger L2 effect for speakers who had been living in migration less than five years than for those who had been there for twelve years or more (Beganović, 2006). This suggests that attrition might be an 'up and down' process, and is probably evident more strongly in those situations where a lot of effort has to go into the development and acquisition of the second language (as is also suggested in the framework of *multicompetence*, see Herdina and Jessner, 2002).

In this respect, there is some converging evidence from different investigations, suggesting that the first decade is crucial, in particular the period between five and ten years after emigration. For example, a comparison of two Turkish families in the Netherlands suggested a reversal of language dominance between five and fifteen years after migration (Huls and van de Mond, 1992). It has even been suggested that those speakers who manage to maintain their L1 during these first years will remain stable afterwards (de Bot and Clyne, 1994). This supposition is borne out by the fact that attrition studies investigating subjects with a period of residence of more than ten years generally find little or no time effects (Ammerlaan, 1996: 209; Brown, 2001: 31; de Bot and Clyne, 1994: 17; Gürel, 2002: 170; Tsimpli *et al.*, 2004), and it has further been suggested that length of residence (LOR) may only have an effect for those speakers who use their L1 very infrequently (de Bot, Gommans and Rossing, 1991: 94; Soesman, 1997: 190).

A general problem in the investigation of LOR is that it will invariably correlate with age: as people live in migration longer, they get older. As they get older, they may become slower or less efficient on some of the tasks which are usually employed to detect language attrition, such as reaction time paradigms or grammaticality judgment tasks. We should therefore be particularly careful when investigating the impact of length of time, and meticulously control for age, for example by comparing the attriters with non-attrited control speakers of the same age.

CONCLUSION

In this chapter, I have attempted to sketch the impact that personal background factors can have on the process of L1 attrition. Of these, the age at the time of migration to date appears to be the most important predicting factor for the degree to which a native language can attrite. Whether a speaker migrates before or after puberty has such drastic consequences for the loss of first language knowledge that the two processes should not even be called by the same name: the term 'attrition' should only be used to refer to language change among post-puberty migrants, while younger speakers are 'incomplete acquirers'.

General assumptions about other background factors which we often find in language attrition, such as old age (language reversion) and time (the gradual deterioration over the entire migration span), on the other hand, should be treated with extreme caution. There are very few experimental findings to date which suggest that these factors actually impact on language attrition in the way that is usually predicted.

NOTE

Take another look at our two speakers, Gertrud U. and Albert L. These two cases suggest very strongly that, while background factors may impact to some degree on the attritional process, they certainly cannot account for all of it: on all of the variables discussed in this chapter, the two speakers are nearly identical:

- both of them were fairly young at the time of emigration (13 years old)
- both lived in an English-speaking environment for about six decades
- both of them were around seventy at the time that they were interviewed.

In order to account for the dramatic differences found in their linguistic data, we therefore have to look elsewhere.

7 The role of L1 input and output

Does it help prevent L1 attrition if you go on using the language on a regular basis? What kinds of language use are necessary? This chapter will explore how L1 use relates to L1 attrition.

Cast your mind back to some of the differences between the excerpt from the narratives of Gertrud U. and Albert L. In part I above, I pointed out that they were different from each other on a range of features (see Table 7.1).

When you see this kind of difference between two speakers who have lived in emigration for more or less the same number of years, the first intuition about how these differences came about is likely to be that Albert L. had probably had more opportunities to 'practise' his German over the years than Gertrud U.

It is an apparently reasonable and natural assumption that speakers who continue to use a language remain fluent in it while speakers who don't forget it. Human knowledge and memory need to be maintained to prevent them from deteriorating: the more often knowledge is called upon, the easier it becomes to recall. If, on the other hand, a certain memory is not activated for a long time, it will eventually become difficult to retrieve. This mechanism is at the heart of the tenet '*use it or lose it*', which in turn is one of the basic assumptions in language attrition research: lack of contact leads to attrition whereas using the L1, preferably on a daily basis, prevents loss – that is a widely held and often repeated view (e.g. Cook, 2005; Paradis, 2007), and one which

Table 7.1 *A comparison of Gertrud U. and Albert L.'s L1 proficiency*

	Gertrud U.	Albert L.
Lexical diversity	reduced	extensive
Morphosyntactic complexity	reduced	high
Number of errors	high	low
Foreign accent	pronounced	untraceable

appears obvious and intuitively convincing. The problem with obvious and intuitively convincing assumptions about language is that experimental and empirical data often tell a less straightforward story.

There is little direct evidence that the degree to which a language system will attrite depends on the amount to which the language is being used in everyday life. Only two studies report that speakers who used their L1 on an extremely infrequent basis showed more attrition over time (de Bot *et al.*, 1991 and Köpke, 1999). On the other hand, another study found a *negative* correlation, suggesting that the attriters who used their L1 on a daily basis actually had more difficulty completing some tasks (Jaspaert and Kroon, 1989).

TIP

When findings are contradictory, it is often helpful to first have a good look at the underlying methodologies. Measuring the amount of use a person makes of a certain language is a complex matter. What situations would you include under the heading 'amount of use'? And how would you measure it?

Interestingly, all three of the studies cited above attempted to reduce the 'language use' factor to one *dichotomous* variable – that is, a variable with only two values. De Bot *et al.* (1991) classified their subjects into two groups: one that had a partner with the same L1 (Dutch) and also claimed to have contact with other Dutch speakers at least once a week, and one who had no such frequent contacts. Köpke asked her subjects to quantify (in percentages) the proportion of conversations they had in their L1 and L2 in three settings (at work, with their partner, and with their children) and averaged the responses per informant. The resulting percentage allowed her to classify her subjects into two groups: one which used the L2 almost exclusively, and one which used the L2 predominantly (Köpke, 1999: 152). Jaspaert and Kroon's (1989) criterion is identical with one of de Bot *et al.*'s measurements: they use the native language of the partner as the sole indication of the degree of L1 use.

Such dichotomous measures probably constitute an unwarranted simplification of a set of relationships and speech situations. The question we have to ask ourselves is what we mean by 'language use', and if it is legitimate to merely average out the answers to many diverse questions, since this factor refers to such a complex pattern of behaviour in everyday interaction. Virtually everything we do, think or feel is in some way dependent on language. We talk to our partner, to our children, to our pets, to our boss and colleagues, to strangers in the street, to our friends, to ourselves and to our computers. We use language to count, to pray, to write our diary, to swear, to sing, to dream; we read, we watch TV. . . Can we quantify the amount of L1 use in all of these situations, and then average them together to calculate one neat little number which tells us that one migrant uses the L1 'more' than another?

I would argue that we need a more fine-grained approach, and that this should first of all distinguish three types of L1 'use', all of which may impact to some degree on language attrition:

- interactive language use (spoken and written communication with others)
- non-interactive exposure (reading, media)
- inner language (thought, dreams, diary writing, counting/maths etc.)

INTERACTIVE L1 USE

NOTE

Mentally go through the past two hours (or, if you want a longer time span, through yesterday). Who did you speak to? What were the topics? What languages did you use? What different speech styles did you use? What did you want from the people you were speaking to? What did you want those people to think about you? How did that translate into how you were using language?

When we communicate with others, only one function of the language is to encode and convey propositional information – that is, information related to the topic of conversation. Whether we are aware of this or not, whenever we talk, we constantly put out signals about who we are. Through the way we use language, we can signal to our interlocutor(s) that we like them, that we belong to the same group as they do (or want to) – or we can use it to create distance and convey that we are members of an entirely different group. In different speech situations, our use of language will therefore vary considerably.

NOTE

For the first twelve years of my life, I was a speaker of the Southern German dialect of Swabian; after that my family moved to a city near the Dutch border and I quickly lost the Swabian dialect (since it turned out to be a source of great amusement for my new classmates) and became a speaker of a fairly standard variety of German.

A few years ago, I returned to the city where I was born to attend the funeral of a relative. All family members who still live in the region, including a cousin that I was close to when we were little, continue to speak the dialect. To my amazement, I found that it had become virtually impossible for me to communicate with my relatives – not because I had any problems understanding them, but because I could not find an appropriate speech mode. Speaking my usual standard variety of German made me feel like I was trying to be posh or show off – Ms Ph.D. demonstrating that she's better than the little people. On the other hand, while I could probably have managed a passable imitation of the dialect given a bit of practice, that would have made me feel like a fake, an impostor – or worse, like a bad comedian 'doing the voices'. There was no way out of the dilemma. I simply kept my mouth shut.

Interpersonal and interactive factors such as prestige and solidarity play a crucial role in determining how our language use varies from one context to the next: speakers adapt their speech behaviour according to speech situation and interlocutor. In this context the standard variety is typically used in situations where prestige is important, whereas situations where solidarity is a chief factor often call for the use of more non-standard or vernacular varieties (dialects, sociolects). If you want to come across as someone who is competent, impressive or professional, you will probably use the grammar-book standard. If, on the other hand, you want to be liked, to establish or maintain a personal bond and to signal your solidarity with the person(s) you are talking to, you may use a dialect, slang or an in-group vernacular.

Among bilingual speakers, this also means that in informal situations, there typically is more language mixing, more L2 interference, and more code-switching. In a more formal context, for example in the use of the first language for professional purposes, the speaker will take more care to avoid such phenomena. It is therefore important when we attempt to measure 'amount of L1 use' to make a distinction between formal and informal speech situations, as speakers who frequently use the L1 formally are probably more aware of CLI phenomena than speakers who are habitually comfortable with code-switching, code-mixing and interlanguage.

NOTE

François Grosjean (2001) points out that in investigations of bilingualism, it is crucial to take into account the issue of *language mode*: in some speech situations, one of a bilingual's languages may be very highly activated, while the other one is almost entirely 'switched off'. This is what he refers to as *monolingual mode language use*. In such situations – for example in conversations between two native speakers of German in Germany – very little code-switching can be expected, even though both speakers may also be fluent speakers of English. In *bilingual mode language use*, on the other hand, both languages are highly active, and speakers fluently code-switch from one to the other.

In between these two types is the *intermediate mode*: a situation where there are external cues that may trigger the activation of the language that is not currently being used, but where the speakers resist using this. Such a situation could occur, for example, among migrant members of a German language club in Canada. They all know that the other interlocutors are fluent speakers of English, but since it is the purpose of the club to maintain and cultivate German, code-switching and language mixing will be frowned upon. Similarly, a German language teacher in an English-speaking environment would probably want to resist switching into English, in order to encourage the students to resist also.

It is important to distinguish in what language mode attriters usually speak and hear their L1, as this may impact on the degree of code-switching, code-mixing and cross-linguistic interference which we can find in their data.

In some speech situations, it may be important to a potential attriter to come across as a fully competent native speaker of the L1, while in others, he or she may cultivate a foreign accent or code-switch to underline expatriate identity. The use of the first language may also create an immediate bond between speakers, since it is a marker of an important commonality and can create a feeling of solidarity and even intimacy. Such a situation is described in a letter from a former citizen of Düsseldorf (who, like Gertrud U. and Albert L., escaped Nazi persecution), who says:

(37)
Mit jüdischen Flüchtlingen so wie ich spricht man nur Englisch
weil man ganz zu 'persönlich' vor kommt direkt Deutsch zu sprechen
With Jewish refugees, such as myself, I only use English
as it would seem excessively 'personal' to speak German straight away

We can therefore expect that the manner in which potential attriters use their first language may vary according to the speech situation. This suggests that any investigation of language attrition cannot confine itself to the quantity of the contacts (how often is the L1 spoken?), but has to take into account their quality (with whom and in what settings is it spoken?). In other words, the contacts should be classified and analysed according to speech situations and interlocutors, as the emotional role which each contact plays for the attriter may be more important than the mere frequency with which the contact occurs. The formality of the speech situation is important in this respect, and the use of the L1 for work purposes should be treated as a variable which is kept separate from the use of the L1 with friends or family.

NOTE

Keep in mind that 'amount of L1 use' cannot be independently and objectively measured – you cannot hang a tape recorder around someone's neck and monitor their language behaviour over weeks, months or years. This means that you have to rely on your participants' self-evaluations and assessments, and those may be coloured and distorted by their own values, beliefs and expectations. Among my own data are two participants who are brother and sister. I asked them both which language they used with their only sibling. The man claimed that they always spoke their first language (German) with each other – the woman said they never did.

However, there is another angle to language use and the different degrees of language erosion or change we can find among bilingual speakers. Imagine the case of a married couple whose native language is German, who emigrated together to the United States and continue to use their L1 between themselves, but beyond that have little or no contact with other speakers of that language: all their friends are American. Compare that to the situation of someone who is married to an American and uses only English at home, but who is very active in a German club and belongs to a close-knit group of German friends. If you investigate the language use of these speakers after a few decades, it is quite likely that you will find a substantially higher amount of attrition in the married couple, although they probably use German more often. The explanation for this can be found in what has been called *Social Network Theory*.

This theory is based on the recognition that, in order to describe and explain language behaviour and language change, it may be important to take into account not only particular speech situations, but to get an overall idea of the social contacts which a speaker has, and of how important these are. Social networks attempt to plot 'the sum of

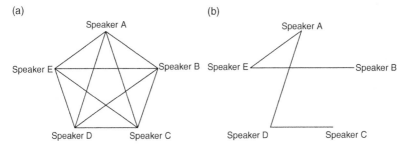

Figure 7.1 (a) Dense and (b) loose sociolinguistic networks

relationships which an individual has contracted with others' (Milroy, 1987: 105). It is the characteristics of these networks – the types and frequencies of contacts that exist between individuals and the position which individuals hold within the network – that will have an important impact on the stability of the language variety which is used by that group of speakers.

Social Networks are typically described on two levels: *density* and *multiplexity*. The network of a particular person is *dense* when all members of the network know each other (e.g. within a family), and *loose* when person A knows person B and person C, but these two do not know each other (see Figure 7.1). *Multiplexity* refers to the extent of different contacts network members have with each other. Members of a multiplex network might, for example, be cousins, neighbours, colleagues and friends at the same time, while in a less multiplex network, members know each other in one 'function' only. The more dense and multiplex a particular network, the more stable (i.e. resistant to change) the variety used within it will typically be. Such a network is referred to as *close-knit*. In looser networks, on the other hand, changes are adopted more easily and spread more quickly (Milroy, 1987).

Applying this framework to multilingual settings, where it is not only a gradient of the dialects of one language that will be used in different speech situations, but where the network includes speakers of different languages, is complex. Migrant communities can vary dramatically as to the density and multiplexity of their L1 network. In the present-day setting of Urban Multilingualism, there are a number of migrant populations – e.g. Chinese in some Northern American cities or Turks in some European countries – where the network is very close-knit and where there are few contacts outside their own speech community. In such networks, the L1 will probably be maintained with relatively little influence from L2, due to the strength of the contacts and also through group pressure to keep the language 'uncorrupted'.

On the other hand, there are speech communities whose members tend to blend into the host community and shift to the host language relatively fast. The Dutch are typically considered an example of this, to the degree that they have been labelled 'invisible migrants' (Hulsen, de Bot and Weltens, 2002: 28). Dutch migrants will often not even teach their own first language to their children, but use the language of the environment as the family language from the start. In such a setting, there will typically be few L1 contacts, and those will tend to be one-dimensional as opposed to multiplex (friends back at home, a work colleague etc.), which in theory will render the L1 more vulnerable to change under the influence of L2.

A German migrant in Canada, whose husband is also German, describes this process of language mixing and language change:

(38)
Wir haben die Sprachen sehr viel durcheinander gekriegt.
Wenn uns geschwind ein Wort gefehlt hat,
dann haben wir eins in Englisch eingesetzt,
und das ist eigentlich nicht schön.
Das hat dann das Resultat von einer typischen Immigrantensprache, furchtbar.
We did mix up the languages a lot.
Whenever we couldn't quickly think of a word
we'd put in an English one,
and that's not really very nice.
It leads to this typical immigrant language, ghastly.

Since the social pressure not to code-switch or to avoid L2 interference will be much lower in such informal settings, these types of contact may even accelerate language attrition in what Grosjean and Py (1991) referred to as a vicious circle: migrants who have very limited contacts with other speakers of their first language, such as the hypothetical German couple mentioned earlier, having lived in emigration for decades, may gradually become insecure about their L1 proficiency. If they are not certain what is 'correct' any more, they may rely more heavily on data in the input to augment their own intuitions. But if the language they are exposed to also contains non-targetlike constructions, these may not only be accepted as correct but also integrated into the repertoire of the other speaker and used again, thereby in turn reinforcing the mixed system of the other interlocutor.

If, on the other hand, the network consists of a larger number of people, all of whom have frequent contacts with each other, that may provide a safeguard against these kinds of changes – particularly in a setting such as a language club whose members may have a highly prescriptive attitude towards keeping the language 'intact' and frown upon 'sloppy' language use and code-switching.

These considerations suggest that Social Network Theory might provide a valuable handle on investigations and quantifications of the puzzling factor of interactive L1 use for language attrition. So far, only one study has confirmed this assumption in an experimental setting: in the case of Dutch migrants in New Zealand, the role of Social Networks for language maintenance and attrition was demonstrated by Hulsen (2000), who found that those speakers who had more L1 contacts, particularly in their primary network (those contacts who are most important in everyday life), had fewer word-finding difficulties than those migrants who used the L1 mainly with speakers who played a less important role in daily interactions.

TIP

Investigations into the role of L1 use for language attrition should make sure that they take into account not only how often a potential attriter uses the language, but also the type of situation (formal or informal), the number of people the language is spoken with, and the characteristics of the L1 social network. Quality may in this case be more important than quantity.

NON-INTERACTIVE EXPOSURE: BOOKS AND THE MEDIA

When questioned about how often he still spoke German, Albert L. replied that 'obviously and naturally' he used English almost exclusively in daily life. However, he pointed out, he very much enjoyed reading German newspapers and watching German TV – adding with a hint of nostalgia 'es ist ja eben doch immer noch meine alte "Muttersprache"' [when all is said and done, German still remains my true 'mother tongue']. Like many other migrants, Albert L. considers exposure to printed and audiovisual media not only a way of keeping up some links with his home country and culture, but also an important means of maintaining his L1. This may indeed be the case, particularly in situations such as the one pointed out above where small or loosely knit L1 networks lead to linguistic insecurity. After all, this kind of input can probably be considered as comparatively reliable in terms of 'correctness', and may help a speaker maintain a certain level of competence.

The impact of passive exposure on language maintenance may even be more straightforward than that of interactive language use, since in this case, the language is used largely for communicative purposes and much less as a marker of symbolic identity. However, the question to what degree (largely receptive) *input* is enough to maintain a language system, or whether more productive *output* and *interaction* are also needed has yet to be resolved. In investigations of second language acquisition, this question is a hotly debated topic. According to the so-called Input Hypothesis

> humans acquire language in only one way – by understanding messages, or by receiving 'comprehensible input' . . . We move from *i*, our current level, to *i* + *1*, the next level . . . by understanding input containing *i* + *1* (Krashen, 1985: 2).

This statement is probably one of the most controversial ones in SLA research, and the question to what degree interactive language use facilitates acquisition more than passive exposure (or is even indispensable to it) is treated at book length by, among others, Carroll (2001), Ellis (1999) and Gass (1997).

With respect to attrition, the question should then be whether non-interactive 'comprehensible input' can prevent a potential language attriter from moving from his or her current level *i* to *i* – *1*. An important finding in this respect is the fact that more advanced language learners are more able to profit from comprehensible input and learn through context (Cummins, 1979; Neuman and Koskinen, 1992). Since the proficiency of L1 attriters, particularly in the early stages of the attritional process, is typically very advanced by SLA standards, this might suggest that they can profit more from this kind of input than second language learners.

However, at present there is not a single investigation on language attrition which takes this factor into account. Methodologically, to investigate the effect of exposure to printed, audiovisual or electronic media on language attrition would be quite a challenge, since their accessibility has changed so dramatically over the past decades. Today, most households have access to the internet, where newspapers, television and radio broadcasts and other texts in most languages can be accessed cheaply or for free, and those who wish to can receive TV and radio programmes from their home countries via a satellite dish. This is quite a contrast to the situation which migrants encountered fifty years ago, when getting hold of books or newspapers from home was a difficult and expensive undertaking. It would not be easy to determine in what way and to what degree this change has interacted with attritional processes which typically take decades.

NOTE

In the project which I refer to here as Schmid (2007), I looked at German speakers in Canada and in the Netherlands. In Canada, there was one TV channel broadcasting a German programme once a week for half an hour, while in the Netherlands many German TV channels are widely available through regular cable services (and have been for a long time). Similarly, German newspapers, journals, books and other media can be bought at every newsstand in the Netherlands, but were often difficult to get hold of in Canada. However, a comparison between the two groups, or between individuals who said that they watched a lot of German TV or read a great deal in German, did not reveal substantial differences. This type of input may therefore be less important than one might think.

THE LANGUAGE OF THOUGHT AND EMOTION

We use language not only to exchange information, but also to communicate in ways which are predominantly (or exclusively) expressive as opposed to representational or informative, for example when we talk to babies and animals, or when we swear. We also use language for a range of other inner functions, such as thinking, praying, counting or doing maths, dreaming, writing a diary, memoirs or shopping lists, and so on. The way in which bilinguals deploy their languages in these situations is complex.

NOTE

Above, I asked you to think back to how you used language over the past 24 hours. It is highly likely that, in thinking back, you only remembered those contexts where you spoke to another person. But what did you do when you spilled your coffee on your computer keyboard? What language did you use when you calculated your share of the bill after you'd had a drink with some friends after work?

When the constraint to be understood by interlocutors is lifted, bilinguals tend to avail themselves relatively freely of the languages at their disposal. As a native speaker of German, living in the Netherlands, working in an English department and being married to a native English speaker, I am frequently asked 'What language do you think in?'

In partial answer, I usually produce one of the crumpled shopping lists which live (and appear to multiply) in my pockets, and which tend to consist, more or less at random, of items in all three languages. There seems to be little or no consistency across lists: today *milk* may appear as Dutch 'melk', tomorrow as German 'Milch' (although I have noticed a tendency to use whichever language offers the shortest word for a particular item).

Different explanations have been proposed for which language bilinguals select in thinking or subvocalizing thought ('now where did I put that?'), and often this selection is ascribed to 'the person, the topic, or the situation being thought about' (Grosjean, 1982: 276). The same goes for language 'choice' in dreams. A large-scale quantitative investigation of Spanish–English bilinguals (Vaid and Menon, 2000) suggests that different inner functions of language are influenced by different factors: in this study, the best predictor of the language of thinking to oneself was the amount of L2 exposure, while speakers reported dreaming mostly in the language which they rated as their dominant one.

On the other hand, sometimes a particular language may be linked intrinsically with one's own experience of a particular situation: it has, for example, been reported that bilinguals tend to use the language for mental calculation in which they received instruction in this at school (Grosjean, 1982: 275; Vaid and Menon, 2000).[1] The language of religion and praying also often appears to be the one in which the speaker was first exposed to these concepts.

A particular language may thus be very deeply linked with certain functions because of the linguistic context of the first exposure, and this may become evident where emotional functions are concerned. For many bilinguals, the language which was predominantly spoken in their early childhood remains the language most appropriate to deeply emotional situations. A letter from another German-Jewish refugee contains the statement: 'the more emotional the topic of conversation, the more strongly biased I am to use German.'

This link between emotionality and language choice has been demonstrated by Aneta Pavlenko and Jean-Marc Dewaele in a large-scale web-based investigation of (among other things) emotionally laden language use among multilinguals (e.g. Dewaele, 2004a, 2004b; Pavlenko, 2005). This study confirmed the impression that for many speakers terms such as swear and taboo words and expressions of love appear to carry the most emotional weight in their first language (Dewaele, 2004a, 2006). One of their informants very succinctly expresses the commonly held perception that swearing in your L2 is 'less bad': 'I prefer to express anger in my L2 . . . because I do not hear the weight of my words so everything comes out quite easily' (cit. after Dewaele, 2004a: 95), while an L1 speaker of Finnish states: 'If I would happen to hit myself with a hammer the words coming out of my mouth would definitely be in Finnish' (cit. after Dewaele, 2004a: 94f.). All in all, many multilinguals seem to find their first language more appropriately expresses strong emotions, irrespective of which language they use most in daily life.

How deeply felt this emotional link can be is evident in the case of Gertrud U. In stark contrast to the fond nostalgia which Albert L. expresses for his native German, she generally wants no part of it any longer. Her first experience of hearing her L1 spoken again, when she returned to Germany after the war to work for the Allied Armed Forces, was traumatic:

(39)
aber das war das erste Mal, daß ich ähm Deutsche sah
die waren ähm # die arbeiteten auf dem Dock
und da- und ich hörte sie sprechen Deutsch
und ich dachte
ich kann das nicht tun
ich kann nicht dort zurückgehen
es ist zu schwer für mich
but that was the first time that I ehm saw Germans
they were ehm # they were working in the dock
and then- and I heard them speaking German
and I thought
I cannot do this
I cannot go back there
it is too difficult for me

With the encouragement of her commanding officer, she eventually managed to overcome her feeling of panic, but her emotional detachment from the German language remained with her all her life. With one exception: when she became a mother, and later a grandmother, talking and singing to the infants in German came naturally and effortlessly to her:

(40)
I sing and talk to my grandchildren in German when they were/are very small babies, just like I did to my children (the only thing that will immediately stop my 11 month old twins from crying is when I sing 'Schlaf Kindchen schlaf' [a well-known German lullaby]). The fact that I naturally, without conscious effort, sing and talk in German to my babies, is probably indicative of long-buried memories of my parents and my own childhood.

What is suggested by such self-reports is that internal functions of language are probably not invariably associated with one language system, but can change with language habits and language learning or attrition. Speakers who report that their first language is no longer their 'best' or dominant one typically also report an increased use of the second language for all of the functions named above (Dewaele, 2004b). One could imagine that in the process of the attrition of a first language, one internal function after the other may be 'stripped away' and move over to the L2, as was the case for Gertrud U., who eventually came to associate the use of the L1 only with her 'long buried' earliest and most primal experiences.

We may therefore expect the process of L1 attrition to be accompanied by an overall reduction of the use of the L1 for internal speech. The difference between this type of L1 use and the two types discussed above (interactive and receptive L1 use) is probably that, while the latter are *input* which can actively help to prevent attrition, a reduction in internal L1 use is probably merely *indicative* of the attritional process, an outcome of the reduced accessibility of L1 words and structures. This factor may therefore possibly serve as a yardstick of the degree of attrition an individual has undergone, but not as a predictor variable which will in itself influence the attritional process.

TIP

In assessing the impact of L1 exposure and use on L1 attrition, it may be wise to distinguish the following three types:

• L1 use where there is *both* input and output (interactive L1 use)
• L1 use where there is *only* input (reading, watching TV)
• L1 use where there is *only* output (inner language)

CONCLUSION

In some way or other, we use language virtually every waking moment, and even some of the time when we are asleep. The proportion of this linguistic activity which is actual conversation is surprisingly small: apparently we only talk to other people for about half an hour a day on average (Cook, 1998). Other types of language 'use' such as passive exposure and internal language therefore probably outweigh the interactive use at least quantitatively. However, their role for L1 maintenance may be less important than types of use which imply both input and output. This should be considered very carefully before we can test the impact of different types of L1 use on the language attrition process.

Findings from L2 acquisition suggest that there may be a further factor which interacts in very important ways with the amount of exposure of whichever type a particular speaker or learner has with a given language. There is a dreadful old joke of the light-bulb genre:

Q: How many therapists does it take to change a light bulb?
A: Only one, but the light bulb really has to *want* to change.

In a similar vein, the answer to the question 'How much exposure does a speaker need in order to learn a language (or in order not to forget a language)?' might be that the amount of exposure may not be all that important, as long as the speaker *wants* to learn or to maintain it. This factor has been termed the *affective filter*: when someone has little motivation to learn a language or feels anxious about it, that person puts up a 'filter' which does not allow the comprehensible input to pass through and prevents language acquisition from occurring (Krashen, 1985: 3). It is highly likely that a similar emotional process applies to language attrition. The opportunity to use a language, the willingness to do so and the attitudes and emotions which a speaker has towards this language are interacting variables in the language attrition process.

8 Attitudes and identities

> In what way does the attitude a speaker has towards his or her L1 impact on language attrition? In this chapter, we will consider issues of identity and emotional affiliation, and how these factors shape and constrain the attritional process.

I mentioned above that migration is invariably a life-changing, and often a traumatic experience. Whatever the situation and circumstances which led to the start of life in a new country might have been, they will interact with the migrant's personality to bring about a particular outlook and a change in identity. A new start is always an opportunity to redefine oneself, although the range of options may be wider in some contexts than in others.

One limitation that almost all migrants experience to some degree is that migration makes you a foreigner, that is to say, an outsider. How a person responds to that, whether she wants to shed that status as quickly as possible and 'blend in', or whether the feeling of difference is accepted and embraced, can play an important role towards predicting how successful the acquisition of the new language will be. These factors can be equally important in predicting success or failure in language maintenance.

MIGRATION, IDENTITY AND BILINGUAL DEVELOPMENT

The circumstances of migration are as diverse and manifold as there are migrants. No two instances of migration will be the same – nor will the role of language. Language is one of the most important markers of identity which human beings have at their disposal. It is through language that we signal to others which group we belong to, that we create solidarity and distance.

The role of second language acquisition for the construction of identity, particularly among migrants, has received much attention in recent decades. The wish to belong to a certain group is often among the most important predictors of success in L2 acquisition: a new migrant to the Netherlands who has a deeply felt love and admiration for Dutch society, and a desire to be as Dutch as possible, will probably eventually become better at speaking Dutch than someone who is perfectly comfortable with their present identity, thinks the Netherlands is a quaint little country filled with tulips, high tech and soft drugs, but has to learn some Dutch because they have to spend a couple of years in Rotterdam for their work.

The question of what happens to the first language of a bilingual speaker or a migrant is the other side of this coin, and we might expect that those factors which influence eventual success in foreign language learning may also impact on first language maintenance or attrition. The assumption would then be that a migrant who has a strong motivation to integrate into the host society will experience more attrition than someone who is comfortable with remaining a foreigner and something of an outsider – all other things being equal. All other things, however, are seldom equal: both in language acquisition and in language attrition, attitudes can interact with other factors in ways which are complex and difficult to predict.

Throughout this book, our companions have been two native speakers of German who had been living in an English-speaking environment for almost sixty years. Both were thirteen years old when they escaped the Nazi terror, and neither used German regularly in their daily lives. And yet it was clear that, while Albert L. would probably be recognized as a native German in virtually any encounter with other Germans, Gertrud U. might more likely be perceived to be a native American with a somewhat limited L2 proficiency in German.

NOTE

I asked Gertrud U. and Albert L. how they themselves felt about German. Albert L. remarked that it had remained his mother tongue to this day. Gertrud U., on the other hand, left no room for doubt: 'America is my country, and English is my language', she stated categorically.

These two speakers are quite extreme cases. However, any investigation of attrited populations will find a large range of proficiency, and conclude that for some speakers the attritional process has been much more dramatic than for others. As the quote at the beginning of this section (p. 69) illustrates, this difference is usually ascribed to 'personal circumstances'. That seems a reasonable assumption, but it is also quite vague. What 'personal circumstances' are we talking about? And how can we investigate them? The case of our two German speakers illustrates the fact that more has to be taken into account than the purely 'objective' recorded facts. We need to try and understand the practical and emotional circumstances which surrounded the migration and the time spent in the new country if we want to understand the linguistic outcomes of the attritional process.

ATTITUDE AND MOTIVATION

> When we were young we found it very offensive (*'abstossend'* ['repulsive', MSS] sounds better) to speak or even listen to German. (Letter from Charlotte G.)

The assumption that there may be a link between language attrition and issues of attitude and identity is an extension of decades of research on the role of attitudes, motivation and emotions for the development of bilingualism. It has been established that these factors are indeed important in predicting individual success for ultimate attainment in second or foreign language learning (in interaction with other factors, such as intelligence and language aptitude). However, the overwhelming majority of research has focused on the development of the second language, and very little work has been done on the implications for the deterioration or attrition of the first.

There are two important methodological problems that such research faces. The first one is that language attrition is a process which may fluctuate over time, and take years to leave a lasting impact on the linguistic system. What will determine the degree of attrition is probably the attitude a speaker has *at the moment of emigration*. In most investigations of L1 attrition, the first encounter a speaker has with the researcher comes decades later. Attitudes and identities, however, are dynamic, socially constructed and do not remain constant across the course of a person's life. 'Absence makes the heart grow fonder', and a migrant who initially wanted to shed her former identity and blend into the new society might, at a later stage (for example upon retirement) find herself thinking of her native country with nostalgia or even homesickness. The reverse, of course, may also be true – an initially reluctant migrant may come to accept and love her new surroundings, and the memories of 'home' may become increasingly distant or meaningless.

These changes are unpredictable, and they need not be unidirectional: the same person could experience both of these changes of heart in different periods of her life. To adequately capture the dynamic interaction of attitude and attrition, the process would have to be monitored longitudinally, and over decades.

Secondly, attitudes are not entities which are observable in themselves, they have to be *elicited* through expression. This makes them a tricky subject of investigation, as people's statements tend to reflect their prescriptively held beliefs – what they think they should feel or say – more than the actual ones (Baker, 1992: 15; Ellis, 1994: 20). Most speakers will feel somewhat constrained in clearly expressing their feelings, for fear of saying something that might be deemed inappropriate, or of offending the investigator (who in most instances will be a native speaker of the L1 in question). Even Gertrud U. apparently feels apologetic:

(41)
und dann waren wir in Berlin #
und ähm # ich hatte # ich *really I* da da hab ich wirklich die Deutschen sehr gehaßt #
ahm ah es war sehr schwer für mich auch
mi- mit denen ich wollte gar nichts mit denen zu tun haben.
Aber das ist ähm # vielleicht verständlich.
and then we were in Berlin #
and ahm # I had # I really I then then I really hated the Germans very much, #
ahm ah it was very difficult for me and
wi- with them I didn't want to have anything to do with them.
But that is ahm # perhaps understandable.

Both of these issues may be less problematic in the investigation of attitudes for SLA than for L1 attrition: in this setting there is usually less of a time-lag and the opinions a learner holds towards their second language are often a less intimate and therefore less sensitive issue than those held towards the language of early childhood (particularly in instructed second language learning).

IDENTITY AND IDENTIFICATION

Migrants who enter a new society are often viewed as outsiders by the mainstream population: they may have different habits, they may look different, they may speak a different language – they do not belong to 'our' group. The classification of ourselves and others into in-groups and out-groups is one of the most basic mechanisms in human interaction and social identity: group membership is how we define ourselves. In some instances, we can choose the groups which we want to belong to, and we will probably pick those which have characteristics that we evaluate positively, because belonging to such a group will have a positive impact on our self-esteem. In other instances, however, group membership is externally ascribed, and this process can present a great threat to personal identity (e.g. Tajfel, 1982).

NOTE

The case of German Jews under the Nazi regime is one of the most extreme cases of externally ascribed identity. Before 1933, 'being German' was a far more important aspect of personal identity for many than 'being Jewish'. Most families, particularly in the upper middle classes, had long since abandoned all Jewish beliefs, rituals and traditions, celebrating Christmas instead of Hanukkah and Easter instead of Passover. Jack Sanders, who emigrated in 1938, sums it up: 'I always felt I was a German. It was Hitler who taught me I was a Jew.' Similarly, a migrant may think that she is a scientist, a mother, a marathon runner, a feminist – but upon her arrival in her new country, she will discover that she has suddenly become a Turk, and that this is the most salient feature that those around her will perceive in her.

When we consign those around us to out-groups, we apply stereotypes. We see the groups that we do not belong to as relatively homogeneous, while we assume that our own group is stratified, that it contains people who have far more features which make them different than features which make them alike. In other groups, we tend to perceive (or imagine) mainly those features which the group members have in common. This mechanism is at the heart of phenomena such as racism, xenophobia and prejudicing in general, and it can be threatening or damaging to the self-image of those who are thus stereotyped.

The way in which groups – particularly ethnic groups – are stereo-typed by the majority depends on a number of factor groups:

- Firstly, different ethnicities are assigned different prestige levels. The more different the minority is from the majority – culturally, economically and in their physical appearance – the more they will typically be downgraded.
- Secondly, demographic factors are of importance: how big is the overall size of a particular population of migrants? Do they form close-knit enclaves, or are they widespread throughout the over-all community? Is there considerable exogamy (marriage outside the ethnic group), or do members of the ethnic community

prefer intermarriage? Is the birth rate higher (or lower) than in the host population?

- Thirdly, it is important to take into account whether particular communities of migrants have institutional support in the form of government representation, newspapers or radio/TV stations, lobby groups and so on.

Together, these factors constitute what has been referred to as the *Ethnolinguistic Vitality* (EV) of a particular ethnic community. Groups with low EV tend to blend into the host society fairly quickly, giving up their cultural habits as well as their language; while ethnolinguistic groups with a high EV index can remain stable for generations (Giles, Bourhis and Taylor, 1977).

ATTITUDES, IDENTITY AND LANGUAGE ATTRITION

Since factors such as attitude, motivation and identity have a demonstrable impact on the development of a second language, language attrition research has long been fascinated with the idea that the converse might also be true: if wanting to learn something (or wanting to be part of a community of speakers) can help with acquisition, can wanting to forget something (or wanting to no longer be part of a speech community) accelerate attrition? The psychological process of suppressing unwanted or traumatic memories is well known, but can it also apply with respect to a linguistic system; that is, knowledge that is represented in quite a different way?

NOTE

Remember that research into the impact of attitudes on language attrition is very difficult for the following reasons:

1. Attitudes cannot be directly observed, so research has to rely on self-reports which may be unreliable
2. Attitudes are subject to change across the lifespan

One of the first larger studies that attempted to investigate this phenomenon was Margit Waas' investigation on the L1 attrition of German in Australia (Waas, 1996), which applied a two-way classification of identity along two criteria: residential status ('permanent resident' vs 'naturalized citizen') and 'ethnic affiliation', measured by systematic exposure to German in daily life. This classification did not yield significant results when correlated with performance on a linguistic test. A more rigorous framework of ethnic identity is applied in Yağmur (1997) and Hulsen (2000) who use Ethnolinguistic Vitality Theory (EVT) in their respective investigations of Turkish in Australia and Dutch in New Zealand. Here, too, no significant impact of the predictor variables of subjective EV could be established.

The findings from these three studies illustrate that socio- and ethnolinguistic frameworks which rely on subjects' self-reports about their use of and attitude towards their L1 may not be adequate tools for the prediction of the linguistic aspects of language attrition: subjective evaluation at the current point in time cannot establish a link between attrition and concepts such as identity. This may conceivably be attributable to the fact that people's identities, affiliations and self-concepts do not remain stable across their lifespan (Breakwell, 1986: 18). Obviously, if a connection between attitudes or identities and attrition is to be found, it would have to be looked for in the moment of emigration, i.e. at the possible onset of attrition.

Furthermore, EVT is highly problematic when applied to only one group of migrants: it was pointed out above that the EV of any particular ethnic minority is dependent largely on group factors, which will be more or less stable for all group members. If we want to understand the extent to which identity and EV determine language maintenance and attrition, different groups of migrants in a similar setting will have to be compared. An attempt to conduct such an investigation can be found in the study which comprises the two speakers, Gertrud U. and Albert L., with whom you are familiar by now.

The issue of attitude and identity is probably what is at the root of the difference between the L1 proficiency of Gertrud U. and Albert L. We have seen that, in most important aspects, these speakers are quite similar with respect to the amount of L1 input they have. Neither of them has close friends or family members with whom they speak German on a regular basis, and apparently, this has been the case ever since their emigration. However, on the rare occasions Albert L. has to use his German, this is an activity which he enjoys. Gertrud U., on the other hand, indicates that for a long time she has had strongly negative feelings associated with the German language.

NOTE

It is interesting to see that Gertrud U.'s negative feelings appear to have been triggered by exposure to the language itself, not by the mere concept or memory of Germany: when she was presented with the opportunity, in 1945, to go to Germany and work there, she was open to this idea in the abstract. It was only when she reached the border and actually heard German spoken again for the first time in years that she felt panic and revulsion, and during the two years she spent in Berlin she avoided contact with German speakers as far as possible.

A superficial analysis may find it hard to account for such different attitudes among two speakers who apparently had quite similar experiences. Gertrud U. and Albert L. both escaped from Germany without their parents. Groups of concerned citizens, mainly in the UK and the US, were responsible for these escape routes for children, as emigration was becoming difficult for German Jews (both because of the ferocious taxes and fines imposed by the Nazi government and because other countries considered the stream of Jewish refugees increasingly unwelcome). Initially, these were mainly individual efforts, but after the pogrom in 1938, when the nature of the threat could no longer be ignored, a number of international organizations achieved the rescue of some 10,000 children up to the outbreak of World War II in September 1939.[1]

Upon arrival in England, Gertrud U. was passed from one reluctant foster family to the next, and Albert L. was sent to a boarding school. It is hard to imagine how devastating these experiences must have been, for both of them. Both found themselves, at age 13, alone, in a country where they did not speak the language. Both were placed in the care of foster families and boarding schools where they felt unwelcome and unwanted. Both must have felt lost, and terrified. And after the war had broken out, their situation worsened in a terrible historical irony: having been deprived of their German citizenship and identity by the Nazis, they were now considered dangerous enemies by the English – because they were German. As a male, Albert L. was confined to an internment camp on the Isle of Man, while Gertrud U. was made to feel keenly that the people around her resented her – paradoxically both because she was German and because her caregivers feared that, in the case of a German invasion, there might be repercussions for those who had given shelter to a Jew.

It is hardly surprising that Gertrud U., like many other German Jews who suffered similar traumata, took the deliberate and conscious decision that she wanted nothing to do with Germany, the Germans, or the German language any more. On the other hand, Albert L. also represents a large group of German Jews who, after the war, felt no need to disassociate themselves from their German origins. To

some degree, such different reactions are, of course, individually conditioned: one person responds differently to the same set of circumstances than another. However, in the case of Gertrud U. and Albert
L. there is one important difference which may go some way towards
explaining why these two young refugees took such different paths:
Albert L. emigrated in 1934, at a relatively early stage of the Nazi
regime, while Gertrud U. only just made it out of Germany before
the outbreak of World War II, in 1939.

The events which took place in the years between the departure
of Albert L. and that of Gertrud U. must have indelibly stamped all
those who experienced them, but were particularly traumatic for
young children. Among these events was the passing of the laws of
Nuremberg on 1 September 1935. These laws for the first time provided
a definition of people of 'German or related blood' (i.e. 'Aryans') and
those of 'foreign blood', and thereby created a legal basis for all the
segregation measurements that were to follow.

NOTE

It is difficult to imagine to what extent German-Jewish children must
have been impressed by this message that they were 'different' and
'inferior' and by the vague and unsettling image that this was
something that 'ran in their blood'. Ilse M., another refugee from
Düsseldorf, told me how she once begged her uncle, a doctor, to put a
drop of her blood under the microscope and show her how it was
different from other people's.

Albert L., having left Germany early on, had no similar first-hand
experience of being thus shunted to the fringes of society or of having
the integrity of his blood thrown into question. Neither did he experience the subsequent anti-Semitic laws and local regulations which
were being passed almost on a daily basis and were designed to deprive
German Jews of their property and their dignity (Walk, 1981). Gertrud U.
witnessed all these events. She could no longer attend the public school
and had to go to a Jewish school. She was told by her parents that she
should never talk to anyone in public, not even to members of her own
family, for fear of being overheard. On the night of 9 November 1938,
her home – like those of thousands of German Jews – was invaded and
destroyed by the SS, and her father and grandfather were arrested and
taken to the concentration camp Buchenwald.

Many refugees who had suffered through these and similar experiences renounced their German identity. As in the case of Gertrud U.,

that decision often implied a break with the language: 'When the war broke out, I vowed I would not speak, write nor read German ever again, another former citizen of Düsseldorf wrote to me. Others who, like Albert L., had been lucky enough to leave the country at an earlier stage, generally did not feel the need for such a radical break. In a nutshell, for earlier emigrants, to be German still meant retaining a proud cultural tradition and heritage, comprising thinkers and artists such as Bach, Goethe and Heine, as part of their birthright – while for later refugees who had felt their personal identity, their physical integrity and their life threatened, Germany symbolized the perpetrators of genocide and terror to an extent that eradicated all positive connotations.

Decades later, the results of this split were clearly manifest in language proficiency: like Albert L., many German Jews who left Germany in the early stages of the Nazi regime were able to preserve an astonishing level of L1 proficiency even sixty years later. On the other hand, speakers like Gertrud U., who did not want to be German any longer, had acquired all the characteristics of an L2 speaker and were only able to express themselves in German with great difficulty (Schmid, 2002).

CONCLUSION

There appear to be a number of factors which will impact in different ways on the process of L1 attrition. Frequent use (interactive or receptive) of a particular language may help to maintain the native language system intact, and so may a positive attitude towards the language or the speech community. On the other hand, none of these factors may be enough in themselves, and not all exposure to the language may be helpful. A small, loose-knit L1 social network may even have a detrimental effect and accelerate language change. Most importantly, however, the opportunity to use a language and the willingness to do so are factors which interact in complex ways to determine the process of language attrition. As yet, our understanding of this interaction is quite limited.

PART III
Conducting research on language attrition – preliminary considerations

In Part I of this book, you were introduced to the phenomenon of language attrition. Chapters 3–5 describe how attrition can manifest itself in a first language – in what way the lexical, grammatical, phonological and pragmatic repertoire of a speaker may be affected. In Part II, an overview was given of the extralinguistic individual, social and attitudinal factors which may influence this process. The question now is how to translate this theoretical knowledge into practical research, how to design and set up a study, how to carry it out, and how to classify, analyse and interpret your data. Part III summarizes the issues that you need to consider when you conduct your own investigation of language attrition.

PRELIMINARY CONSIDERATIONS

> Alice . . . went on: 'Would you tell me, please, which way I ought to go from here?'
> 'That depends a good deal on where you want to get to,' said the Cat.
> 'I don't much care where' said Alice.
> 'Then it doesn't matter which way you go,' said the Cat.
> '– so long as I get *somewhere*,' Alice added as an explanation.
> 'Oh, you're sure to do that,' said the Cat, 'if you only walk long enough.' (Lewis Carroll, *Alice's Adventures in Wonderland*)

This exchange between Alice and the Cheshire Cat is a good illustration of the way in which research on language attrition has often been approached. In many studies no explicit aim or target of the investigation was set beforehand, nor were the means of getting to this target clearly specified. That is understandable to some degree: if you are planning to conduct your own study, you will be champing at the bit to go out there and collect your data – and you may think that you are bound to get *somewhere* if you only walk long enough. However, formulating your questions, hypotheses and requirements precisely at this stage will save you major headaches later, and probably make your findings easier to interpret and the answers more reliable.

In order to formulate testable research questions and hypotheses you will need to be maximally specific about these issues, and get the best possible advice on all of them. The following chapters will help you address some of these preliminaries.

9 The test populations: participant characteristics and acquisition

To test attrition, you need attriters, and you usually also need 'controls', speakers who are similar to the attriters in terms of age, gender etc. but still live in the country where their L1 is spoken. How do you set about finding groups of such speakers? What do you need to keep in mind when you select them? This chapter will acquaint you with some of these considerations.

The first question you have to ask is what your experimental population is going to look like. Try to formulate as clearly as possible the subject characteristics that you are looking for. As you saw in Part II, a daunting number of external factors can impact on the process of language attrition, and these may often interact in unexpected or unpredictable ways. Such characteristics of the participants in an experiment, which may influence the outcome variables but which the researcher cannot or does not attempt to manipulate (for example, we cannot make a subject older or younger than she is, nor can we change how often she has spoken her first language or how long ago she emigrated), are called *independent variables* or *predictors*.

Be thorough

The fact that attrition is conditioned by so many predictors confronts the researcher with the dilemma of which factors to include in the research design, and which to exclude through controlling them. It is impossible to investigate everything. How many factors you can investigate depends largely on the size of your sample.

TIP

When you plan your investigation, a good rule of thumb is that you should have at least fifteen subjects for each of the external criteria which you want to investigate. If you want to look at the impact of age at emigration, length of residence, the use of the first language for professional purposes, and the attitude towards that language, that gives you four factors (assuming you can manage to reduce the complex factor of 'attitude' to just one variable), and so your *experimental group*[1] should contain at least sixty speakers. You will then also need a *control group* or *reference group* of the same size. You can see how quickly a growing number of predictors inflates the number of subjects you need.

It is therefore of vital importance that you try to eliminate any impact of those predictors which you do not want to investigate. That is, there should be *as little variation as possible* along those factors in your sample. For example, if you do not intend to make the age at emigration a part of your research question, you should try to ensure that all subjects had a certain minimum age when they emigrated. Likewise, if you are not concerned with the impact of the frequency of use of the L1, it would be wise to try and find subjects who speak it equally frequently or rarely.

On the other hand, the predictors which you do want to investigate should, if possible, be *evenly distributed* in your data. If you intend to investigate the impact of length of residence, different emigration spans should be equally represented among your subjects: it would not be good to have three subjects who have a length of residence of less than five years and forty-seven who emigrated more than four decades ago.

And thirdly, for those factors on which you cannot contrast the experimental and the control group, you should strive to *match* them as evenly as possible: factors such as age, educational level and sex should be represented equally in both groups, as should the regions of their origin (in order to achieve the same distribution of dialects). Again, the ideal way is to keep these factors constant – but you will be hard pressed to find an attriting population that is composed entirely of (for example) 45–50-year-old university-educated females. The next best way to achieve matching is to establish a control group where each of your experimental subjects is matched, one to one, with a control group subject of (more or less) the same age, the same educational level, the same dialect and the same sex.

BASELINE REQUIREMENTS

On the basis of what, to date, is known about language attrition, there are a number of baseline requirements which every study should meet with respect to the participants that are selected:

- *Age at onset*: if you do not want to investigate the impact of this factor, your study should not include participants who were younger than 17 years at the moment of migration. This threshold should ensure that this variable will not have a confounding effect on your data.

  If you do intend to study this predictor, keep in mind that the impact of pre-puberty vs post-puberty migration appears to have a radical impact on the attritional process (see above) but is very much under-researched to date. Any investigation of Critical Period effects in language attrition would therefore be well advised to use age of onset as the only predictor variable, keeping all other external factors constant (as far as possible).

- *Length of residence*: many studies have taken the cautious option of establishing a minimum length of residence of ten or fifteen years, as it seems unclear to date how attrition progresses in the first ten years or so after migration. If you are looking for relatively stable effects which are not the outcome of a highly active development of an L2, it may be wise to follow this lead. Again, if you are interested in the development over the first ten years, you should probably make this your priority and try to control other factors.

- *Age*: first of all, it is important to keep in mind that age will almost invariably correlate with length of residence in your population – the longer people have lived in migration, the older they get. Because of this correlation, you cannot use both factors – length of residence *and* age – as predictors in the same study, and any effect that you find with respect to one you should always also consider a possible outcome of the other. Secondly, because many tasks become less efficient as people grow older, and because of the impact of bilingualism on cognitive ageing, it is probably wise not to investigate speakers who are older than 65. That, however, is often difficult in attrition studies.

- *Linguistic habits prior to migration*: here it is of vital importance that all of your speakers (attriters and controls) should have a comparable background. Most studies of language attrition to date investigate speakers who were predominantly monolingual until their emigration. They may have had some instruction in other languages, but did not use those languages regularly in their daily lives. However, for some populations of migrants, this is not possible. For example, if you want to investigate migrants from virtually any country on the African continent, it will be impossible to find participants who were not exposed to at least two (and often five or more) languages from birth or early childhood. Conducting research on speakers with such a background necessitates extremely careful deliberation and is probably far more complex and difficult than investigating boringly monolingual Europeans (the fact that many African languages do not have a written tradition is only one of the complicating factors here). But then, of course, the most difficult tasks are also often the most interesting, and practical problems in themselves should not be considered a reason not to do them.

These basic requirements should be kept in mind when recruiting subjects for attrition studies. Other criteria, such as *amount of contact with the L1*, are for the researcher him- or herself to determine – some research designs will be targeted towards people with as little exposure to their native language as possible, while other investigators may be particularly interested in the impact of intensity of use and therefore have to cast their net a bit wider. Bear in mind that, if you want to add extra criteria, it is wise to get that information from potential participants as early as possible, in order to achieve an even distribution of these predictors across your sample.

Before you begin recruiting your participants, you should therefore establish:

- *exclusion criteria*, e.g. minimum age at migration, minimum length of residence, maximum age, restrictions or requirements for amount of contact with L1. Depending on your theoretical and methodological background, you may want to include other factors here. In many psycho- or neurolinguistic investigations, for example, the population is limited to right-handed individuals of a certain gender. You may also want to screen your participants' medical background, to make sure, for example, that none of them has ever suffered a stroke or any other illness which may lead to linguistic impairment. Much of this information you will, of course, need to obtain from both your experimental and your control population.
- *matching criteria* which are to be distributed evenly across experimental and control group (e.g. age, sex, education).
- *relevant predictors* which should be *distributed normally* in the experimental population (e.g. length of residence, attitudes, amount of contact with L1 in certain settings).

- *non-relevant predictors* which should, as far as possible, be kept constant across the experimental population.

TIP

In many countries, ethical considerations and limitations on the types of research you are allowed to do, and the kind of information you are allowed to ask for, are becoming stricter. You should try to find out at an early stage what kinds of permission you need to get from the ethical commission of your institution, funding body or country in order to gather these types of information. In some settings, you may not even be allowed to ask for any details pertaining to your participants' medical history, or pay them for participating.

All of this may sound straightforward and obvious in theory, but the practical difficulties of finding potential participants for an attrition study often mean that the researcher has to compromise on some of these issues. Even more so than in other areas of applied linguistics, methodological compromise is often a frustrating constraint for attrition research. Having established what your ideal population should look like, you may find that your lofty criteria are impossible to maintain in the actual fieldwork, and that you consequently end up with a much smaller group of participants than you had hoped for. Attriters do not tend to hang around in convenient, ready-made age- and education-matched populations, the way L2 students do in foreign language classes. And this observation brings us to the question of how to find participants – one of the biggest practical problems for any attrition study.

PARTICIPANT ACQUISITION (AND A NOTE OF CAUTION)

Making your way into the linguistic community which you want to investigate can be difficult, but once you have made the first contacts it will probably become easier. Speakers often have other contacts within the community and may help you to find more participants – a method referred to as 'snowball sampling'. In fact, once you have met the first participants, you will probably be surprised, if not over-whelmed, by the degree of warmth, friendliness and help with which you are met. During my own fieldwork, I was the grateful recipient of meals, packed lunches, lifts to my next appointment, and generous efforts to help me overcome any glitches and problems which I had encountered, from failing equipment to cancelled appointments.

TIP

The best initial way of finding participants is to advertise in both regular newspapers and, where they exist, in expat media. In order to find the latter, you should contact the embassy or consulate of the country your speakers come from (the address will be on the internet). They will be happy to provide you with the addresses of clubs, organizations, radio stations, newspapers or any other bodies which may exist. You can then write to these, asking them to circulate your request for participants among their members/audience.

In order not to alert potential participants to the intent of the study, I have found it useful to make the claim that I was investigating language change and therefore looking for people who, having lived outside the country, had 'missed out' on some of it. Here is an example of such an ad:

Research on German language change:
Participants wanted for linguistic experiment!

It has long been established by linguistic science that all human languages are undergoing a constant process of change. For many languages, this change has been speeded up considerably over the past years by technological innovations such as the internet. Where the German language is concerned, an additional impetus was provided by the historical process of the reunification. We would like to investigate this, and are looking for Germans in the Vancouver area who have been living in Canada for at least the past 15 years (or longer).

There is no required specialized knowledge – we're looking for you, whether you speak German on a daily basis or virtually never.

The experiment will take around 2½ hours and will take place at a location of your choice between June 15th and July 31st. Participants will receive $30.

If you are interested, please contact:

TIP

A word of warning: you may get more than you bargained for. A disgruntled potential participant, who had tried twice to leave a message on the answering machine of a Ph.D. student of mine, once wrote a letter of complaint to the rector of our university. The student had received over 800 calls after circulating a request for control group participants, and her answering machine was *hors de combat* for weeks. Getting the matter sorted out took some serious grovelling on our part.

It is advisable

- not to give out private phone numbers
- to keep very good track of who has contacted you and
- to send everyone who has responded nice and polite letters, whether you will include them as participants or not

Once word is out, you will probably be able to find enough speakers willing to participate in your experiment. The blessing as well as the curse of language attrition studies is the intuitive appeal of the topic. Researchers who investigate level-ordered morphology or articulatory phonetics will probably rarely find that their friends and family, or even colleagues who work in different areas of linguistics, show great interest or enthusiasm for their work. If you tell anyone that you are studying language attrition, you'll find yourself with a much more receptive audience. Even if you are professing to merely investigate language change, migrants will often be eager to have their L1 skills looked at.

Be sensitive ▓▓▓▓▓▓▓▓▓▓▓▓▓▓▓▓▓▓▓▓▓▓▓▓▓▓▓▓▓▓▓▓

There is a reason for the intuitive appeal of our topic. Within our frame of experience of language, attrition is often perceived to be an unnatural process. Any other situation in which we experience language, particularly when it comes to a change within our own linguistic repertoire, is a social one: L1 acquisition, L2 learning, communication, language for creative purposes, and so on. Wherever we encounter language, it is inseparably linked to contact with other human beings. Language is arguably what makes us part of a community or a relationship.

Attrition, on the other hand, is felt most keenly where it is associated with loneliness or isolation. Although a migrant may be an active member of an L2 community in which she has a large circle of friends, there is often a sense of loss or nostalgia with respect to the L1 community. Attrition can represent the tangible symptom of this disconnectedness and severance. Someone who has lived halfway across the globe from their family and childhood friends may encounter an inexplicable feeling of estrangement when they meet them again after many years (this feeling is often shared by the ones who had stayed behind), and although there can be many cultural reasons for this estrangement, the experience that you can no longer interact as spontaneously and naturally in your L1 as before can serve as the point where such feelings can be concentrated. A familiarity that had been taken for granted has been lost, and to pin that loss on language can serve as a way to protect the speaker from explanations that may be more threatening to her identity.

Since attrition can act as a psychological 'buffer', focusing and representing some of the minor or major traumata almost invariably experienced by an emigrant, it is often a very sensitive issue, and this is something that the researcher has to keep in mind.

NOTE

There is the danger that your experiments bring home to the subjects in a new and possibly dramatic way the degree to which their language has deteriorated. I once made the rather naïve mistake of sending informants a transcript and CD of their autobiographical interview. I thought they might be pleased to have it, and most of them were. One, however, sent me an irate reply, saying he sounded like a retarded child, which had insulted him a great deal. 'My German is much better than that!' he ended the letter. While such cases are rare, particularly among post-puberty immigrants for whom attrition is typically minimal, it is important to be prepared for the eventuality and to offer support and reassurance. If an informant is getting agitated and upset about their performance during an experiment, the researcher has to be able to imperceptibly and immediately switch to an easier level, in order to avoid causing pain and psychological damage.

By proposing to investigate what has happened to someone's L1, you are (perhaps unwittingly) sending out the signal that you are interested in whatever this L1 may represent for your participants. Migration takes a great deal of energy and courage, even under the most favourable of circumstances, for example a move to a country with a similar cultural setting and background for career reasons. No matter how great the benefits – prestige, income, new friends – there will always be costs: distance, estrangement, occasional homesickness. And in today's world only a tiny proportion of migrants have moved under the most favourable of circumstances. Many of the subjects may feel that you are the person with whom they can share the pain about these losses. And yes, there will be tears.

TIP

You are not only responsible for protecting your informants, you are also responsible for protecting yourself. The role you play will mean that many of the people you encounter are willing to bond with you immediately. While this can be a rewarding and satisfying experience in many ways, a succession of personal encounters during which so much is entrusted to you is eventually exhausting. Keep this in mind when arranging your research schedule, and allow yourself as much time between experiments as you can. In purely practical terms, try not to make more than two appointments in a day, and keep at least one day a week free for the purpose of recovery.

Be organized ▬▬▬▬▬▬▬▬▬▬▬▬▬▬▬▬▬▬▬▬▬▬▬▬▬

Planning the actual experiments both chronologically and geographically is a nightmare. For months my office was papered with enlarged copies of maps that had little coloured pins stuck in them. Get a good map as early as possible, and make a lot of copies that you can write on. I have found it helpful to sort my list of participants' addresses by postcode, in order to be able to plan appointments in the same region for the same day. Never rely exclusively on SatNav, but take a map along with you as a back-up, and look up where you are going on the map before you set out. Always make a courtesy phone call the evening before your appointment, confirming the time and place – it helps avoiding awkward situations when you turn up on the doorstep of someone who has forgotten all about you.

WHO TO COMPARE THEM AGAINST: POINT OF REFERENCE

When you investigate L1 attrition, what you are looking for is some kind of *change* to your participants' L1. This critically implies that you need to have baseline data in order for this change to show up.

NOTE

Let us assume, for the sake of argument, that your hypothesis is that men will suffer more attrition than women, as they tend to work outside the home and therefore have more contact with the L2 than women, who will probably bring up their children using their first language (please note that all of these assumptions can and should be challenged!). In order to test this hypothesis, you might administer some test to a group of male and female attriters. If the women do outperform the men, will this allow the conclusion that your assumption was right?

The answer to this question is, of course, no – because how can we know whether the women would not have done better on the test even before they emigrated? In other words, how can we make sure that a difference we find within our group of attriters is really the outcome of the attritional process, and has not been a factor of their sociolinguistic difference all along? There are two possible ways of establishing this: by means of a longitudinal study, which tests the same participants at several points in time, or by means of a control group. Both methods have their advantages and drawbacks.

Longitudinal studies

In a longitudinal design, also known as a pre-/post-design, the same group of people is tested on at least two occasions, typically before and after some event or treatment. In the case of language attrition this would involve investigating the proficiency of a sample of people before they emigrate (time A) and then again after the time span within which we assume attrition to take place has elapsed (time B). In theory, this looks like the best and 'cleanest' way of establishing a point of reference, as it allows us to track the change in proficiency of individual speakers over time. In practice, however, such a set-up is rife with difficulties.

The first difficulty in designing a longitudinal investigation is practical: attrition takes a long time. In order to conduct such a study, a researcher would first have to convince some funding institution to finance a research project which will only yield results after ten years or so. She would then have to find a group of speakers who were about to emigrate or had just emigrated, and who were willing to participate in her tests. That in itself would be no mean feat.

NOTE

Find a person who is planning to move to a different country, and you will probably find someone on the verge of a nervous breakdown, whose mind is full of visas, removal companies, jobs, passports, aeroplanes, what to do with the goldfish, and so on. Convincing this person to spend a few hours on a linguistic experiment will be a difficult task. Finding a group of such people large enough to satisfy the requirements of statistical analysis will be close to impossible.

Furthermore, caution dictates that our researcher find a group at least three times the size of the one she will eventually need. That is because people have a lot of inconvenient habits. They move, they marry and change their names, they decide they do not like the country they have gone to and move back (or somewhere else where a different language is spoken), they do not answer letters, and some have even been known to die. After ten years, you will be lucky to still find a third of your subjects – and then it is possible that the ones you locate will no longer make up a group that satisfies your requirements for a random sample. What if the only people you manage to track down are, say, highly educated men?

The second point to be made here is methodological. In order to be able to compare the results from time A and time B, you have to use more or less the same test design. This means, however, that there is the danger of a *training effect*: people typically perform better on any test the second time around.

> **NOTE**
>
> A longitudinal design, particularly one with more than two test moments, brings with itself the possibility of preventing the very phenomenon that you are looking for: your attriters may not attrite because of the training and reinforcement your tests are providing for their L1.

Thirdly, such a design crucially relies on the assumption that there will be no L2 influence on L1 at time A. This, however, is anything but certain. Even instructed L2 acquisition in an L1 setting, e.g. an intensive language course or evening classes, has been shown to affect proficiency and performance in L1. And given that our subjects are about to emigrate at time A, or have done so very recently, is it not highly likely that at least some of them will have been preparing themselves for this step by some form of studying the L2?

All of this implies that it may be a better, easier and cleaner choice to try and find a reference population back in the country of origin, against which our attriters can be compared: a *control group*. Finding a suitable control group is easier from a practical point of view than overcoming the problems mentioned for longitudinal designs mentioned above, and very few longitudinal attrition studies exist. Those investigations which do attempt a longitudinal design are almost exclusively *case studies* with very few subjects, and are either based on corpora of letters written across a long time span or treat a comparatively short attrition period.

> **NOTE**
>
> The only truly longitudinal quantitative investigation of a group of potential attriters was conducted in Australia by Michael Clyne, who interviewed the same group of speakers of Dutch three times: in 1971, in 1989 and again in 2005. The first time the interviews were

conducted, there were indeed signs of L1 attrition. However, the subsequent sampling did not reveal any further deterioration. Whether this is an indication that attrition happens early on during the emigration span and then progresses no further, or of a training effect of the investigation such as I have pointed out here (or of something else), is impossible to determine.

Control groups

A control group is a sample established for the purpose of comparison: a population of speakers who are similar to the experimental population in all aspects except the one which you assume will have caused the change that you are looking for.

TIP

The number of participants in the experimental group and the control group should be equal, and the distribution of all matching criteria (female–male speakers, educational levels, age, and other demographic factors) should be kept constant across the groups. In this manner, if a difference between experimental and control group is observed, it is highly likely that this difference is the outcome of the one factor on which your groups differ – in our case, residence in a foreign country.

Establishing a control group comes with its own set of problems. The first one of these is the issue of matching: your two groups should ideally be matched on all factors except the one that you are investigating. In other words, you should have two groups whose background is exactly the same, except that one group has emigrated while the other has not. The problem here is that emigration is a very disruptive event and will almost invariably affect many other aspects of a person's life. While a minority of people may relocate because they have been offered a better job elsewhere, emigration is not usually a good career move. This means that good judgment has to be applied in making difficult choices on matching criteria.

NOTE

Take the example, which occurred in one of my studies, of a German law graduate and judge who falls in love with a Canadian. She moves to Canada with him, where her German law degree is useless, and henceforth works as a secretary. Should the control group subject she is matched to be a judge or a secretary? What about a Kurdish doctor who is seeking political asylum in the Netherlands and, as an asylum seeker, is barred from working altogether?

Secondly, all languages change all the time. The researcher thus has to be aware of the possibility that a difference he or she may detect between the experimental and control group is the outcome of a linguistic change that the control group has undergone and the experimental group has 'missed out' on. It is therefore a good and prudent safeguard to use diachronic data and documentations of recent developments in the L1 as a second measuring stick where such data are available.

While it is essential for the researcher to keep these complicating factors in mind when setting up the experiment and when interpreting the findings, the difficulties pointed out above concerning longitudinal studies still make a control group the only feasible point of reference in a large-scale investigation of language attrition.

That is all very well, I hear you cry – but what exactly do you mean by 'large scale'? Ten subjects? Thirty? Fifty? 500? And do I really have to do something large scale anyway? Can I not just have a very good look at my Russian neighbour or my Turkish–English bilingual daughter instead? Or, for that matter, at myself ??

HOW MANY? THE ISSUE OF SAMPLE SIZE

A basic distinction of experimental linguistics, and one which has (unfortunately) not always been taken into account in attrition studies, is the one between *qualitative* and *quantitative research*. Broadly speaking, quantitative analyses are those investigations which:

- diverge from a specific and testable hypothesis
- translate this hypothesis into an experimental design
- apply this design to a sizeable group of participants, drawn from the larger population by *random sampling*
- interpret the results by means of statistical analysis
- are replicable
- can be generalized to the larger population from which the sample was drawn

Qualitative investigations, on the other hand, are more explorative in character. They typically concern longitudinal case studies of a very limited number of participants, and are appropriate in situations where 'the researchers do not set out to test hypotheses, but rather to observe what is present with their focus, and consequently the data, free to vary during the course of the observation' (Larsen-Freeman and Long, 1991: 11).

NOTE

While in quantitative research idiosyncratic or individual variation of patterns of language learning or language attrition are masked, and those tendencies which persist across the group are exposed, qualitative research always has to keep in mind the possibility that a finding may be coincidental and typical only of the person who was investigated.

A case in point

The distinction between qualitative and quantitative research and methods is a vital one, as can be illustrated on the basis of an investigation of the L1 attrition of German morphosyntactic features carried out by Evelyn Altenberg. This study formulates a rigorous hypothesis ('which aspects of first language grammar are most vulnerable to attrition' (1991: 189), and aims to test this by means of three experiments: two grammaticality judgment tasks (on word order and idiomatic verb use) and a fill-in task where bare nouns were presented, and the subject was asked to provide the gender-marked article and plural form, in order to investigate gender assignment and plural allomorphy. Clearly, the point of departure here was an appropriate one for a quantitative study. However, the experiments in question were performed by only two speakers – moreover, they were a married couple and had lived in an L2 environment together for forty years. As Altenberg herself points out, 'these three tasks were preliminary studies, their finding must be interpreted cautiously and their limitations are obvious: future research of this type will require more subjects, more tokens, and possibly a monolingual control group' (p. 203).

Unfortunately, Altenberg's study has, so far, not been replicated with such a wider design. Instead, her cautionary note has been ignored by many researchers (including myself) who wildly overgeneralized her findings and quoted them as evidence for a range of phenomena, such as that similarity between L1 and L2 are a necessary condition for L2-induced L1 attrition (e.g. Bardovi-Harlig and Stringer, 2010: 5; Beganović, 2006: 9; Gürel, 2008: 444), that L1 attrition is subject to cross-linguistic influence (Gross, 2004: 283; Isurin, 2000: 151), that lexical information is more vulnerable to attrition than morphological rules (Ross, 2002: 8), in particular where selectional restrictions are concerned (Schmid, 2002: 32 – *mea culpa*) and that German L1 attrition affects case and number features but not negative placement (Sorace, 2005: 67). While many of these statements may be true, and some of them almost certainly are, Altenberg's findings certainly do not license any of these conclusions.

On the other hand, where it is properly done, there is no reason why a qualitative and a quantitative approach should not be combined within the same study. In such an event, however, it is recommended that you familiarize yourself very thoroughly with the underlying principles of qualitative research (good places to start reading are Davis and Lazaraton, 1995 and Larsen-Freeman and Long, 1991).

Sample size and quantitative analyses

If you do decide to conduct a quantitative analysis – remember: you need a testable hypothesis and a replicable research design – you will then be faced with the choice of how many subjects you want to include. The naïve view here is 'the more the better', but this has to be tempered by a number of other considerations. Firstly, as linguists we are constrained by the fact that our investigations are extremely time consuming, particularly where they involve the elicitation, collection, transcription and analysis of free-spoken data.

NOTE

If you are a social scientist who uses survey data collected through questionnaires which take a few minutes for the participants to fill in, and not much longer to enter into the database, you can afford to turn up your nose at population sizes with less than four figures. If you get the advice of someone with this type of scientific background, they will probably tell you that, in order for your findings to be valid, you should investigate no less than 5 per cent of your entire target population. For experimental linguistic research, this is quite simply not feasible.

There is a second reason why huge group sizes may not even be desirable. The purpose of statistical analysis is to assess whether a difference found between two (or more) populations is likely to be due to chance. A *significant* difference is one where this likelihood is less than 5 per cent (in other words, it is 95 per cent – or more – likely that a similar difference would be found in the population at large, this is what we indicate by saying that '$p < 0.05$'). However, a *significant* difference is not necessarily a *large* difference, merely a relatively *consistent* one. The larger your sample, the smaller the differences between the groups have to be in order for the statistical tests to return a significant result. In other words, in small groups, the danger of a 'false positive' (or, as statisticians call it, a Type I error) is less than in very large groups.

Yes, yes, I hear you shout, with mounting frustration in your voice – but *how many*??? In the language sciences, populations of thirty are generally accepted as an adequate number to conduct a statistical analysis on (that is, thirty experimental and thirty control subjects). It may not be possible for you to find that many subjects – but in that case, you should be aware that you may have problems in getting your findings accepted and published. If you do have to go for less than thirty, you should spell out very clearly the constraints which were responsible. If you are interested in a large number of extralinguistic factors, you will need more subjects: as I said above, most statistical models stipulate that you have at least ten to fifteen cases for each predictor variable you want to test.

Assuming that you have established contact with the required number of participants conforming to your criteria (ideally plus a safety margin in case you experience data loss, have to end an experiment early, etc.) and have your meetings planned out, you can begin the actual fieldwork: you can start looking for signs of L1 attrition. That brings us to the question of what to test.

10   Types of linguistic knowledge

Attrition is a linguistic phenomenon, so in order to investigate it, we need to look at language. That seems fairly obvious, but language is not something we can go out and collect like butterflies or plant samples. As researchers, we need to take some kind of action in order to *elicit* the data that we want to look at. This chapter will discuss various ways of doing this, and also go into their respective advantages or disadvantages.

Chapter 9 acquainted you with the *independent variables* or *predictors* which play a role in the process of L1 attrition. These are the external factors which may impact on the processes of language attrition that we observe among bilingual migrants. In chapter 10, aspects of *dependent variables* will be discussed. These are those elements in an experiment which the researcher attempts to elicit, and which we expect will change or have changed as a result of differences in the predictors. Your dependent variables are therefore those linguistic features for which you expect to find differences between the experimental and the control population as a result of the process of attrition (their vocabulary or specific fields of it, their grammar, etc.). Again, you will make life a great deal easier for yourself if you try to be as specific as possible as to which linguistic features, and which aspects of these features, you are planning to investigate.

TIP

Although there are a number of investigations of language attrition which attempt to paint a general and overall impression of the process of change or deterioration, the more specific you are about your research questions, the more straightforward it will be to design your study and to interpret your findings. It is easier to test 'gender concord in plural noun phrases in French' than it is to test 'grammatical gender', it is easier to test 'grammatical gender' than it is to test 'inflectional morphology', it is easier to test 'inflectional morphology' than it is to test 'how much people still know about their L1'.

Similarly, be specific about *why* you want to investigate a particular linguistic feature. If you are going to test (to stick with the previous example) gender concord in plural noun phrases in French, there will be a reason why you suppose that this grammatical construction will be vulnerable to attrition. 'Because it is difficult to learn' may be a start, but is not an adequate explanation. What are the theoretical assumptions underlying your prediction? What model of language learning, language use, language knowledge, language production or language processing will you adopt? What predictions does this model make for the L1 acquisition, L2 acquisition, pathological decay and L1 attrition of the linguistic feature you are interested in?

This implies that where dependent variables are concerned, the path that you have to choose will depend not only on where you want to go, but also on where you are coming from. Different theoretical frameworks will allow you to make predictions with respect to the development or deterioration of different variables. For example, if you are planning to conduct an investigation within the theoretical model of Government and Binding (e.g. Haegeman, 1991), you will have to test specific areas of syntactic knowledge, namely pronouns or reflexives. Within which theoretical school or framework (generative linguistics, cognitive linguistics, usage-based approaches, psycholinguistics, contact linguistics . . .) you conduct your analysis is your own choice. However, it is important that you make this choice, and that you are aware of the theoretical implications of your research questions before you begin your investigation.

L2 DEVELOPMENT AS THE IMPLICIT MODEL FOR L1 ATTRITION

In this context, it is important to keep in mind that most theories about bilingual development focus on the L2 as the developing system. The predictions which they make are therefore based on assumptions about the nature of language knowledge which do not necessarily hold true for L1 attrition. For example, since in late bilingualism second languages are acquired at a point at which the native language has already been firmly established in the mind and is deeply entrenched through long-term and frequent use, the grammatical system of the L2 is usually thought to be influenced by L1 rules and principles to a certain degree.

In L1 attrition, it is then often assumed that this cross-linguistic influence can become reversed, and that the grammatical knowledge of an attriter's native language can develop traits that are more similar to that of an L2 system. However, theories about bilingualism may not be reversible in such a simplistic way, since they are based not merely on which language is used or represented dominantly, but also on how and when the languages have been acquired. Second language learning, particularly among older speakers (adolescents or adults), is different in many ways from first language acquisition among children – and this suggests that an attriter, who has learned the L1 as a native speaker from birth, will be different with respect to the knowledge and use of this language from someone who has learned the same language later in life.

IMPLICIT AND EXPLICIT KNOWLEDGE

NOTE

When I was in high school, I studied classical Latin. The goal of the instruction was not to learn how to speak the language, but to be able to translate passages of text written around 2,000 years ago into my first language. Tackling a sentence was an exercise in identifying words which, even though they might appear at a great distance from each other, had to belong together since their endings indicated the same case, gender and number (in the case of nominal elements such as adjectives or nouns) or person, number, tense, mood and so on (in the case of verb phrases). Understanding of meaning was only possible after the hunt for grammatical constituents, such as the finite verb, the subject and the object, had been successful.

This example illustrates the application of a type of knowledge which is entirely *explicit*: I would go through the sentence, identifying words one by one, determining their function in the sentence based on their inflectional endings (which would correspond to an entry in the tables of declension or conjugation which I had memorized) and their meaning based on the lexical stem (which I would look up in the dictionary).

Speakers of morphologically complex languages may be blissfully ignorant of terms such as *genitive masculine plural, third person singular pluperfect passive* or *ablative absolute*. This, however, does not impair their ability to automatically use and instantly understand sentences using all of these daunting forms. In fact, when they are exposed to any utterance in their native language they cannot choose *not* to understand it (something which I could do with no difficulty whatsoever, by simply not applying my rote-learned rules to the words on the page). Such a knowledge of a native language is referred to as *implicit*.

Speakers can know many aspects of language – in particular those aspects which we would think of as 'grammatical' – *implicitly* or *explicitly*. The distinction is based on how the language was learned and affects how these aspects are represented in memory[1] and used in production and understanding. Implicit knowledge is typical of the grammar of a language that has been acquired during childhood: when children acquire language, they do not focus on the learning process, nor are they even aware of it. They are exposed to linguistic input – from their parents, caregivers or peers – while their conscious mind is focused on doing other things. The grammatical knowledge that is built up in this way is not open to introspection or verbalization, and it is used automatically.

Languages which are learned at an older age, in particular through instruction, are acquired in a very different manner: second language learners are aware of their learning process and consciously analyse the grammatical structures they are attempting to acquire. Of course, this consciousness is strongest in instructed L2 learning, but even immersion learners bring their cognitive skills to bear on the linguistic structures they are exposed to. As a consequence, knowledge of L2 grammar is (at least initially) *explicit*. Explicit knowledge is available for introspection, and its use is controlled, not automatic, in production or understanding. Whether the learning process changes because we lose the ability for entirely implicit grammar-building at a certain age or because our other cognitive and analytical skills have become so strong that we cannot disable them and expose ourselves to linguistic input naïvely is a matter of controversy.

In language production and processing, the main difference between implicit and explicit knowledge is thus that the former is applied *automatically* while the latter is always *controlled*. This means that an L2 learner may be able to rattle off aspects of L2 grammar, such as a list of prepositions governing the assignment of certain cases. However, when the same speaker constructs a sentence containing one of these prepositions, a wrong case may be chosen if attention is focused elsewhere (e.g. on lexical access). A native speaker may not be able to produce a complete list of the prepositions which take the accusative case, but will usually automatically assign the correct case in language production, and notice grammatical violations in speech produced by others.

Success in L2 learning therefore depends on fast and routine application of knowledge which is explicit. Whether L2 grammar can ever become fully implicit is a matter of some debate, but there are indications that, at least for some aspects of grammatical knowledge, implicit representations can also be built up over time (Paradis, 2008). This state of dual knowledge is probably similar to what happens when you attempt to learn a complex motor skill, such as playing an instrument or touch-typing: at first, notes or letters have to be consciously translated into a command such as 'press down the third finger on the left hand in a certain manner'. After a while, these commands become faster, and at a certain point, automatic knowledge can gradually take over. While you are still relying on both knowledge systems to some degree, hopeless confusion can ensue if, in the middle of typing a sentence or playing a passage of music you become aware, all of a sudden, of what your fingers are doing and conscious control attempts to take over.

This means that second language learners are likely to do best on any grammatical task when there is no time pressure, and when they have the leisure to consciously work out the appropriate linguistic forms based on their explicit knowledge. For L1 attriters, the situation may be rather different: while there is evidence that automatic processes can eventually come to replace controlled ones, the reverse is probably not true. If implicitly represented grammatical rules have become inaccessible over the attrition period, the attriters do not have the consciously learned and explicitly represented knowledge of the L2 speaker to fall back on. However, what they do have is explicit knowledge of the L2 rules. It is therefore possible that, on tasks for which they are under no time constraint, attriters may draw more heavily on such explicit knowledge to 'fill the gaps', and actually do worse than on a more naturalistic task which forces them to apply their automatic and implicit language knowledge.

NOTE

Like many other Germanic languages, Dutch historically has three noun genders (masculine, feminine and neuter), but masculine and feminine have been conflated into a single class, common. The masculine–feminine distinction survives only in anaphoric pronouns, and as many native speakers do not know any longer whether a certain common noun is masculine or feminine, they tend to avoid these (Audring, 2009). I once asked a number of colleagues to supply the missing pronoun in sentences such as *De deur is op slot, ik kan _____ niet openen*. ('The door is locked, I cannot open [it].') Virtually all my informants used either demonstratives, which do not distinguish masculine and feminine (*ik kan deze niet openen* 'I cannot open this one'), or repeated the full noun phrase ('The door is locked, I cannot open the door'). Only one speaker did supply anaphoric pronouns. These, however, deviated from the dictionary-defined genders of some of the nouns. When I asked him how he had made his choice, he told me he had no idea what the correct gender was in Dutch – so he had based his judgment on his L2, Italian!

It is important to keep the distinction between implicit and explicit knowledge in mind when designing your experiments, as most tasks which are available to test bilinguals have been developed in the context of L2 acquisition studies. They may therefore be more suitable for the application of explicit knowledge – and while an L2 learner may do better on such tasks than in free spoken interaction, the attriter may actually do worse. Such a finding may be interesting; but caution should be applied in interpreting it as evidence that an attriter has 'lost' a certain part of her grammatical knowledge: if someone makes a mistake on an explicit grammatical task, but can use the relevant feature without problem in free speech, we should reflect carefully on what this says about the state of her linguistic knowledge.

In other words, what you may find depends crucially on the tasks that you choose to use, so you should be very careful in selecting them.

ONLINE AND OFFLINE TASKS

One of the most difficult and most important steps in your research design will be to decide which tasks you will use. Once you have selected one (or several) linguistic variable(s) on which your study will focus, and considered whether you are interested in implicit or explicit representation and use, you will have to decide in what manner you will try to manipulate your participants into using, constructing or responding to the linguistic structures in which you are interested. The nature of different types of linguistic knowledge – implicit or explicit – obviously has a huge impact on task selection.

> An implicit task is one which attempts to access internally represented knowledge without requiring the subject to become consciously aware of that knowledge. In contrast, an explicit task is one which requires the subject consciously to access particular types of knowledge in the process of carrying out the task. (Tyler, 1992: 159)

Generally speaking, linguistic research therefore distinguishes *online* tasks, which tap into implicit knowledge, and *offline* tasks, in which the participant applies explicit knowledge: online tasks are the ones which attempt to simulate implicit language use or processing, by trying to get the participants to apply more or less the same kinds of mechanisms which they would in naturalistic language use. This means that online tasks are designed not to allow for the application of explicit metalinguistic knowledge or introspection. This is often done by putting participants under time pressure. For example, an online task might present a sentence on a screen word by word at a very fast rate (a method referred to as *rapid serial visual presentation* or RSVP) or require the subject to make a decision on whether a sentence is grammatically correct as quickly as possible. In an offline task, on the other hand, no such time pressures are applied and the participant has the opportunity to consciously reflect on her answers. In other words, online tasks attempt to measure implicit knowledge, while in offline tasks, both implicit and explicit knowledge may be drawn upon.

For second language learners, who potentially possess both types of linguistic knowledge, offline tasks may therefore be advantageous: removing the time pressure and allowing them, if necessary, to consciously work out a certain linguistic rule can make it possible for them to correctly construct a complex expression, or to judge it as good or bad, even if they might not have been able to do this in a 'normal' discourse situation. Again, the situation might be different for an attriter, who may never have consciously acquired the underlying grammatical rules of his or her language.

NOTE

Take a piece of paper and write down, in your first language and in capital letters, the word 'cinnamon'. Now look at this word continuously for a period of thirty seconds. You will probably notice that, after a while, the word begins to look odd. Even though you know perfectly well that you wrote it down correctly in the first instance, you will start questioning it. The same thing may happen if you look at a perfectly normal sentence and then allow yourself the time to question whether it is correct or not.

SPOKEN AND WRITTEN LANGUAGE

The implicit/explicit and online/offline distinction impacts in particular on the format, or mode, of the testing; that is, on whether investigations take place in the written or in the spoken form. Written language gives a speaker far more opportunities to apply explicit knowledge than spoken interaction: writing is slower than speaking, and long pauses in the language production process do not impair the flow of information in the same way that frequent hesitations may do in spoken interaction. While writing, a language user can try out various constructions on a separate sheet, go back and make corrections, and so on. Many L2 learners therefore do better on written than on spoken tasks. Since explicit L2 instruction often focuses strongly on written language, many of the tests which are used in this context use the written mode. This is also a matter of convenience, as written tests can be performed by a large group of participants at the same time, which is impossible for spoken language, and they are also easier to score.

Such considerations, as well as the fact that written tests are widely used and easily available, may make it tempting to apply them for investigations of L1 attrition. However, an attriter's performance on a written task may not be representative of her overall state of linguistic knowledge. It is possible, for example, that someone keeps on using their L1 as a home language, and will therefore be fluent and accurate in spoken use, but has had minimal exposure to written language (books, newspapers or even letters) for a long period of time. There are a number of studies which investigate a longitudinal corpus of letters written by an attriter over a period of several decades (e.g. Hutz, 2004; Jaspaert and Kroon, 1992) and draw their conclusions about the grammatical knowledge which these language users have retained or lost over the attrition period. However, it is possible that an investigation of spoken data produced by the same attriters might have yielded entirely different results.

PRODUCTION, COMPREHENSION AND PROCESSING

A further consideration in this respect concerns what it is that you want your participants to do. Do you want them to actively *produce* the linguistic structures in which you are interested (whether in an offline setting in an explicit task, or online in free production), or to test their response to linguistic material to which they are passively *exposed*? In some cases, it may seem easier to choose the latter option, as it can be extraordinarily difficult (and tedious) to manipulate a speaker into using a certain linguistic structure. Say, for example, that you are interested in relative clauses – a highly complex structure in some languages, for example Turkish. While it is very possible that certain speakers will begin to develop problems using this structure over a long period of attrition, relative clauses are easy to avoid in free speech. Furthermore speakers can be very resourceful in devising ways of not using linguistic features about which they may be uncertain. This means that, if you simply rely on letting your participants talk, you may end up not having enough instances of the structure in which you are interested.

Many studies therefore try to devise ways which make the use of certain structures unavoidable. For example, Kutlay Yağmur attempted to elicit Turkish relative clauses by presenting their different sentence constituents to his informants in scrambled word order, and asking them to rearrange them into a coherent sentence. So the input that the participants received would look something like this:

(42)
(a) duran vazo   çarpmasıyla masanın üstünde düşüp kırıldı   topun
    was standing the ball hit   the vase which fell down and broke when

They would then be expected to form the following sentence from these building blocks:

(42)
(b) Masanın üstünde duran vazo topun çarpmasıyla düşüp kırıldı.
    The vase which was standing on the table fell down and broke when the ball hit.

Such a task may indeed be an option to force speakers into producing a certain type of syntactic structure. However, the nature of this production process can seem very contrived and artificial, requiring speakers to manipulate language in a way that they are totally unused to. It is therefore possible that such tasks do not tap directly into the actual knowledge associated with the online production of relative clauses in normal speech, but into some other (explicit) component of linguistic knowledge. Depending on the linguistic structure that you are after, it may be possible to manipulate your speakers' behaviour in a more subtle manner, for instance by asking questions which are phrased in a certain way. Other structures may be more difficult to avoid in free speech, so that simply getting people to talk will not necessarily provide the evidence that you need.

On the other hand, you may be interested in properties of language which are impossible to investigate simply on the basis of language use or free speech. For example, some researchers have focused on the way in which different languages resolve potential ambiguities. Consider the following sentence:

(43)
(a) I just saw the sister of the actress who is pregnant.

There are two possible interpretations here: (a) the actress is pregnant, (b) her sister is pregnant. In English, the preferred option is to 'attach' the relative clause (*who is pregnant*) to the second NP in the complex clause – that is, to read the sentence to mean that *the actress* is the one who is pregnant. This means that (43b) is easier to comprehend than (43c):

(43)
(b) I just saw the brother of the actress who is pregnant.
(c) I just saw the sister of the actor who is pregnant.

Some languages, for example Spanish, have a different preference with regard to such structures, so that (44a) would typically be taken to indicate that it is *the sister* who is pregnant (Dussias, 2004). Spanish speakers therefore have more difficulty with sentence (44b) than with (44c).

(44)
(a) Acabo de ver a la hermana de la actriz que está embarazada.
   I just saw the sister of the actress who is pregnant.
(b) Acabo de ver al hermano de la actriz que está embarazada.
   I just saw the brother of the actress who is pregnant.
(c) Acabo de ver a la hermana del actor que está embarazada.
   I just saw the sister of the actor who is pregnant.

You will find some more examples below on the resolution of potentially ambiguous structures, as well as on ways to test them. The interesting question for our purpose is whether attriters can change with regard to the preference they apply in interpreting such structures. In other words, will Spanish speakers who have lived in an English-speaking environment for a long time begin to take sentence (44a) to mean that it is *the actress* who is pregnant, and consequently find (44c) more difficult to comprehend than (44b)?

In order to find answers to these kinds of questions, it is often not enough to look at *production* data alone, but to investigate the way in which participants *respond* to and *process* input to which they are exposed. Possible ways in which this can be achieved will be discussed below.

CONCLUSION

Before you can get started on actually designing your test battery, it is vital to be clear on what the tasks which you are planning to use actually investigate: are you truly going to test 'the knowledge of grammatical gender concord', or merely how this knowledge translates to behaviour within a certain language mode, situational context, and format? Might your informants have performed totally differently on another type of task, or in free speech? Is their performance constrained by other factors, such as their own educational level and their familiarity with explicit rules? Will some speakers, for example language teachers, do particularly well on a certain type of task because they tend to set similar exercises to their students?

A good way of controlling for this is to try and use a range of different types of tasks which will allow you to compare each individual speaker's performance on the linguistic structures that you are interested in across these settings. The following chapter will familiarize you with a number of such experiments that have been used in previous studies of language attrition. I will try to point out the advantages and disadvantages of each of these tasks, and show you various alternatives of how to construct, present, score and analyse them.

Some of these experiments can be carried out with no more than pen and paper. However, you will probably minimally need a laptop computer on which you can present stimuli such as film sequences, and a good recording device. The best available technology has a very short shelf life these days, so I will not advise you on what kinds of devices to use here (the equipment I used five years ago – a minidisc recorder – has already become obsolete and turned out to be a very bad choice with hindsight). But do keep in mind that even a slight improvement in recording quality can save you many hours of work and frustration when it comes to transcribing the data. The difference of a few hundred euros may seem large when you buy it – but if it means two months less time spent on figuring out what people are saying, it will be well worth it.

Other experiments critically rely on a laboratory. You can conduct a reaction time study on a laptop with the suitable soft- and hardware, but the equipment you need to conduct an eye-tracking, EEG or fMRI study is usually not portable. This means that feasibility is a huge consideration: will you be able to get lab time in minimally two countries (for attriters and controls) and find enough speakers who satisfy your subject characteristics and live close enough to travel there in order to participate in the experiment? Last but not least, will you be able to afford the lab time and reimburse the participants for their travelling expenses?

PART IV
Experimental designs for attrition research – the language attrition test battery

When Barbara Köpke and I first became interested in the study of language attrition, we felt that one of the main problems of the field was the fact that there was no consistent methodology available for attrition studies. It seemed that everyone who had ever looked at attrition had invented their own approach, tests and questionnaires. This not only seemed like a huge waste of time but also contributed to the fact that little overall progress was made in the common understanding of how attrition takes place: no two findings could be compared to each other, and so nothing could ever be generalized beyond the scope of an individual investigation. We therefore decided to target our collective effort at providing a methodological framework that people would be able to adapt to different languages and different contexts.

The data collection instruments and experiments presented in this section are the outcome of these efforts. They were largely developed between 2003 and 2009 in the European Graduate Network on Language Attrition, a group of young researchers and Ph.D. and M.A. students working on language attrition in a variety of languages and settings. This group met on a regular basis and during those meetings we selected various tests and evaluated their potential for application in language attrition research. This means that for all of the tasks described here, previous findings from attrition in a range of first languages are available.

To some extent, your own experiments will depend on your research questions, and those research questions will depend on the languages you are investigating and the theoretical framework within which you will conduct your investigation. However, it may be advantageous both for yourself and for others if you try to use at least some of the tests and instruments that have been applied in other studies. In this way, you may be able to compare your findings with results obtained from other attriting populations, and this can help you get a better impression of the actual loss which has taken place among your speakers.

NOTE

Of course, you are free not only to select or reject but also to modify and change any and all of the tasks described here. If you do that, however, you should be very much aware not only of why you are doing it, but also of the consequences it may have for your results. What may seem to be relatively minor modifications to the experimental procedure, which you decide to make for the sake of convenience, can have huge ramifications for the claims that your findings allow you to make. One example of this, described in more detail below, concerns the way you present the stimulus sentences in a grammaticality judgment task, and how you invite your participants to respond to them: if you simply ask them to tell you whether or not these sentences are correct, you are conducting an experiment that is entirely different from one where you urge them to make that judgment *as fast as they can*.

You should also keep in mind that some of the procedures described here rely crucially on very specialized and expensive equipment and may not be feasible to implement outside a laboratory context. As ever, you will have to make a choice which strikes the appropriate balance between scientific rigour and practicality.

There are different types of data which you may want to collect from your potential attriters. Formal tasks targeting the production and processing of specific linguistic variables can help you assess what part of the linguistic repertoire of the speakers has become impaired. If you are interested in how language attrition has affected the mental lexicon, you may want to employ a *Picture Naming* or *Picture Word Matching Task* or a *Verbal Fluency Task*. If your interest is more in the area of grammar and you have concrete and directed hypotheses about which part of the grammatical system may have been affected by the attritional process, you may want to employ a *grammaticality* or *truth value judgment* task. If you want to study morphological processes, you may want to invite your participants to inflect real or made-up words (the latter task is called a *Wug-test* or *nonce word paradigm*). And if the focus of your interest is syntax, a *sentence production task* may be a suitable instrument. There are also tasks which elicit more general and more holistic information about the overall proficiency level which a speaker retains in his or her L1, such as the well-known *C-Test*.

Given the considerations I raised in the previous section with respect to different types of knowledge and responses to various tasks, it is advisable for investigations of language attrition to include free spoken data. Such data come with their own set of problems and considerations: they are extremely time-consuming and complicated to process and analyse, but well worth it.

TIP

I strongly recommend that you do not base your research on one type of data alone, but ideally try to spread your test battery over all of them.

The following chapters will give you a general introduction to the tasks that have previously been used in attrition research. At the end of each chapter, you will find a short overview of the task in question, the types of knowledge it tests, the types of data you can elicit with it, the equipment requirements for carrying it out, and some suggested further reading.

11 Lexical tasks

The bilingual mental lexicon is often named as the most vulnerable area of linguistic knowledge in language attrition. This chapter will show you some ways in which you may investigate whether *lexical access* and *lexical knowledge* have indeed attrited.

PICTURE NAMING TASK

The Picture Naming Task (PNT) is a psycholinguistic experiment in which participants are presented with pictures and asked to name them as quickly as possible. The purpose of the task is to measure the speed and accuracy with which participants are able to accomplish the naming. This means that the data you obtain are relatively easy and straightforward to analyse: you simply calculate the average reaction time (RT) of the correctly named items and the proportion of accurate responses for each individual.

When constructing such an experiment, however, there are a number of issues that you should be aware of. The first is where to find the pictures that will be used as stimuli. This is an important consideration, not only for the PNT but for any experiment which uses picture stimuli. The temptation may be to use images which are widely available, for example on the internet. However, you should keep in mind that there may be serious issues of copyright. Just because someone has published an image on a website does not mean that there are no proprietary rights to it or that it can be freely reproduced. It may be that the owner of the website has the intellectual rights to the image, or (more likely) that it was posted violating the rights of the original owner. Either way, once you attempt to publish your findings you will have to include examples of your stimuli, and if there are copyright issues, you will encounter significant problems in doing that.

There are therefore two options: either to use images which you have drawn yourself (or had someone draw for you) or to go with stimuli which were developed for the purpose of scientific research and which are available for free or for a small fee. Many studies use a set of *standardized line drawings* developed by Joan Gay Snodgrass and Mary Vanderwart. The original article in which these pictures are presented and described (Snodgrass and Vanderwart, 1980) also presents information on their familiarity. This information allows the experimenter to distinguish between highly familiar objects, which should be easy to name, and unfamiliar items with which speakers may be expected to encounter more difficulties.

The full set of pictures contains 260 line drawings, such as the one of an aeroplane represented in Figure 11.1, and currently costs around US$200. They can be purchased from Life Science Associates (http://lifesciassoc.home.pipeline.com) in different file formats. Once you have acquired them, you have the right to use them in your publications provided that you give the proper reference, as I am doing here.

You should make a selection of items which are evenly distributed across high, medium and low familiarities (PNT experiments typically use around sixty to a hundred picture stimuli) and which you find instantly recognizable. Within our team, there was some debate, for example, as to whether the potato didn't look more like a stone. The best principle to adopt here is 'when in doubt, leave it out'. A second consideration that is important to keep in mind is the issue of *cognates*: items which are similar across languages, such as English *cat* and Dutch *kat*. There is a great deal of evidence that bilinguals are

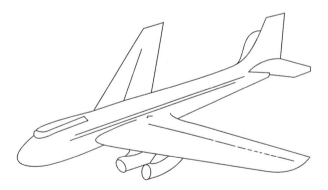

Figure 11.1 An example of a stimulus item in a Picture Naming Task ('aeroplane'), using an image from the Snodgrass and Vanderwart, 1980 set (Copyright 2009 Life Science Associates)

faster in naming words which are cognate in their two languages and slower in naming items which are not. You should therefore either make sure that the set of pictures you select contains no cognates, or that you have an equal number of cognates and non-cognates per familiarity category.

The second practical difficulty is how to administer the presentation of the pictures and measure the RTs. Some previous studies have employed a manual manner of presentation through flash-cards, timing the responses by means of a hand-held device (e.g. Isurin, 2000). This method is unreliable, as it adds your own response delay (activating the timer synchronously with presenting the stimulus and stopping it again as soon as you hear the participant say the correct word) to the reaction time which you are attempting to measure.

At a pinch, you may have to take recourse to the solution used by Ammerlaan (1996), who had the pictures presented on a computer screen. The appearance of the picture was accompanied by a beep, and the entire experiment was audio-taped, so that he could measure the time between the onset of the beep and the participant's response. This is a more reliable, albeit highly time-consuming way of measuring RTs.

The easiest and most reliable way of administering this experiment is by means of specialized software such as *E-Prime*. Familiarizing yourself with how to use this program to set up an experiment may take a little time, and the software is not cheap. There are shareware alternatives, such as *Superlab*, *NESU* or *DmDX* which you can use if your institution does not have an *E-Prime* licence. The advantage of *E-Prime*, however, is that it is the accepted standard for psycholinguistic and psychological experiments.

You can record the response times by means of a *Serial Response Box* (SRB), a device which you attach to your computer and which can accurately measure how long a participant takes between seeing a certain stimulus and performing a certain action, such as pressing a button on the SRB. There are different types of such devices, e.g. with only two buttons for 'yes' and 'no', or with several buttons for a graded response.

If you do not have such a box, the program can also record responses given by pressing pre-defined keys on the keyboard. For example, you can designate two keys on your keyboard (e.g. C and M) as the 'yes' or 'no' trigger. In this case, it is advisable to make a cardboard cover for the keyboard, leaving only these two keys open, and putting a red and a green sticker on the keys themselves. Between trials, the participants can either leave one finger on each key, or place the finger they use to press the key (right for right-handed participants, left for left-handed ones) at a position which is equidistant to both keys. Both the accuracy of the judgment and the time it took are then recorded by means of the software package you are using.

If you are using an SRB you can also connect a microphone to the device and use it as a voice key, so that the program will measure the time between the presentation of the picture and the onset of the spoken response. For each participant and each picture the response time will be automatically entered into a table, which you can then export to your database software. Beware of the readings, however: the voice key will pick up anything, including hesitation markers (ehm. . .), coughs, throat-clearing etc., and it is important to determine beforehand how far from a person's mouth the microphone should be placed in order to minimize the impact of such distracting factors but still pick up the responses reliably. You should monitor the experiment very carefully and note down for yourself wherever you feel that the response which was picked up was the actual item, or something else. You can facilitate this by setting the program to display the picture only until a response has been detected and then make it disappear.

The voice key only records the fact that an answer has been made, not whether or not it was accurate. It is therefore important to record the experiment so that you can later determine which of the pictures were named correctly.

Task:	Picture naming
Linguistic area:	Mental lexicon
Type of knowledge:	Lexical access/word retrieval
Type of data:	Accuracy in naming, reaction times (RTs)
System requirements:	Computer for presentation
	Pictures (e.g. standardized set of line drawings (Snodgrass and Vanderwart, 1980), available from Life Science Associates, http://lifesciassoc.home.pipeline.com)
	Software for timing responses (E-Prime, available from www.pstnet.com; or appropriate shareware alternative such as NESU www.mpi.nl/world/tg/experiments/nesu.html or DmDX, www.u.arizona.edu/~jforster/dmdx.htm)
	Hardware: Serial Response Box, Voice-Key Activation, available from www.pstnet.com
Investigations of attrition using a PNT:	Ammerlaan, 1996; Hulsen, 2000; Isurin, 2000; Yilmaz, in prep.

Further reading:	Bates *et al.*, 2003; Johnson, Paivio and Clark, 1996
Advantages:	Easy to construct and score, does not rely on written material
Disadvantages:	Many studies do not find any differences in naming times or in accuracy between attriters and controls

PICTURE WORD MATCHING TASK

In some studies, the PNT has been modified to trigger not the *recall* of a word but its *recognition* by matching the picture with a lexical item in a Picture Word Matching Task (PWMT). This is achieved either by presenting the participant with a picture and a word at the same time, requiring him or her to indicate whether the word correctly identifies the picture, or by giving a multiple-choice set of alternatives from which the correct item is to be selected. You can present one picture and four words (of which one is the target and three are distracters), or one word and four pictures.

Presenting a single word together with one or several pictures has the advantage that you do not have to rely on written language for the presentation. As was pointed out above, many of the world's languages do not have a written system. If you want to investigate L1 attrition effects in such languages, you have to rely on tasks which make no use of written language. In such cases you can make recordings of individual stimuli and present these together with the picture(s). The task for the participant is then to press the 'yes' or 'no' button on the SRB, depending on whether the picture presented is correctly identified by the word he or she hears at the same moment; or to click on the picture amongst of a set of alternatives which belongs to the word that is presented auditorily.

In such a *multiple choice* or *forced choice* option of the PWMT the four alternatives usually comprise the correct item ('target'), a semantically related alternative, a phonologically related alternative, and an unrelated distracter. So, the screen you present might look like the one represented in Figure 11.2, and you would request the participants to either click on the target or say it out loud as quickly as they can.

The PWMT allows you to test whether the participants are able to recognize a certain word, even if they may not be able to name it in a PNT, as it does not require the participant to self-activate the relevant

TREE   BEAR

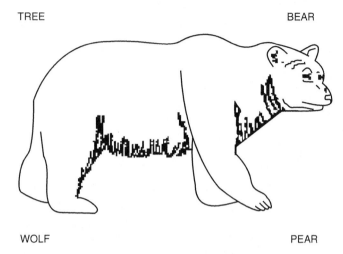

WOLF   PEAR

Figure 11.2 An example of a stimulus item in a Picture Word Matching Task, using an image from the Snodgrass and Vanderwart (1980) set (Copyright 2009 Life Science Associates) with the correct lexical item ('bear'), a semantically related distracter ('wolf'), a phonologically related distracter ('pear') and an unrelated distracter ('tree')

lexical item from memory: recognition of a word is easier than recall, as it requires less activation effort. The PWMT is otherwise constructed, presented and timed similarly to the PNT.

In attriting populations who emigrated after puberty, a general version of the PWMT by means of the standardized Snodgrass and Vanderwart picture set is probably a task that is too easy, so that there may be a *ceiling effect*. Hulsen (2000), for example, finds no difference either in RTs or in accuracy between her adult attriters and her control population. However, the PWMT may have some application in testing specific areas of lexical knowledge which differ considerably between the L1 and the L2.

Task:	Picture Word Matching
Linguistic area:	Mental lexicon
Type of knowledge:	Lexical access/word recognition
Type of data:	Accuracy in matching, reaction times (RTs)
System requirements:	see PNT
Investigations of attrition using this task:	Ammerlaan, 1996; Hulsen, 2000

Further reading:	De Bot and Stoessel, 2000; Green, 1986; Hermans, 2000
Advantages:	Easy to construct and score
Disadvantages:	Accuracy scores usually do not differ between attriters and controls

PNT AND PWMT FOR SPECIFIC LEXICAL AREAS

It is possible to use the PNT and the PWMT to investigate lexical fields in which the L1 and the L2 differ specifically in order to find instances of CLI. This task is particularly interesting for research into issues of *categorization*, which can differ across languages. An example of this is presented by Pavlenko (2011), who demonstrates that the lexical sub-categorization of the overall category 'containers from which you can drink' varies across languages and is subject to cross-linguistic interference for bilinguals. In American English, for example, the main factor on which naming is based appears to be the material from which the container is made (glass, porcelain, ceramic, Styrofoam etc.), somewhat tempered by its function (used to drink hot vs cold beverages), while for Russian speakers, the shape of the container (round, cylindrical, with or without a handle) as well as its function play a more important role than the material.

Pavlenko presented her subjects with a total of sixty photographs (which she had taken herself), some showing very typical instances of a certain category, such as a cup, a mug or a glass, and some showing rather untypical examples. This study establishes, firstly, that native American English and native Russian speakers differ with respect to the criteria on which they base their categorization of an object – for example, some of the objects that English speakers refer to as a 'cup' are called a *chashka* by the native Russians, others are referred to as *stakan* and yet others are called *riumka*. However, for L1 Russian speakers who have lived in the US, the categorization principles appear to have changed to some extent. For example, a roundish porcelain cup without a handle was preferentially called *riumka* by the monolingual Russian speakers in Russia, while the bilingual Russian–English speakers in the US tended to call it a *chashka*.

Pavlenko's survey is an example of how a PNT can establish very subtle changes in the L1 mental lexicon of language attriters which would probably not have been evident in other types of task. The underlying principles of classifying a certain object as a member of one category (for example, a 'cup' vs a 'mug') can be relatively vaguely defined and can vary across languages (and across their dialects). In order to explore how such categorization mechanisms can encroach from one language onto the other, tasks of this nature have to be employed.

Pavlenko's study is interesting for another reason: she uses an *internet-based survey* in order to elicit her data, something which had not previously been done in investigations of language attrition. Given the practical difficulties involved in participant selection, internet-based experiments can be an attractive, inexpensive and time-saving alternative to face-to-face interviews. There are, of course, always drawbacks to consider – precise measurements of reaction times are impossible in web-based applications, the writing systems can differ (as they do between Russian and English) so that the experimental group may have to transliterate their responses while the control group can use their native writing system, and so on. Nevertheless, if your resources are limited, you may want to develop experiments which can be administered at a distance. In particular, this may be an eminently suitable method for a pilot-study.

VERBAL FLUENCY TASK

The last task for the investigation of the mental lexicon which will be discussed here is the *Verbal Fluency Task* (VFT), sometimes also called *Fluency in Controlled Association* (FiCA). This is a task which is very simple to construct and administer and requires no specialized equipment beyond a stopwatch and a recorder. The participant is given a certain period of time, usually 60 or 90 seconds, to name as many items within a certain category as he or she can. The instructions given run something like this: 'Now I would like to see how many animals you can name within 60 seconds. You could start with the word *dog*.'

While some researchers have managed to write down the items as the informant produces them, I recommend taping the experiment – sometimes the speaker will go into a spurt of productivity beyond your ability to keep up. Simply counting the items that are being produced is not an option: often speakers will repeat items that they have named earlier, and such repetitions should be eliminated from the overall count.

There are two types of the VFT: *formal* verbal fluency, where the participant is asked to name words starting with a certain letter, and *semantic* verbal fluency, where the items to be named belong to a certain category, such as animals, fruit, foods, items in a supermarket and so on. Both types of VFTs are used frequently in research on lexical access difficulties related to brain damage, aphasia, dementia etc., where they have been shown to be highly reliable indicators of early deterioration. For language attrition research, the semantic VFT has, so far, been the preferred option. However, formal VFTs may yield interesting and valuable findings in an attritional setting, in particular as there is typically more variation within healthy populations in formal than in semantic VFTs. On the other hand, formal tasks can be problematic in some languages and for some letters – think, for example, of *t* in English, which can be the first letter in words starting with a variety of different speech sounds, such as /t/ or /θ/, which may confuse participants.

If you want to use the formal version of the VFT, you should choose two or three stimulus letters. It is usually recommended to use the *most frequent word-initial letters* of the language which you are investigating, in order to give your participants the widest possible range of lexical items to choose from. If there are no previous investigations using the VFT for your language, you can establish the frequency roughly by looking at the number of entries in a dictionary which start with each individual letter, or by investigating electronic corpora – however, beware of letters which are used in the representations of different phonemes. Since the number of responses which you can elicit with any individual letter will vary, it is important that all your participants are given the same stimuli, although you may vary the order in which you present them.

For the semantic verbal fluency task, there are now a considerable number of studies on language attrition which have used two stimuli: 'animals' and 'fruit and vegetables'. However, these categories are not unproblematic for a number of reasons: firstly, they are to some degree culture-specific and may therefore prompt code-switching. Many migrants to Canada, for example, attempted to name animals which are highly frequent and familiar in that context, but unfamiliar in the European setting where they came from, such as 'moose' or 'racoon', and named them in the L2. While such phenomena in themselves might be indicative of language attrition, code-switches could trigger further L2 items and therefore distort the picture of overall productivity. Furthermore, the speaker may get stuck on trying to think of the L1 translation of this item, and therefore be less productive than someone who does not attempt this. To some extent, there may be similar issues in the 'fruit and vegetable' category, which furthermore typically elicits a higher number of responses from women than from men. It is therefore important to give careful consideration to the stimulus categories which you will use (in particular because average productivity varies widely across different categories) and anticipate whether such problems might occur in your population.

Task:	Verbal Fluency Task
Linguistic area:	Mental lexicon
Type of knowledge:	Lexical access
Type of data:	Number of responses given within a certain time span (averaged across tasks)
System requirements:	Recording device, stopwatch
Investigations of attrition using this task:	Dostert, 2009; Hulsen, 2000; Keijzer, 2007; Schmid, 2007; Yağmur, 1997
Further reading:	Goodglass and Kaplan, 1983; Roberts and Le Dorze, 1998
Advantages:	Easy to use, most studies find significant differences between attriters and controls
Disadvantages:	Scores often do not correlate with other measures of lexical access (PNT, lexical diversity in free speech, fluency in free speech)

12   Grammaticality judgment tasks

Grammaticality judgments are a very popular task in attrition research. This chapter will look at different ways in which these tasks can be set up and used.

Grammaticality or acceptability judgment tasks (henceforth GJT[1]) are among the most widely used instruments in research on language acquisition, bilingualism, second language learning and language attrition. As the name implies, such tasks present stimulus sentences to participants, inviting them to rate these as grammatically acceptable or unacceptable. Due to the popularity of the GJT it has been adapted and applied in a number of very different ways. This means that if you decide to use such a task, you have to be particularly careful with respect to the methodological choices you make. This does not only apply to the way in which you choose and construct your stimuli but even more importantly to how you present them, how you invite the judgments, and how you record and time responses.

CONSTRUCTION OF THE GJT

The answer to the question of which grammatical features to incorporate in a judgment task depends, of course, on what you want to find out. If your research question is very specific as to the investigation of a particular feature (for example if you are looking at the attrition of Finnish case marking in an English-speaking environment), this choice will be relatively easy. If your approach is more inductive, deciding which grammatical structures you want to test can become complicated. Either way, it is a good idea to base the selection of linguistic variables on previously existing studies of the attrition of this particular language, and to incorporate those features that were found to be problematic for attriters in other situations, e.g. when they were speaking naturally. If there is no such literature, the next best thing is to turn to research on L1 and L2 acquisition of that language. Which features are difficult for children to learn, and why? Which features are difficult for foreigners to learn, and why?

Make sure you present each of the features in which you are interested multiple times in both correct and incorrect formats, and also to include a sufficient number of filler items. There should be at least as many *distracters* (grammatical and ungrammatical sentences containing different constructions) as there are *targets*. A carelessly constructed task with too few distracters can make it possible for the participants to work out what feature you are after, and that may lead to a confusion of explicit and implicit knowledge. You should also always pre-test the GJT on at least ten (unattrited) native speakers to make sure it will elicit the corrections you want. Often your pre-test subjects will stumble over things which you would never have expected to be problematic.

Before the actual test, you should give your participants a number of example or training items in order to demonstrate what the procedure is all about. Here you should also include some items which will illustrate to the participants that they are supposed to judge the formal, i.e. grammatical, correctness of the sentence, not whether or not it is true.

NOTE

I had a number of participants reject perfectly well-formed sentences, such as *I am not afraid of snakes*, saying 'No, that is not correct – I am afraid of them.' On the other hand, a clearly ungrammatical sentence was accepted by a much larger number of participants, both in the experimental and the control group, than any similar sentence, and I think this was due to the fact that it touched on a sensitive issue (extra-marital affairs). Be very careful not to include anything in your test that might in any way be considered taboo or offensive.

PRESENTATION

One of the most important decisions you will have to make with respect to the GJT is how to present your stimulus sentences to your participants. This is important since it impacts on how you will invite their responses: do you allow them time to reflect on whether or not the sentence is correct, or do you require them to respond as quickly as possible, i.e. give their very first gut reaction?

Received wisdom has it that the former type of task – untimed – is an *offline* task and measures explicit knowledge about the grammatical structure, while a timed task is *online* and taps into implicit knowledge. However, this distinction – although widely used and generally accepted – is not entirely unproblematic. Recall the definition of implicit/explicit tasks given above:

> An implicit task is one which attempts to access internally represented knowledge without requiring the subject to become consciously aware of that knowledge. In contrast, an explicit task is one which requires the subject consciously to access particular types of knowledge in the process of carrying out the task. (Tyler, 1992: 159)

If you invite your participants to judge whether or not a particular sentence is grammatical, that judgment will *always* require them to reflect, at some level, on the structure that they have just heard, and not simply to process it as they would any other utterance. In order to get an impression of how the grammatical violation is processed by your participant *before* conscious awareness kicks in, you would have to monitor unconscious or even uncontrolled responses while the sentence is being read, for example by recording eye-movements or an EEG signal (see below).

The concern with online/offline tasks is fairly recent, and you may find that older studies which have used grammaticality judgment tasks do not give detailed information on how their sentences were presented (auditorily, visually) and how the responses were elicited (yes/no or gradient judgments). One of the milestones of attrition research, the volume *First Language Attrition* edited by Herbert W. Seliger and Robert M. Vago in 1991, for example, contains three contributions which describe studies using grammaticality judgments but do not describe their procedures. Reading between the lines it seems likely that they used a pen-and-paper method and untimed responses (Altenberg, 1991, who does state that the responses ranged from 1 (totally unacceptable) to 5 (totally acceptable); de Bot *et al.*, 1991; Seliger, 1991). This method of elicitation was the norm at that time, although some studies already preferred gradient judgments (e.g. Grosjean and Py, 1991, who used a 7-point Likert scale) to binary yes/no answers.

Studies which time responses and require subjects to answer as quickly as they can are more recent (e.g. Köpke, 1999, 2002; Pelc, 2001). If you do plan on using a grammaticality judgment task, be aware that a careful description of your task as well as a motivation of your choice to use a certain type of construction, a certain mode of presentation and a certain way to elicit responses is an absolute necessity. In the following, I shall present the various options, proceeding from the most explicit/offline to the most implicit/online condition.

Pen-and-paper method

This is the most low-tech way of administering a GJT. You simply give your participants a list of sentences on paper and ask them to record their judgment for each item. This method has its practical advantages, for example if your fieldwork includes travelling in regions where you may not always have a chance to find an electrical socket to plug your computer into, or where the power supply is unreliable. However, there are drawbacks: in reading grammatical and ungrammatical sentences, people will often unconsciously apply a correction, particularly if the two versions are very like each other.

For example, one of my ungrammatical sentences elicited a surprisingly high rate of acceptance in my (pen and paper) pre-testing procedure. This was despite the fact that the violation it included, word order in the context of negation, is quite uncommon and unambiguously ungrammatical. This puzzled me, until I realized that the violation depended solely on the order of two short words which largely contain the same letters. (45a) is the ungrammatical version which I had included in the test, (45b) presents the correct alternative (the two crucial words are set in bold here):

(45)
(a) Der Koffer ist zu voll, ich kann *__nicht ihn__ zumachen.
(b) Der Koffer ist zu voll, ich kann __ihn nicht__ zumachen.
   The suitcase is too full, I cannot shut it.

The pre-test comprised seventy-eight participants, all of whom were first-year university students of German and native speakers of that language. Ten of these speakers accepted (45a) as a correct sentence – more than twice as many acceptances as I received for any other incorrect item used in the test. I assumed that this was not so much the outcome of the respondents being unable to recognize this structure as a violation but of relatively careless reading. I therefore decided in my actual experiment to present sentences visually and auditorily at the same time. The outcome of the experiment corroborated my intuition: only one participant, from a total of 159 (53 control group speakers and 106 attriters), did not judge sentence (45a) as grammatically incorrect upon having both read and heard it.

I recommend this *double mode of presentation* for untimed (offline) versions of the GJT. At a pinch, you can achieve it by reading the sentences out yourself while the participants have the written version in front of them. That, however, does not exclude the possibility that you give some of your participants stronger clues than others through your intonation, nor that you might stumble while reading some of the sentences. If you are tired (as you will be!), you yourself may even inadvertently 'correct' the sentence which you read out.

It is therefore advisable to have a native speaker with a standard accent practise both correct and incorrect sentences until they sound natural, then tape them and present them at the same time as the written version on your computer. The participants can pace themselves through the presentation by pressing a button once they have made their judgment, and you can record the judgments on paper as you go along. You may also want to ask them to correct the sentences they object to, in order to see whether the judgment is based on the target features.

NOTE

You should always use a voice other than your own for such recordings. Since you are the researcher, a university-educated language expert, your participants may assume that you know about language far better than they themselves do (this is particularly true for attriters, who may have come to doubt their own proficiency), so they may tend to accept everything you say as correct per definition.

Task:	Untimed (offline) grammaticality judgment task
Linguistic area:	This task is typically used to investigate morphosyntax
Type of knowledge:	Explicit application of grammatical rules
Type of data:	Accuracy judgments
System requirements:	None for pen-and-paper version, laptop computer with presentation software for simultaneous presentation of written and spoken sentences
Investigations of attrition using this task:	Altenberg, 1991; de Bot *et al.*, 1991; Grosjean and Py, 1991; Seliger, 1991
Further reading:	Altenberg and Vago, 2004; Schütze, 1996
Advantages:	Can investigate specific areas of grammar
Disadvantages:	Some studies find no significant difference between attriters and controls

Speeded GJT

It is often assumed that while the untimed task described above measures explicit knowledge, GJTs can also tap into implicit knowledge, provided that the judgment is forced as quickly as possible after the presentation of the sentence. In principle, such a test can then again elicit two types of data: accuracy in detecting ungrammatical structures and response time. However, timing in this context is a highly complex issue: if you start measuring the RT from the moment that the sentence is presented on the screen, there will be a delay which is affected by sentence length, word length, sentence complexity and possibly a number of other variables, and will thus vary per stimulus.

In order to circumvent this, many studies employ the method of presenting each word individually for a certain length of time, often 250 milliseconds (ms) plus 17 ms for each letter of the word, to allow extra reading time for longer words. This is called *rapid serial visual presentation* or RSVP. So, in the case of (45a) above, the first word, *der* 'the', would be presented for $250 + 3 \times 17 = 301$ ms, the second word, *Koffer* 'suitcase', for $250 + 6 \times 17 = 352$ ms, and so on (see Figure 12.1).

Before the words start appearing on the screen, a fixation point, i.e. a star or a cross, is presented in the middle of the screen at the location where the words are about to appear. After the last word has disappeared, the participant is required to press the 'correct' or 'incorrect' button as quickly as possible.

The advantage of this method is that it allows you to measure reaction times either from the moment that the participant has read the entire sentence or from the point in the sentence at which it can unambiguously be identified as ungrammatical. However, it is possible that accuracy and response times may be influenced, not only by the knowledge of grammatical rules (implicit or explicit) but also by the participant's working memory span. It has been shown that RSVP

Order of presentation	1	2	3	4	5	6	7	8	9	10
Word on screen	der	Koffer	ist	zu	voll	ich	kann	nicht	ihn	zumachen
On-screen time (ms)	301	352	301	284	318	301	318	335	301	386

Figure 12.1 A schematic representation of word-by-word presentation of a sentence in a speeded GJT

is similar to normal reading for short sentences, but as the sentence gets longer, the system can overload quickly, causing a breakdown of comprehension. If you decide to present your sentences in this manner, it may therefore be a good idea to also include a standard working memory test in your test battery, for example the Digit Span Test included in the Wechsler Adult Intelligence Scale (WAIS), in order to determine if there is a correlation between the two measures.

If you are concerned with implicit grammatical knowledge, you may decide to simply ignore the issue of reaction times, as Köpke (1999) did. You still put your participants under time pressure, urging them to make their choice as quickly as possible, but for your analysis you only consider the accuracy of these judgments and disregard their speed.

Task:	Speeded grammaticality judgment task
Type of knowledge:	Implicit grammatical knowledge
Type of data:	Accuracy judgments
System requirements:	Computer for presentation
	Software for timing responses (E-Prime or shareware alternatives, see above under PNT)
Investigations of attrition using this task:	Köpke, 1999
Further reading:	On GJT Schütze, 1996; on RSVP Masson, 1983
Advantages:	Appears to elicit more reliable differences between attriters and controls than untimed GJTs
Disadvantages:	Requires specific hard- and software

Self-paced reading

In this task, the stimulus is again presented one word at a time, but it is up to the participants to 'forward' through the sentence. Every time they press a button, the next word will appear, and this response will be timed by means of the appropriate software. After the sentence has finished, the participant is again invited to judge whether it was grammatically correct or not.

In the schematic representation of (45a) above, presented in Figure 12.2, the line between the 9th and the 10th word symbolizes the point in the sentence at which it can unambiguously be identified as ungrammatical: until the word *nicht*, there is still the possibility that it might be concluded without any violation, e.g. (45c).

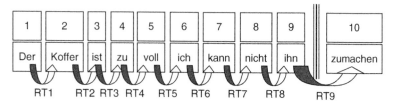

Figure 12.2 A schematic representation of word-by-word presentation of a sentence in a self-paced reading task

(45)

(c) Der Koffer ist zu voll, ich kann nicht noch mehr hineintun.
   The suitcase is too full, I cannot get anything more in it.

In self-paced reading, we assume that when participants detect an error, they will slow down because of the increased processing effort of trying to make sense of the deviant construction. It would therefore be expected that speakers who have internalized the rules governing German word order in negation would have a delay on RT9 in comparison with a similar sentence which does not contain a violation. This method has an advantage over both the untimed method and the speeded GJT, as it can provide insights into *where* the participant first encounters a problem. Again, if you apply this type of measurement, you should be aware that short-term memory might be an issue. However, in this case that problem can be circumvented by allowing the text to appear *cumulatively*, so that each new word appears next to the previous ones in the position where it would be in normal reading.

Presentation of a sentence in this manner should then be followed either by a comprehension question (e.g. 'Ist der Koffer voll?' – *Is the suitcase full?*) or by an overt judgment of the sentence's grammaticality. This ensures that the participants will actually read the sentence, and not just click through the words as fast as they can once they begin to get bored.

Task:	Self-paced reading task
Type of knowledge:	Processing of implicit grammatical rules
Type of data:	Accuracy judgments, response times when forwarding from grammatical vs violating stimuli
System requirements:	See speeded GJT
Investigations of attrition using this task:	To my knowledge, no studies have been carried out so far using this paradigm

Further reading:	Ferreira and Henderson, 1990
Advantages:	Can provide insight into the specific locations at which grammatical problems are encountered
Disadvantages:	Requires specific hard- and software, results may be influenced by participants' working memory

Eye-tracking

A different method of gaining insight into the actual mental processes that take place when participants read ungrammatical sentences is by means of investigating on which items in the sentence the eyes are focused during reading, for how long this focus lasts, and in which order they are looked at. In silent reading, short and very rapid gaze movements which are called *saccadic eye movements* alternate with *fixations* on particular regions of the text, typically lasting around 200–250 ms. In other words, what you do when you encounter a written text is read a bit, move your eyes to the next bit, stop and read it, and then move on. There are very systematic tendencies here: readers tend to focus longer on more important words, less frequent or unpredictable words and longer words, while short, frequent and predictable words (particularly function words) are often skipped entirely.

NOTE

A few years ago, the following little exercise was circulated on the internet:

Count the number of times that the letter F appears in the following sentence:
FINISHED FILES ARE THE RESULT OF YEARS OF SCIENTIFIC STUDY COMBINED WITH THE EXPERIENCE OF YEARS.

Most people count 3 occurrences (finished, files and scientific) but overlook the fact that F also occurs in the three instances of the word of, because these belong to the short, frequent words which tend to be skipped.

However, when you encounter a construction which is odd in some way, you will usually pause longer and then move your eyes back to the material you had encountered previously, trying to make sense of the erroneous construction. In order to judge how problematic an item is, there are therefore three things that have to be taken into account:

how long is the item focused on during the *first pass*, how often do readers move their eyes backwards to previous material (this backward saccadic movement is called *regression*) and what is the total time they spend reading the item in question (i.e. the sum of the duration of the first and all subsequent fixations). This technique can therefore provide more detailed information about processing strategies than self-paced reading, which only provides insight into how long a reader takes before progressing to the next word.

Traditionally, eye-tracking has most often been used to monitor processing of ambiguous structures – the so-called *garden-path* type of sentence. Such sentences are biased towards one interpretation until a certain point, at which it becomes clear that this cannot be correct. For example, consider the sentence 'The horse raced past the barn.' Here, the word *raced* is clearly the finite verb of the main clause. However, in the construction 'The horse raced past the barn fell' *raced* begins an embedded relative clause in the passive, and *fell* is the verb of the main, matrix clause. In other words, the sentence could also have read 'The horse [which was raced past the barn] fell (while the horse [which was walked slowly] made it safely to the stables).' Readers of such garden-path sentences typically pause when they encounter the ambiguity and then regress to previous regions of the text in a process called *garden-path recovery*.

Similarly, sentences which contain grammatical abnormalities, such as 'The cats won't *eating* the food we put on the porch' elicit eye-movements back to previous regions of the text in comparison with a 'normal' sentence such as 'The cats won't *eat* the food we put on the porch.' Note that, since factors such as word length or frequency impact on reading times, as was pointed out above, it is vital in the construction of a reading task that these factors should be balanced equally across grammatical and ungrammatical (or normal and garden-path) sentences.

The only investigation of language attrition using the eye-tracking technique to date is Paola E. Dussias' 2004 investigation of relative clause attachment in Spanish–English bilinguals. Recall the sentences quoted above:

(46)
(a) Acabo de ver a la hermana de la actriz que está embarazada.
   I just saw the sister of the actress who is pregnant.

English speakers would tend to interpret (46a) to mean that it is *the actress* who is pregnant (low attachment), while for Spanish speakers the referent is more likely *the sister* (high attachment). This means that

Spanish speakers will encounter problems with a sentence such as the one in (46b) which is unproblematic in English, while (46c) would be more difficult for the English speakers.

(46)
(b) Acabo de ver al hermano de la actriz que está embarazada.
I just saw the brother of the actress who is pregnant.
(c) Acabo de ver a la hermana del actor que está embarazada.
I just saw the sister of the actor who is pregnant.

Dussias (2004) and Dussias and Sagarra (2007) monitored the eye-movements of Spanish monolinguals and Spanish–English bilinguals when they were reading such structures. They found that, while the monolinguals behaved in the expected way, with longer fixation times on the item which disambiguates the referent of the relative clause – in this case, the adjective 'pregnant' – in sentences of the type (46), the bilinguals had apparently come to adopt the English preference for low attachment and took longer to read structures of the type (46c).

The eye-tracking technique can thus provide very interesting insights into subtle changes in the interpretation of sentences. Some of these changes might be too fine-grained to appear in surface grammaticality judgments. Unfortunately, this method uses relatively expensive equipment which usually is situated in a laboratory (although there are now some eyetrackers which are portable). It also requires very specialized knowledge and highly sophisticated statistical analysis. However, for researchers who have access to the necessary equipment and expertise, eye-tracking is certainly a promising method for further investigations of language attrition.

Task:	Eye-tracking while reading, followed by grammaticality judgment
Type of knowledge:	Processing of implicit grammatical rules
Type of data:	Saccadic eye movements, accuracy judgments
System requirements:	Eye-tracker (head-mounted or free standing) with computer system for monitoring gaze movements, specialized software for the recording of the data
Investigations of attrition using this task:	Dussias, 2004; Dussias and Sagarra, 2007
Further reading:	Eye-movements in resolving syntactic ambiguities: Dussias, 2010; eye-movements

	in response to unambiguous anomalies: Ni, Fodor, Crain and Shankweiler, 1998.
Advantages:	Can provide insight into the specific locations at which grammatical problems are encountered
Disadvantages:	Requires specialized and expensive hardware and software and knowledge

EEG measures and event-related potentials (ERPs)

The final manner of investigating the processing of grammatical vs ungrammatical sentences which will be discussed here is by way of monitoring voltage changes in electroencephalogram (EEG) readings during the presentation of stimulus sentences. Whenever we encounter information, electrical activity takes place in our brain as synapses communicate with each other, and this activity can be measured by means of electrodes. These electrodes are integrated into a cap which is placed on the scalp and sends the readings to the computer controlling the experiment and presenting the stimuli. The readings of neural activity which occurs as processing unfolds after a particular stimulus is encountered are called event-related potentials (ERPs).

ERPs can provide online, millisecond-by-millisecond insights into what is going on in the brain as certain stimuli are presented. For the purpose of investigating implicit grammatical knowledge, ERPs can be used to compare the neural activity which takes place when someone reads or hears a well-formed sentence with the response to a sentence containing a grammatical violation. Depending on the type of violation, a number of different ERP components have been found. Where syntactic violations are concerned, the best-known component is the so-called P600. The P here stands for 'positivity' and the 600 refers to the number of milliseconds which typically elapse between the moment at which the deviant stimulus is presented and the moment where a peak can be observed in the EEG signal.

Figure 12.3, which originates from an investigation by Hanneke Loerts, illustrates such an effect. In her study, words were presented serially for 240 ms on a computer screen, followed by a 240-ms pause before the presentation of the next word. Some of the stimuli used were grammatical, as illustrated in (47a), others contained a violation (47b).

(47)
(a) He walks down the street to the café.
(b) *He walk down the street to the café.

The electric signal was measured from the point where the violation could be detected in the ungrammatical sentence (in this example the onset of the word *walk*). The solid black line in Figure 12.3 represents the signal from the electrode labelled Pz (posterior central, that is at the back of the skull and in the middle) in those cases where the sentences were grammatical (negative activity is usually plotted upwards of the x-axis (horizontal), positive activity is plotted downwards). The dotted line shows the activity when the sentence contained a grammatical violation. You can see that the two lines start diverging around 500 ms, and that the peak of the response to the violation is reached around 700 ms.

In other words, the P600 is a peak in the signal which takes place ca. 600 ms after the violation has been presented. This effect is found very reliably in response to ungrammatical sentences and is mainly distributed over the electrodes which are placed in posterior (back) central and right locations of the head.

ERPs have often been used in order to investigate implicit grammatical knowledge of L2 learners in an attempt to determine whether their responses can ever become truly native-like. They can provide

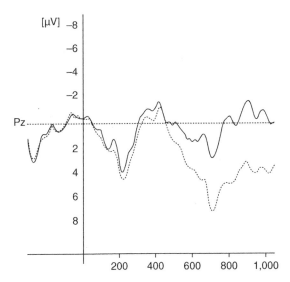

Figure 12.3 EEG reading upon the presentation of a grammatical (solid line) and ungrammatical (dotted line) stimulus sentence. I am grateful to Hanneke Loerts for providing this picture.

insights into such processing issues and the difference between L2 learners' implicit and explicit grammatical knowledge, particularly if the ERP reading is combined with an accuracy judgment at the end of the sentence. So far, no one has attempted to use ERPs in investigations of L1 attrition (a description of an ongoing project can be found on www.let.rug.nl/languageattrition/projects).

Working with the ERP technique requires more training and expertise than most of the methods presented above. Furthermore, it crucially depends on access to laboratory facilities. The technology needed to take ERP readings is not normally portable (although mobile labs are being developed), so you will need all your participants to come to you. If you are going to take readings in two countries – for the experimental and the control group – you will also have to make sure that the technology used in both laboratories is comparable. In addition, you may be required to pay for the lab time, certainly in the country where you are a visitor, and an hour's use of an EEG lab will typically cost between €75 and €100. If your university has some kind of formal or informal partnership programme with the institution abroad, or if you can interest a scientist there in working with you, you may be able to negotiate on this. However, you should be aware that the technical and financial difficulties to overcome if you are planning to use the ERP technique will probably be larger than with most alternatives.

Task:	Event-related potentials (ERPs) in response to grammatical violations
Type of knowledge:	Processing of implicit grammatical rules
Type of data:	EEG readings
System requirements:	EEG laboratory
Investigations of attrition using this task:	The ERP technique has not yet been applied to investigations of language attrition (but see www.let.rug.nl/languageattrition/projects)
Further reading:	Luck, 2005; van Hell and Tokowicz, 2010
Advantages:	Can provide insight into how grammatical processing unfolds across time upon the presentation of the stimulus
Disadvantages:	Requires access to an EEG laboratory and very specialized knowledge for designing and carrying out the experiment as well as for the analysis of the data

NOTE

Where the presentation of your stimuli for the GJT and the elicitation of the responses are concerned, you have a range of options. These options determine which type of knowledge you investigate: if you use untimed, offline judgments, you are investigating *explicit* grammatical knowledge. Speeded tasks, eye-tracking, self-paced readings and ERPs, on the other hand, are considered online tasks which can tap into *implicit* knowledge.

Types of judgments

A second important issue to consider when using grammaticality judgment tasks is in what form you will invite the responses. There are three options here:

1. Binary judgments (yes/no)
2. Scaled judgments (Likert)
3. Magnitude estimation

Binary judgments merely require your participants to state categorically whether the sentence they have just heard/read is grammatically acceptable or not. If you are planning to use some form of speeded judgment task, that is the only option. However, if you are going to allow your participants time to think about their judgment – either in the offline version of the task, or in combination with some other online measure such as self-paced reading, eyetracking or ERP, you may want to consider a more fine-grained measure of acceptability judgment.

Investigations of L2 linguistic knowledge often use scaled judgments, allowing to capture the *relative* acceptability of a sentence. Here, the participant is presented with a number of options (usually five or seven) ranging from *completely grammatical* to *completely ungrammatical*, as illustrated in (48):

(48)
Der Koffer ist zu voll, ich kann nicht ihn zumachen.

completely   completely
grammatical   ungrammatical

This method tries to reflect the fact that acceptability is a gradient phenomenon: some sentences are *marginally acceptable* to most speakers, or can be made acceptable if the sentence is embedded in some specific context. Other sentences will constitute an unambiguous violation for most or all speakers, regardless of the context.

One problem with such scaled (Likert) options is that they may be employed slightly differently by different populations. In particular when the judgments are elicited from both native speakers and L2 learners or L1 attriters, the latter groups may use them not so much as a scale of acceptability but as a *confidence* scale. In other words, an L2 learner may think 'This sentence looks bad to me – but what do I know, I am just a foreigner . . .' and therefore avoid the extreme ends of the scale altogether. The same may be true for L1 attriters who have come to doubt the reliability of their own intuition. Furthermore, with these kinds of scaled judgments one can never be sure that each option is the same distance from its neighbours. The boxes are typically assigned numerical values ('1' for 'totally correct', 7 for 'totally incorrect'), but when a participant picks a '4', this does not necessarily imply that this sentence is four times as bad as a perfectly acceptable one. It means that calculating averages across judgments is problematic (although it is common practice to do so). I will address these specific problems below when I discuss types of data (chapter 16).

A different manner of eliciting gradient judgments, where neither of these two problems occurs, is called *magnitude estimation* (ME). This is a technique which was originally developed in the area of psychophysics, for example to measure impressions such as how loud a given stimulus is. In this experiment, subjects would be presented with a certain mid-range stimulus (e.g. a sound that was neither very loud nor very soft), and asked to assign it a number that would represent its loudness. This initial number is therefore individual: one participant might give it a 10, the next a 20, and so on. A range of other stimuli is then presented which the participant has to rate *in relation to* the original one. So, if the stimulus appears to be twice as loud, the reference number (10 or 20 in our case) is to be multiplied by two, if it is ten times as loud, by ten.

In experiments which use MEs to elicit linguistic judgments, participants are often trained on non-linguistic stimuli beforehand to familiarize them with the idea of this scale. For example, you may present your speakers with lines of different length and require them to rate their lengths in the fashion described above. This procedure is recommended by Bard, Robertson and Sorace (1996), who used twelve lines, ranging between 2 mm and 98 mm, starting with a stimulus of around 50 mm.

Since for ME judgments each participant establishes their own individual range of values, the problem of non-native speakers avoiding the extremes of the pre-established Likert Scale does not occur. Once

Table 12.1 *A hypothetical example of ME responses on a grammaticality judgment task*

	Sentence 1	Sentence 2	Sentence 3	Sentence 4	Sentence 5
Participant A	35	70	350	140	210
Participant B	20	100	200	500	300
Participant C	1	5	15	10	15
Participant D	−20	0	100	80	60

all judgments are elicited, you can recalculate them yourself to a standardized scale (so that you can compare the judgments between your participants) by setting the highest number as 100 and the lowest as zero. For the sake of illustration, say that you have a GJ task which includes five sentences, and that four participants have completed this task (of course any real task would have more sentences and a larger number of participants). Table 12.1 gives the values which each of these hypothetical participants have assigned each sentence.

As you can see, there is a rough tendency towards agreement: all participants give the lowest value to sentence 1, and rate sentences 3–5 relatively high, although not everyone has the maximum rating for the same sentence. The different scales, however, make the individual responses very hard to compare, as you can see in Figure 12.4 when they are put in a graph.

Obviously, you cannot compare these ratings or calculate averages either for the individual sentences or for the individual participants. What we need to do, therefore, is to recalculate the scale for each participant, so that they all have a 0 for the sentence that they had rated the lowest (sentence 1), Participants A and D have 100 for sentence 3, Participant B for sentence 4 and Participant C for sentences 3 and 5. The remaining values should then be distributed proportionally across this scale (see Figure 12.5).

The formula to calculate this is actually much less complicated than it may look. You first need to determine the minimum and maximum of the scale which each participant has applied. For example, in the case of Participant A, the minimum is 35 and the maximum is 350. For each individual value in the table, you subtract the scale minimum from the value, and then divide the result by the maximum minus the minimum. So, to recalculate a value X, you need to apply the following formula, as in Table 12.2.

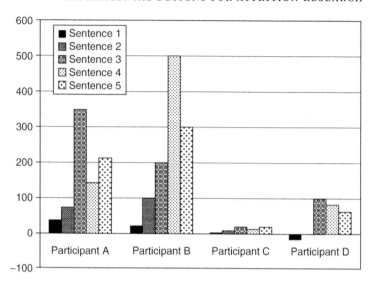

Figure 12.4 A graphic representation of a hypothetical sample of ME ratings

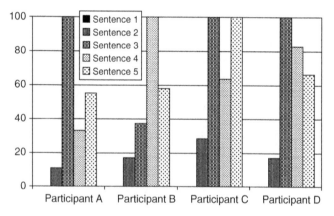

Figure 12.5 A graphic representation of a hypothetical sample of ME ratings, recalculated to a scale of 0–100

$$(X - \text{ScaleMinimum})/(\text{ScaleMaximum} - \text{ScaleMinimum})$$

As you can see, this operation recalculates the original values to a proportional scale between 0 and 1. In order to increase this scale to

Table 12.2 *Recalculation of ME responses from Participant A*

Sentence 1	Sentence 2	Sentence 3	Sentence 4	Sentence 5
$=\frac{(35-35)}{(350-35)}$	$=\frac{(70-35)}{(350-35)}$	$=\frac{(350-35)}{(350-35)}$	$=\frac{(140-35)}{(350-35)}$	$=\frac{(210-35)}{(350-35)}$
$=\frac{0}{315}$	$=\frac{35}{315}$	$=\frac{315}{315}$	$=\frac{105}{315}$	$=\frac{175}{315}$
$=0.00$	$=0.11$	$=1.00$	$=0.33$	$=0.56$

Table 12.3 *Recalculation of ME responses to a scale of 0 to 100*

	Sentence 1	Sentence 2	Sentence 3	Sentence 4	Sentence 5
Participant A	$=\frac{(35-35)}{\left(\frac{(350-35)}{100}\right)}$	$=\frac{(70-35)}{\left(\frac{(350-35)}{100}\right)}$	$=\frac{(350-35)}{\left(\frac{(350-35)}{100}\right)}$	$=\frac{(140-35)}{\left(\frac{(350-35)}{100}\right)}$	$=\frac{(210-35)}{\left(\frac{(350-35)}{100}\right)}$
	$=\frac{0}{\left(\frac{315}{100}\right)}$	$=\frac{35}{\left(\frac{315}{100}\right)}$	$=\frac{315}{\left(\frac{315}{100}\right)}$	$=\frac{105}{\left(\frac{315}{100}\right)}$	$=\frac{175}{\left(\frac{315}{100}\right)}$
	$=\frac{0}{3.15}$	$=\frac{35}{3.15}$	$=\frac{315}{3.15}$	$=\frac{105}{3.15}$	$=\frac{175}{3.15}$
	$=0.00$	$=11.11$	$=100.00$	$=33.33$	$=55.56$
Participant B	$=\frac{(20-20)}{\left(\frac{(500-20)}{100}\right)}$	$=\frac{(100-20)}{\left(\frac{(500-20)}{100}\right)}$	$=\frac{(200-20)}{\left(\frac{(500-20)}{100}\right)}$	$=\frac{(500-20)}{\left(\frac{(500-20)}{100}\right)}$	$=\frac{(300-20)}{\left(\frac{(500-20)}{100}\right)}$
	$=\frac{0}{\left(\frac{480}{100}\right)}$	$=\frac{80}{\left(\frac{480}{100}\right)}$	$=\frac{180}{\left(\frac{480}{100}\right)}$	$=\frac{480}{\left(\frac{480}{100}\right)}$	$=\frac{280}{\left(\frac{480}{100}\right)}$
	$=\frac{0}{4.8}$	$=\frac{80}{4.8}$	$=\frac{180}{4.8}$	$=\frac{480}{4.8}$	$=\frac{280}{4.8}$
	$=0.00$	$=16.67$	$=37.50$	$=100.00$	$=58.33$
Participant C	$=\frac{(1-1)}{\left(\frac{(15-1)}{100}\right)}$	$=\frac{(5-1)}{\left(\frac{(15-1)}{100}\right)}$	$=\frac{(15-1)}{\left(\frac{(15-1)}{100}\right)}$	$=\frac{(10-1)}{\left(\frac{(15-1)}{100}\right)}$	$=\frac{(15-1)}{\left(\frac{(15-1)}{100}\right)}$
	$=\frac{0}{\left(\frac{14}{100}\right)}$	$=\frac{4}{\left(\frac{14}{100}\right)}$	$=\frac{14}{\left(\frac{14}{100}\right)}$	$=\frac{9}{\left(\frac{14}{100}\right)}$	$=\frac{14}{\left(\frac{14}{100}\right)}$
	$=\frac{0}{0.14}$	$=\frac{4}{0.14}$	$=\frac{14}{0.14}$	$=\frac{9}{0.14}$	$=\frac{14}{0.14}$
	$=0.00$	$=28.57$	$=100.00$	$=64.29$	$=100.00$
Participant D	$=\frac{((-20)-(-20))}{\left(\frac{(100-(-20))}{100}\right)}$	$=\frac{(0-(-20))}{\left(\frac{(100-(-20))}{100}\right)}$	$=\frac{(100-(-20))}{\left(\frac{(100-(-20))}{100}\right)}$	$=\frac{(80-(-20))}{\left(\frac{(100-(-20))}{100}\right)}$	$=\frac{(60-(-20))}{\left(\frac{(100-(-20))}{100}\right)}$
	$=\frac{((-20)+20)}{\left(\frac{(100+20)}{100}\right)}$	$=\frac{(0+20)}{\left(\frac{(100+20)}{100}\right)}$	$=\frac{(100+20)}{\left(\frac{(100+20)}{100}\right)}$	$=\frac{(80+20)}{\left(\frac{(100+20)}{100}\right)}$	$=\frac{(60+20)}{\left(\frac{(100+20)}{100}\right)}$
	$=\frac{0}{\left(\frac{120}{100}\right)}$	$=\frac{20}{\left(\frac{120}{100}\right)}$	$=\frac{120}{\left(\frac{120}{100}\right)}$	$=\frac{100}{\left(\frac{120}{100}\right)}$	$=\frac{80}{\left(\frac{120}{100}\right)}$
	$=\frac{0}{1.2}$	$=\frac{20}{1.2}$	$=\frac{120}{1.2}$	$=\frac{100}{1.2}$	$=\frac{80}{1.2}$
	$=0.00$	$=16.67$	$=100.00$	$=83.33$	$=66.67$

0 to 100, you need to make one further adjustment in the formula: the divisor has to be divided by 100 (see Table 12.3):

$$(X - \text{ScaleMinimum})/((\text{ScaleMaximum} - \text{ScaleMinimum})/100)$$

If we now put these new values on a graph (see Figure 12.5), we can see that, while the original proportions for each participant are preserved, they are now all neatly on the same scale.

You may now perform mathematical and statistical operations on these recalculated values: you can calculate group averages and standard deviations, perform group comparisons, relate them to extralinguistic variables and so on.

If you think it is important to investigate gradient acceptability judgments, that is, if you want to gain a fine-grained insight into intuitions about the grammaticality of certain features, then using an ME scale may provide you with better data than Likert Scale responses. However, you will have to train your informants on how to establish their ratings beforehand, and for some groups of speakers (particularly elderly speakers with little formal education), this may not always be easy.

If, on the other hand, you do not want to bother with these complications, you are on solid ground as well: there are a number of studies which have specifically compared different types of ratings for the same GJT items – that is, they carried out the same task with three groups of participants, eliciting dichotomous, Likert Scale and ME ratings. These investigations find that there are no overall group differences, and that the added value of scalar judgment is therefore not as great as is commonly believed (Murphy, 2007; Weskott and Fanselow, 2008).

In conclusion, I want to emphasize again that whichever types of judgments you choose to elicit, and however you choose to present your sentences (on paper, on the screen, auditorily, through RSVP), it is crucial that you think about these issues in advance, and that you present your rationale and motivation clearly.

13   Other grammatical tasks

> Grammaticality judgment tasks are probably the most frequently
> used but by no means the only tasks that seek to tap into underlying
> structural linguistic knowledge. This chapter will present some other
> tests that have been used in attrition research.

INTERPRETATION OF AMBIGUOUS SENTENCES

While the GJT is useful for testing grammatical rules and their violations,
there are cases where a straightforward acceptability task may not be
possible: some grammatical structures are perfectly grammatical but
may bias or force different interpretations. Since this preferential interpretation can vary across languages it is a potential source for attrition
effects. One grammatical feature which has been investigated in this
respect is the referential potential of pronouns which I discussed above.
For example, in English, the sentence

(49)
Murat said that he would go to the movies.[1]

can either mean that it is Murat who would go (for example in response to
the question 'What did Murat say?') or that it is someone else (in response
to the question 'Where is Thomas?'). It is common practice to indicate
these possible readings by providing each item in the sentence with a
subscript letter, called an *index*:

(49)
Murat$_i$ said that he$_{i/j}$ would go to the movies.

where the i after *he* and after *Murat* means that the two words can be
co-referential (they mean the same person), while the j indicates that

the pronoun could also refer to someone else (not present in this sentence).

Turkish, on the other hand, has three options for this sentence, which are illustrated in (50a–c) below.

(50)
(a) Murat$_i$ onun$_{*i/j}$ sinemaya gideceğini söyledi.
(b) Murat$_i$ kendisinin$_{i/j}$ sinemaya gideceğini söyledi.
(c) Murat$_i$ Ø$_i$ sinemaya gideceğini söyledi.

In the first sentence, the pronoun *onun* cannot refer to Murat himself, only to another person. The pronoun *kendisi* used in sentence (50b) is ambiguous between Murat and another person. Similar to English, the sentence would likely be interpreted to refer to Murat, unless there is a disambiguating context (e.g. if the sentence is an answer to the question 'Where is Thomas?'). Sentence (40c) does not contain an overt pronoun at all (the literal translation would be 'Murat said that Ø would go to the movies', where the symbol Ø – zero – stands for a phonetically empty form), and the only possible referent for the person who is going to the movies is Murat himself.

Such subtle differences between how sentences can be interpreted across languages are, of course, a potential source of cross-linguistic influence both for L2 learners and for L1 attriters. In order to test how participants interpret these potentially ambiguous constructions, sentences are often either presented together with a picture of the situation, or followed by a comprehension question. This task is called *Picture Verification* or *Sentence Interpretation Task*.

The Turkish structures above are borrowed from the work of Ayşe Gürel (2002), who tested the interpretation of pronominal reference in Turkish by both L1 attriters and L2 learners of this language. In her experiments, participants simultaneously saw a picture and heard a sentence. They were instructed to indicate whether the situation portrayed in the picture matched the sentence. In order to unambiguously identify the characters in the picture, Gürel used the ingenious strategy of having the characters drawn in different colours, and referring to them with names such as *Mehmet Yeşil* (Mehmet Green) or *Ahmet Sarı* (Ahmet Yellow).

Here is an example from Gürel's investigation which she kindly allowed me to use. In this case, participants listened to the sentence 'Ahmet Yellow said that he talked to Ayşe.' At the same time as they heard this, they were shown the picture in Figure 13.1.

Figure 13.1 A stimulus picture for a picture verification task used by
Gürel (2002), reprinted with kind permission of the author

(51)
(a) Ahmet Sarı$_i$ onun$_{*i/j}$ Ayşe'yle konuştuğunu söyledi. (sentence presented
auditorily)
(b) *Ahmet Yellow$_i$ said that he$_{i/j}$ talked to Ayse.*

In the picture, the speaker (Ahmet Yellow, who is wearing a yellow jacket)
is clearly referring to himself as the person who spoke to Ayşe. In the
Turkish sentence given under (51a), this interpretation is not possible, as
the overt pronoun *onun* was used which cannot be co-referential with
Ahmet Yellow. The English sentence (51b), on the other hand, does allow the
interpretation depicted in the picture. It is therefore expected that, while
monolingual Turkish speakers would reject this combination and say
that there is a mismatch between the sentence and the picture, Turkish–
English bilinguals might accept it due to cross-linguistic influence.

While such picture verification tasks may present a convenient
method of tapping into the way in which speakers establish reference,
they are very labour-intensive to construct, and the experimenter
again has to be wary of the copyright issues involved in reproducing

the pictures. Even if you do know someone who can draw the pictures for you specifically or are able to do so yourself, however, picture verification tasks limit you to sentences which describe situations that can easily be depicted. Some studies therefore use more overt sentence interpretation tasks. For example, recall the English and Turkish sentence mentioned above:

(52)
(a) Murat$_i$ onun$_{*i/j}$ sinemaya gideceğini söyledi.
(b) Murat$_i$ kendisinin$_{i/j}$ sinemaya gideceğini söyledi.
(c) Murat$_i$ Ø$_i$ sinemaya gideceğini söyledi.

In addition to her picture verification task, Gürel had her participants read such sentences, and followed them with questions such as:
   Who went to the movies?

(a) Murat
(b) some other person
(c) both

She also used a slightly more elaborate version of the same task, in which the content was not limited to a single sentence but consisted of a little story. Following the story was a sentence, and the participants were asked to judge whether the sentence was true or not:

(53)
Mehmet and his friend, Burak, were going on a business trip on the same day. Mehmet was going to Germany, while Burak was going to England. When they arrived at the airport, they were told that flights to England had been delayed.
Burak onun uçağının gecikeceğini öğrendi.
Burak$_i$ learned that his$_{*i/j}$ flight was delayed.

Again, since *onun* can only refer to a person other than Burak in this sentence, monolingual Turkish participants were expected to judge this sentence as 'false', while Turkish–English bilinguals might accept it due to interference from their L2.

Summary

Three tasks were described above, which attempt to tap into the way in which participants establish the meaning of potentially ambiguous items within a sentence:

1. Picture verification task
2. Sentence interpretation task
3. Story interpretation task

The examples used here concerned the reference of pronominal elements, but similar tasks have been employed to test other areas of language. For example, Montrul (2004) employed a story interpretation task to test the imperfect/preterit distinction in Spanish. The advantage of this type of task is that it allows zooming in on very subtle, language-specific features which would be difficult to investigate otherwise. The disadvantage is that participants may feel that the tasks which they need to perform are somewhat contrived and do not correspond much to what they normally do with language. Due to this somewhat unnatural way of manipulating language, it can also be easy for the participants to work out what the object of the task is, in particular if an experiment uses multiple items which test essentially the same structure (and that, of course, is necessary in order to obtain reliable results).

Task:	Interpretation of ambiguous structures by means of
	(a) picture verification (truth value judgment)
	(b) picture-sentence matching
	(c) sentence interpretation
	(d) story interpretation (truth value judgment)
Type of knowledge:	Meaning potential of grammatical structures
Type of data:	Accuracy of judgment
System requirements:	None
Investigations of attrition using this task:	Gürel, 2002, 2004; Montrul, 2004; Tsimpli *et al.*, 2004
Advantages:	Allows the investigation of very specific structures
Disadvantages:	Involves a relatively unnatural and contrived manner of interpreting linguistic data

INFLECTION OF (NONSENSE) WORDS

If the language you are investigating has a complex system of grammatical morphology, for example a number of different affixes to form the plural form of certain nouns (*plural allomorphy*) or regular and irregular past tense forms for verbs, you may want to test whether your participants have retained the ability to correctly inflect these various items.

Consider the way in which the English language marks the plural of nouns. While there are a handful of unpredictable irregulars which speakers have to learn separately in each instance, such as *child – children*, *fish – fish*, *foot – feet* and so on, the vast majority of English nouns are pluralized by adding some form of -s: nouns which end in a voiced item take a voiced plural -s (*boy – boyz*), if the ending is voiceless, so is the plural (*lamp – lamps*), and where the noun ends in a sibilant (for example, *house*), the -s becomes /-ɪz/ (*houses*).[2]

German, on the other hand, has a more complicated system of plural marking, as any poor soul who has ever attempted to learn German as a foreign language knows to their cost – perhaps even literally, as Mark Twain remarks in his wonderful essay *The Awful German Language*:

> if one is casually referring to a house, *Haus*, or a horse, *Pferd*, or a dog, *Hund*, he spells these words as I have indicated; but if he is referring to them in the Dative case, he sticks on a foolish and unnecessary *e* and spells them *Hause*, *Pferde*, *Hunde*. So, as an added E often signifies the plural, as the S does with us . . . many a new student who could ill afford loss, has bought and paid for two dogs and only got one of them, because he ignorantly bought that dog in the Dative singular when he really supposed he was talking plural.

While I am uncertain as to whether there are any attested cases of a customer mistaking the dative singular of an item they were intending to purchase for a plural, there is no doubt that a single glance at the German plural system may cause any beginner to lose the will to live. Table 13.1 summarizes its horrors.

A system like this, one may have cause to think, should present multiple wonderful opportunities for the attriter. So, how would you set about testing this (apart, that is, from having attriters talk and hoping that they get things wrong)?

There are, in principle, two possibilities. The first is to take some existing words, present them to your participants and ask them to supply the plural. You can do this by simply asking 'What is the plural form of X?', but as there are many people who get nervous in the face of grammatical terms such as *plural*, a better choice is probably to provide sentences such as 'You can have one fish, but if there are two, you have two _____.'

Constructing such a task is more complex and labour-intensive than you might think. Before you set out, you should meticulously acquaint yourself with the rules and processes underlying the distribution and use of the forms in question (not omitting the issue of whether there may be dialectal variants!), and then decide which of the plural allomorphs you want to test. This decision should be guided not only by

Table 13.1 *Overview of plural morphemes in German (based on Köpcke, 1988: 307, his Table 1)*

	Gender		
pl.-morpheme	masculine	feminine	neuter
-e	Fisch/Fische	Kenntnis/ Kenntnisse	Jahr/Jahre
	'fish'	'knowledge'	'year'
-(e)n	Bauer/Bauern	Tür/Türen	Auge/Augen
	'farmer'	'door'	'eye'
-er	Geist/Geister	-	Kind/Kinder
	'ghost'		'child'
-s	Park/Parks	Mutti/Muttis	Auto/Autos
	'park'	'mum'	'car'
-∅	Adler/Adler	-	Fenster/ Fenster
	'eagle'		'window'
umlaut [+ -∅, MSS]	Bruder/Brüder	Tochter/Töchter	Kloster/Klöster
	'brother'	'daughter'	'monastery'
umlaut + -e	Sohn/Söhne	Kuh/Kühe	Floß/Flöße
	'son'	'cow'	'raft'
umlaut + -er	Wald/Wälder	-	Volk/Völker
	'wood'		'people'

the acquisitional patterns – which of the allomorphs appear first in child language, which are overgeneralized longest to other forms, how do second language learners acquire them – but also by their frequency. Furthermore, there may be theoretical concerns which go beyond the mere distributional patterns. To stick with the example above, while only about 5 per cent of all German nouns form their plural in -s, there is a substantial body of literature which suggests that -s, notwithstanding being the least frequent allomorph of all, is actually the default form. These kinds of factors should be considered when choosing items and forms to use in an inflectional task.

A second consideration which may impact strongly on inflectional tasks such as the ones described above is *word frequency*. When you ask a speaker to provide the inflected form of an existing word, you cannot be certain whether a correctly supplied answer is an indication of the speaker producing the form according to the underlying rule, or merely retrieving a fully stored plural lexical item from memory. The latter may be easier to do if the word is a highly frequent one. In order to circumvent this problem and make sure that participants actually apply inflectional processes, some studies have taken the approach of presenting their participants with words which they *cannot* have encountered before: made-up items or pseudowords which comply with the phonological and orthographical conventions of the target language – words that could exist, but don't.

This test was first applied by Jean Berko (later Jean Berko-Gleason) in 1958 in order to study morphological processes in child language acquisition. She drew a number of pictures of fantasy creatures and showed them to the children. The first picture would have one such creature, and the child would be told that the creature was, for example, a *wug* (/wʌg/). This would be followed by a picture of two of the creatures, and the experimenter would say: 'Now there are two of them. There are two _____', upon which the child would be expected to provide the form *wugs* (/wʌgz/) (see Figure. 13.2).

This type of test may provide interesting insights into the processes underlying the rules which a speaker applies for plural allomorphy. Recall the German item, *Hund*, which forms its plural with -e, *Hunde*. A relatively similar-sounding nonsense word, such as *Nund*, might elicit the analogous form *Nunde* or the default plural, *Nunds*. The interesting distinction here is

Figure 13.2 Berko's original stimulus pictures to elicit the form *wugs* (Berko 1958). All the pictures used in this study may be downloaded from http://childes.psy.cmu.edu/topics/ and used in other investigations

whether a speaker forms the plural based on a *schema* or on a *rule*. There is a difference between L1 speakers and L2 learners: L1 speakers have the tendency to base their inflection of novel words on schemata, using existing words as analogues, while L2 learners often stick to rules.

However, we are dealing with German here, so there is – of course – a problem: it is by no means the case that all German words which sound similar to *Hund* form their plural in -e. For example, the plural of *Hand* 'hand', while taking -e, also has a vowel mutation (*umlaut*), namely *Hände*. So does *Mund* 'mouth', but with the allomorph -er: *Münder*. And the relatively recent borrowing *Stunt* 'stunt' (pronounced with a vowel anywhere between ʌ and ʊ) would take the default plural marker -s, to make *Stunts*. This means that *Nund* is probably not a good candidate for testing the schemata-versus-rules question. In other words, if you are going to form nonsense items based on existing lexical forms, make sure that there are no competitors which could serve as the analogue. This can be done by means of so-called rhyming or reverse dictionaries, where words are sorted on the basis not of their initial letters, but their ending (presumably intended for the use of the more desperate poets or their translators).

Inflectional paradigms where there is a great deal of variability, such as the German plural system, and where the precursor for a form is not always easily identifiable (or where there are a number of potential candidates) may therefore not be an ideal environment to conduct a Wug-test, since whatever results you obtain will probably be messy and difficult to interpret. More clear-cut results can be expected in a situation where (a) there is allomorphic variation, (b) there are rules underlying this variation and (c) these rules are of varying complexity. Such a case was investigated by Merel Keijzer (2007) in her study on the attrition of Dutch diminutive formation.

The diminutive system in Dutch is probably unique in a number of ways. Firstly, diminutives are extremely frequent and productive. Diminutive formation is not confined to nouns: adjectives such as *dubbeldik* ('double thick', a type of ice-cream) and even phrases such as *onder ons* ('between us') can take a diminutive suffix. Diminutives can carry a large range of meanings beyond simply denoting some-thing small, from endearment to contempt and from individuation to unimportance. Crucially, there are five different suffixes which are used to form diminutives (-*tje*, -*je*, -*etje*, -*kje* and -*pje*). These are assigned to lexical items based on phonological principles of the stem. The default form, which is also the one that children learn first, is -*tje* (*tafel* 'table' – *tafeltje* 'small table'). Other suffixes are restricted in their distribution – for example, words ending in -ŋ, such as *koning* 'king', take the suffix -kje, while after m the suffix becomes -pje, as in *duim* 'thumb' *duimpje*. Children will therefore first produce forms such as **duimtje* before eventually acquiring the rules underlying the formation of the less frequent forms.

Keijzer invited her participants to provide diminutive suffixes on existing and on made-up items. Since she was investigating adult attriters and controls, she felt that using pictures of fantasy creatures, the way it had been done in Berko's original study, might not be appropriate. Instead, she provided sentence contexts such as:

(54)
Je hebt een **cyclaam**, *maar als het maar een kleintje is, heb je een klein*
_____.
There is a **cyclaam**, but if it is only a very small one, it is a little _____.

This allomorphic paradigm is probably one of the best possible environments for the application of a Wug-test: it concerns an inflectional process which is widely and very frequently used in the L1, but very infrequent and highly marked in the L2 (in Keijzer's case, the L2 was English, a language which makes very little use of diminutive formation). Furthermore, there are clear rules underlying allomorphic variation, and the different allomorphs are acquired in a fixed sequence by children.

Wug-tests have also been applied for items other than nouns. In particular in the verbal paradigm, this may provide interesting results in languages such as English, Dutch or German, which have both a strong and a weak system of verb inflection. For example, English *sing* takes the strong[3] past tense form *sang*, while the past tense of *work* is the suffixed form *work-ed* (this is referred to as the weak conjugation). Dutch and German have a similar paradigm, but while in English the strong conjugation applies only to a relatively small number of very frequently occurring verbs, about half of the Dutch and German verbs are strong.

Keijzer's (2007) investigation also contained a number of sentences with made-up verbs, for which her participants were asked to provide the past tense form. These verbs were based on very frequently occurring strong and weak Dutch verbs for which she changed the initial consonant, for example deriving the nonsense item *nelpen* from *helpen* 'to help'. Her stimuli were constructed as follows:

(55)
Jullie **nelpen** *maar als jullie het gisteren deden dan* _____ *jullie gisteren.*
You are **nelping** but if you did so yesterday, then yesterday you _____.

Dutch *help* is a strong verb, with the past tense *hielpen*, so the expectation was that unattrited L1 speakers might prefer the form *nielpen*. For the attriters, it was assumed that the strictly rule-governed process of past tense formation through suffixation might have taken over, so that they would produce *nelpten* (and this was indeed what Keijzer found).

Presenting attriters and controls with made-up, nonsense words can provide interesting results, and help you to determine whether they have come to rely more on rules than on schemata when they are integrating unknown lexical forms into the grammatical frame of the sentence. However, a practical note of caution is in order here: while Wug-tests have often been shown to work very well in investigations of child language (Berko's original study reports that children were very eager to provide the requested forms), we have found that they may be problematic for adults. Both in Keijzer's investigation and in my own, which used a similar design, participants sometimes did not understand the nature of the task, in particular where the nonsense verbs were concerned. Even though we included a number of training sentences, some of the participants insisted on inserting existing verbs which were contextually appropriate (and bore no resemblance whatsoever to the nonsense forms which they were asked to inflect).

Task:	Inflection of (nonsense) words (Wug-test)
Type of knowledge:	Schemata and rules for inflection
Type of data:	Inflected form
System requirements:	None
Investigations of attrition using this task:	Keijzer, 2007 (existing and nonsense words); Altenberg, 1991 (existing words),
Further reading:	Berko, 1958
Advantages:	Can provide insight into underlying grammatical processes
Disadvantages:	Are sometimes difficult to convey to participants, particularly adults

C-TEST

The last formal task to be discussed here is the so-called *C-Test*. This test was originally designed as a broad measure of overall language proficiency and is a development of the 'cloze test'. In a cloze test, participants are presented with a text from which a number of words have been deleted, and their task is to fill in the missing words. In the C-Test, words are only partially deleted according to a pre-determined schema, but the gaps are more frequent. C-Tests are fairly easy to construct: texts are typically fairly short (around 70 words in length), and they can be taken from published sources such as newspapers or encyclopaedias.

NOTE

At this point, another note on copyright is in order: on the website accompanying this book (www.let.rug.nl/languageattrition/experiments) I have made available a number of texts which I and others have used in investigations of language attrition. For the texts which you will find there, the original publishers very kindly granted me permission to do this. In other cases – for example with respect to a text that was published as a newspaper column in 2003 – this permission was refused, and I was therefore unable to include it with the other materials. I should, of course, have checked this before I used it in my experiments.

In the construction of a C-Test, the first sentence of the text is left intact. Starting with the second sentence, the second half of every second word is removed and replaced by a gap. Compounds, words of one letter, names, numbers or words that have occurred before are skipped from this count, and for words with uneven numbers of letters, one more letter is removed than is left in place. Here is an example of the beginning of such a C-Test (as used by Keijzer 2007): (56a) gives the original version, while (56b) is the gapped version which was actually used in the experiment):

(56)
(a) We all live with other people's expectations of us. These are a reflection of their trying to understand us, . . .
(b) We all live with other people's expectations of us. These a_____ a refl_____ of th_____ trying to under_____ us, . . .

This kind of task requires the participant to make full use of the natural redundancy of a text, which makes it possible to measure not only relatively low-level skills (command of vocabulary, grammar, idioms), but also higher-order skills, such as awareness of intersentential relationships, global reading, etc. Further advantages of the C-Test are that it is based on authentic material and that it is relatively easy to use and to score: any correct response is simply awarded one point. We have found it useful to use five texts with exactly twenty gaps each, so that the maximum possible score was 100, but this is, of course, not necessary.

The C-Test has been extensively studied and found to be a valid and reliable predictor of overall proficiency. In particular, it has been shown among L2 learners that the C-Test is a good measure of proficiency for more advanced learners. This also makes it a good test instrument for L1 attriters. Like all other tests, your C-Test should be piloted on a group of unattrited native speakers. For L2 investigations, the recommendation is to use texts on which natives can attain ca. 95 per cent correct responses. We have found this percentage somewhat high for investigations of L1 attrition, and therefore selected more difficult texts on which natives got 80–90 per cent correct, since we were afraid of a ceiling effect in the attriting groups.

Two things should, however, be kept in mind. Firstly, performance on the C-Test invariably correlates with the educational level of participants: more highly educated speakers will achieve higher scores. If you are planning to use this task, it is therefore of vital importance that you balance the educational level across your experimental and your control groups, and also use it as a covariate (see below, chapter 17). A second, more practical problem, is that tests such as the C-Test which rely extensively and exclusively on written material cannot be adapted to languages that do not have a writing system. Depending on which language(s) you are planning to investigate, you may therefore not be able to use this task. Otherwise, the C-Test is an excellent, widely used and amply documented instrument.

Task:	Completing gapped text
Type of knowledge:	Overall knowledge of the language, full use of redundancies
Type of data:	Proportion of accurate responses
System requirements:	None
Investigations of attrition using this task:	Dostert, 2009; Keijzer, 2007; Schmid, 2007; plus a number of ongoing investigations
Further reading:	Grotjahn, 2010; Klein-Braley, 1985; www.c-test.de
Advantages:	Widely used in both L2 learning and L1 attrition, can provide reliable information about participants' overall proficiency, particularly for relatively advanced learners (and therefore also highly suitable for the investigation of attrition)
Disadvantages:	Results will be influenced by participants' educational level; relies on the presence of a written system

SUMMARY

This chapter has introduced you to various methods of data collection and types of data that are relevant for language attrition studies. The experiments, methods and instruments which I have presented here are tried and tested, as they have been applied in other studies of language attrition. If you use these tasks, you can therefore compare your findings to those of other studies, which may help you with the interpretation and explanation of your findings. I have attempted to give detailed practical information on types of task which you may want to use for the investigation of specific grammatical features and their development in the attritional process.

All of these tasks have advantages and disadvantages, which I have summed up in each case. However, they all have one major advantage and one major disadvantage in common. The advantage is that each task allows you to zoom in specifically on some part of linguistic knowledge. The disadvantage is that it is often difficult to tell what the outcome of the task actually says about this specific bit of the linguistic repertoire.

One of the major problems for language attrition research is that so many studies avail themselves of some controlled task(s) in order to exploit their potential to investigate a particular, localized feature of the lexicon or the grammar. However, the interpretative problem has often been ignored. A researcher who conducts an experiment on an attriting population and a control population, and finds a difference between the two, will typically use these findings to make the claim that the attriting population has 'lost' the full native knowledge of this feature. I hope that the discussion above has shown that such a claim may be unwarranted: it is equally possible that the attriting population has a problem with a particular *task*, not with a grammatical or lexical *feature* as such.

If you are planning to investigate a specific grammatical phenomenon, the only way to make sure that it is this *linguistic feature* which has (or has not) been affected by the attritional process is to test it repeatedly with different tasks – ideally tasks which investigate it in production, understanding and processing. While all the experimental designs described in the present section are useful tools towards this end, I am convinced that the most important thing that *any* investigation of language attrition has to do is to simply get people to speak naturally. Free speech – while being far more labour-intensive to investigate than any of the other kinds of data described here – can provide insights into a speaker's linguistic repertoire which simply cannot be gathered by any other means. That is because free speech has one characteristic that no controlled tasks share: it is what people normally and naturally use language for.

14   Free speech

Formal tasks, such as the ones discussed above, allow the investigator to zoom in on some aspects of the attriting language. Their drawback is that the findings may not be true representations of the actual state of an attriting individual's knowledge or proficiency. The best picture of this can be gained by trying to get your participants to do what they usually do with language: talk. This chapter discusses ways of doing this.

I pointed out above that there are two scenarios for what happens in the process of language attrition. The first assumes that attrition can have *structural* ramifications for first language knowledge: underlying rules can be eroded, the intuitive knowledge on how to use language can be lost, the lexical and grammatical repertoire can shrink. The attriter will therefore have an underlying representation of his or her language which deviates from the knowledge of the non-attrited control speaker. The second scenario assumes that this underlying knowledge is perfectly intact and unaffected by erosion or attrition. However, the attriter has more difficulty *accessing* it: the second language keeps getting in the way, and it becomes more effortful for the speaker to retrieve some of the words or grammatical processes from memory, particularly if he or she has not spoken the language for a long time. On this view, the attriter may use the language differently from the control speaker, simply because something has got to give: attriters have less cognitive resources to devote to getting out the linguistic message, because they need to divert some of these resources to *inhibiting* the L2 and to digging up those bits of knowledge that have become more difficult to access.

The first scenario would predict that the same attriter will have problems with the same areas of knowledge across all kinds of different situations. If the structure of the language has become affected – for example, if the speaker is no longer certain of the underlying rules governing the assignment of the German plural allomorphs discussed above – the same kinds of mistakes should keep recurring, and he or she should be unable to correctly complete inflectional tasks as well as provide accurate grammaticality judgments focusing on this feature. The feature should then also be problematic in free speech.

If, on the other hand, differences in the behaviour of attriters which we can observe in comparison with the control group are the outcome of general cognitive difficulties and limitations, there is no reason why they should be that systematic. On this view, an attriter who is trying to formulate a sentence but has difficulties accessing a number of words that are necessary for this may be focusing very hard on remembering these words or appropriate alternatives, and that particular sentence may then contain grammatical deviations or be uttered with a strong foreign accent. Five minutes later, the same attriter may be able to produce similar grammatical structures with no problems at all, and have a perfectly native accent, since he or she is now talking about something that poses no vocabulary difficulties.

The only way to truly investigate which of these two scenarios applies is to look at free speech, since this is the only linguistic task which requires a speaker to activate all of the subcomponents of language knowledge at the same time. Controlled experimental tasks may provide excellent complementary data to free speech, but they are no substitute.

If you are planning to collect and analyse free speech, there are a number of issues you need to address:

1. How will you elicit your data?
2. How will you transcribe your data?
3. What feature(s) will you code, and how?
4. How will you analyse and quantify the use of these features?

ELICITATION

In order for *free speech* to be *naturalistic speech*, it is important that your informants really use language in the way they would normally do; that is, that they do not feel tongue-tied or put on the spot. This is impossible to achieve entirely. You – the interviewer – are a stranger, a highly educated person, a researcher, an academic. Worse: you are a linguist. You will probably have had the experience at some point that your interlocutors became wary even in perfectly innocuous situations upon hearing that you are interested in language – the 'Oops, better watch my grammar, there's a linguist present!' effect. It is probably unavoidable that your participants will feel the same to some extent, particularly since they are attriters who may feel self-conscious about their language to start with. When collecting naturalistic data, we are always bound to some extent by the observer's paradox, which argues that it is impossible to observe anything in its naturalistic state since the mere act of observation impinges on this state. However, if you yourself are natural and friendly, people will tend to relax and often forget the running microphone.

There are two ways of eliciting free speech: firstly to try and initiate a natural conversation and secondly to give the speaker some kind of descriptive task. For the former, I have very positive experiences with a semi-structured autobiographical interview based on a catalogue of questions you can download from www.let.rug.nl/languageattrition/ SQ. You can find extremely valuable guidelines on how to conduct such an interview in Tagliamonte (2006: ch. 3). For the descriptive task, you may show participants a silent film sequence and ask them to narrate this afterwards.

Various film stimuli have been used in different investigations. Some researchers have opted to film their own – for example, Pavlenko (2003, 2004) used film sequences she herself staged and recorded in order to make her participants talk about particular kinds of emotions evoked by what they had seen. On the other hand, there are a growing number of investigations which use a re-telling task based on a sequence from Charlie Chaplin's 1936 film *Modern Times*. This task was invented and first described by Clive Perdue (1993), and it involves the participant watching and then re-telling a 10-minute excerpt from this film, which starts ca. 33 minutes from the beginning of the movie.[1] This particular stimulus has the advantage that it has been used across a range of different investigations of both L2 acquisition and L1 attrition so that the free speech data collected can be compared across languages and contexts. Participants furthermore have few problems following the plot, and tend to find it funny and entertaining. It typically elicits retellings of anywhere between 5 and 10 minutes (ca. 500–800 words).

The film is widely available on DVD (you will be able to order it over the internet), and as far as I have been able to ascertain, showing it to your informants in a one-on-one experimental setting for research purposes (that is, not with the aim of obtaining any kind of profit) does not violate any copyright restrictions. You should have the DVD in your computer and set to playback at the correct scene prior to the experiment, so you don't have to fiddle around trying to find the starting point. Tell your participants that you would like them to watch a film sequence of ca. 10 minutes, and to tell you afterwards what they have seen. Try to make sure that there are no distractions during this. If there are – for example, should the telephone ring or a child come to claim the parent's attention – stop the film and re-wind it to ca. 30 seconds before the point where the interruption occurred. Immediately after the participant has seen the entire sequence, invite them to narrate what they have seen.[2]

If you are planning to use this task, you should hold back as much as possible while your participants are narrating what they saw. Do not interrupt, even if they get an event or a sequence wrong, or if they forget something (they will usually realize this later and self-correct). If they leave out a major part, you may prompt them for it when they have finished. If you keep interrupting, it will be difficult afterwards to analyse the flow of speech, and also to tell whether you might not have primed them to use certain words or grammatical structures.

TRANSCRIPTION AND CODING OF FREE-SPEECH DATA

Transcribing free-spoken data is a labour-intensive process. Firstly, you will have to decide whether you want to describe the data *orthographically* or *phonetically*. Phonetic transcription is far more time-consuming than orthographic transcription, and should only be used if your research question specifically necessitates it. If you are interested only in more general features, you can still opt to code certain words phonetically in addition to the orthographic representation, for example if they were produced with a strong foreign accent, non-targetlike stress or intonation patterns etc.

Even for purely orthographic transcription, however, you need to adopt a clearly defined *coding system*. It is important from the outset to realize not only *what* you want to code but also *how* to code it. Do you want to include, for example, overlaps between speakers? Interruptions? Specific intonation patterns? Errors? Depending on your research question, you may also be interested in particular grammatical constructions. Say, for example, that you are interested in German plural morphology. You may initially decide that you need to code all noun phrases in the plural, specify which plural allomorph was used, and whether this use was targetlike or not. You may then find, however, that there is a pattern of errors on this feature which does not at all tally with your overall impression of your speakers' proficiency: some otherwise highly proficient speakers may have a lot of mistakes, while people whom you would have ranked on the lower end of the scale have none at all – because they avoid the use of plurals altogether. It may therefore be necessary to code not only all instances of nouns in the plural, but *any* noun, whether singular or plural, in order to see what proportion of them was pluralized.

This example illustrates that, for virtually any phenomenon in free speech, the issue of quantification is a highly complex one. Whenever you want to investigate the distribution of a linguistic feature, you have to ask yourself *in relation to what* you want to assess it. Often the baseline is the total number of words which a speaker has produced – however, you should bear in mind here that a more complex speech style with longer clauses may reduce the total number of potential contexts for some features. The number of clauses or utterances may therefore be a better measure. In other cases, as illustrated by the example of plural allomorphs above, you may have to relate the number of actual occurrences to the total obligatory or potential contexts.

A good template for the analysis of spoken language can be found in what recent approaches to second language learning have labelled the CAF framework: complexity, accuracy and fluency (Housen and Kuiken, 2009; Van Daele, Housen, Kuiken, Pierrard and Vedder, 2007).

Complexity

Complexity may be assessed on the lexical, morphological and syntactic level. Measures of *lexical complexity* or *lexical diversity* are ideally based not only on 'blind' counts of type–token frequencies or related measures such as *D* or the *Uber*-formula (see chapter 4 above), but should also take into account lexical richness profiles. Where *morphological complexity* is concerned, I have pointed out above that it may be necessary to code all obligatory contexts for a specific variable – for example, all linguistic items that have to be marked for case, gender or tense, with the specific variant (nominative, accusative; present, simple past, periphrastic past etc.). In this manner, it is possible not only to see whether the *proportion* of targetlike use of a certain feature differs between attriters and controls, but also whether the *overall application* of this feature has changed.

Similarly, a full picture of *syntactic complexity* can only be gained if a full analysis is conducted on the different types of sentence structures of which the speaker makes use. If you are interested in certain grammatical structures or sentence types, you should code all occurrences here – for example, the distribution of main and subordinate clauses, the order of direct–indirect object, the amount of wh-structures, and so on.

Accuracy ▄▄▄▄▄▄▄▄▄▄▄▄▄▄▄▄▄▄▄▄▄▄▄▄▄▄▄▄▄▄▄▄▄▄▄▄▄▄▄

Errors

In addition to the *overall distribution* of lexical and morphosyntactic variables, you may also want to assess to what extent speakers might, on occasion, have used them inaccurately. However, identifying an 'error' is not a trivial matter. As Tagliamonte (2006) points out, our underlying assumptions of what is 'grammatically correct' is typically based on written language, which often bears little relationship to what people do when they speak. Applying such prescriptive standards as a baseline for accuracy measurements in free speech would lead to a very distorted picture. Tagliamonte gives the example of the variation between *those* and *them* in some varieties of British English: some speakers may prefer the standard variant 'in those days', while others may say 'in them days' (Tagliamonte, 2006: 66). In written language, the latter would probably be considered to constitute an error, while in spoken language it is perfectly acceptable (at least in certain dialects). Similar considerations apply to certain word order patterns. For example, in German, subordinate clauses typically place the finite verb at the end. Consider the alternation between (57a), which uses two independent compounded main clauses, and (57b) with a subordinate clause:

(57)

(a)	Ich	habe	ihm	gesagt	ich	kann	nicht	kommen.
	I	have	him	told	I	can	not	come.

I have told him I can't come.

(b)	Ich	habe	ihm	gesagt	dass	ich	nicht	kommen	kann.
	I	have	him	told	that	I	not	come	can.

I have told him that I can't come.

However, in spoken language, the subordinator *weil* 'because' can be used with both types of word order. This is a source of great controversy: many people object violently to this 'sloppy' use of language and insist on correcting it wherever they encounter it. Linguists, on the other hand, have argued that the use of *weil* with main clause word order constitutes an enrichment of the language, as it is rule-governed and adds a different (more subjective) type of meaning to the expression (see for example Keller, 1995).

For many variants that you will encounter in free speech, whether from attrited or non-attrited populations, it may be extremely difficult to decide whether you will treat them as perfectly good expressions, or whether you will mark them as errors. Three things are important here:

- do not adopt a yard stick that is too prescriptive (allow anything that you think you might structurally encounter)
- take into account the speaker's dialect (things that may not be acceptable in your variety may be in his or hers)
- be totally consistent!

A taxonomy of errors for attrition research

NOTE

For my own work on the attrition of German and Dutch, I have developed the following taxonomy of errors which I have found helpful and workable. You may want to adopt and/or adapt this for your own analyses, or you may want to work out something that is completely different.

Category 0: Code-switching
Category 1: Lexical
Category 2: Semantic
Category 3: Function words (e.g. prepositions)
Category 4: Morphology
    4.1 Case
    4.2 Gender
    4.3 Plural
    4.4 Tense assignment
    4.5 Tense agreement
    4.6 Weak/strong past tense
    4.7 Auxiliary
    4.8 Participle/infinitive
    4.9 Reflexive
Category 5: Morphosyntax
    5.1 Negation
    5.2 Passive
    5.3 Syntactic transfer/structural borrowing
    5.4 Quantifier
Category 6: Word order
Category 7: Obligatory verb placement in Germanic languages
    7.1 Verb second violation
    7.2 Discontinuous word order violation
    7.3 Verb last in subordinate clause violation

False starts

A second consideration that you should make at the outset with respect to accuracy is how you will deal with self-corrections. For example, consider the following stretch of text from a Dutch version of the Chaplin film retelling task:

(58)

meegenomen	naar	uh	de	naar	het	naar	de	gevangenis
taken along	*to*	*uh*	*the*	*to*	*the*	*to*	*the*	*prison*

In this example, the speaker wants to use the word *gevangenis* 'prison'. In Dutch, the definite article has to agree with the gender of the noun. If the noun belongs to the common gender (as is the case for *gevangenis*), the correct article is *de*; if it is neuter, it should be *het*. In this case, the speaker is obviously uncertain: she first (correctly) uses *de*, then switches to *het* and back to *de* again. This means that she eventually does get it right, but how should we treat these false starts?

Again, the choice is yours. Some studies, for example my own 2002 investigation, decide to ignore cases like the ones above where the speaker eventually produces a targetlike form. Others, such as the investigation by Köpke (1999) take them into account as important indicators of a disruption of the speaking process. She places them in the same category as a number of other such disruptors: indicators of not so much *inaccuracy* as *disfluency*.

Fluency

The last aspect of proficiency which is relevant to investigations of attrition is *fluency*. This phenomenon has gained massively in importance over the past years, particularly with respect to second language development (e.g. Hilton, 2008). However, it has been a rather neglected aspect of L1 attrition studies (the only investigations which treat it in some detail are Yukawa, 1997 and Schmid and Beers Fägersten, 2010). What findings there are indicate strongly that in-depth investigations of hesitations and disfluencies can provide much additional insight into the attritional process.

Recall the section on the different types of grammaticality judgment tasks presented above. I demonstrated how, in a self-paced reading task or in the recording of eye-movements, the point of a message where a reader hesitates can provide insight into processing strategies. It can be similarly interesting to investigate at which points during the *formulation* of a message a speaker encounters difficulties and manages this through pausing, using a hesitation marker (*uhm, ahem*), repeating some words or self-correcting.

Schmid and Beers Fägersten (2010) provide a detailed illustration of how to conduct such an analysis, based on the word class of the context where different disfluency markers appear. In this analysis, disfluency markers confirm the impression that the problems which attriters experience in accessing their first language concern mainly *lexical* items (nouns and verbs) and affect *grammatical* phenomena less.

Perceived nativelikeness

Once you have applied all of the above analyses to your data, and gained an impression of each speaker's overall level of complexity, accuracy and fluency, you may feel that the numbers which come out are interesting but to some degree unsatisfying. When we listen to attriters, we often feel that there is something more, some very subtle quality of change, in the spoken language which cannot be captured by *counting* things, however many extra things to count we may come up with.

I have therefore found that one of the most illuminating analyses for free speech concerns quite a simple experiment: to find out how native speakers respond to these data. In order to conduct such an experiment, all you need is excerpts from each of your recordings[3] (these need not be long, 15–20 seconds will suffice). Patch these together, mixing up attriters and controls, to make one large sound file, with a silent pause of 7–10 seconds between each segment, and then make native speakers listen to the whole thing. In the silent pause between speakers, these raters should note down for each speaker whether or not they think that he or she is a native (such an experiment is described in detail by de Leeuw, Schmid and Mennen, 2010). These ratings will allow you to compare whether native speakers perceive your attriters as foreigners or as natives.

CONCLUSION

Free spoken data provide the most naturalistic material for the investigation of language attrition. They allow insights into how exactly a speaker's language and the use of this language have changed over the attrition period, since they are the only type of data which requires the speaker to rapidly integrate all areas of linguistic knowledge in real time. However, in order to be used to their full potential, they have to be coded and analysed extensively: while speakers have to use all levels of linguistic knowledge in free-speech production, they can also develop avoidance strategies for some of the more complex linguistic phenomena. A speaker who is no longer certain about how to form a plural or a relative clause may modify his or her speech patterns accordingly. This means that investigations of language attrition should never rely solely on *deviances* or *speech errors*, but should always take into account, as far as is reasonably possible, the overall distribution of linguistic structures, fluency patterns and perceived nativelikeness.

This makes analyses of free data a highly labour-intensive endeavour, and it is therefore advisable to organize the processes of transcription and coding as efficiently as possible. Good equipment (a top-class recording device, headphones and a foot pedal with which you can control the playback) can help considerably. Furthermore, it is crucial that you are absolutely consistent with respect to the system of transcription and coding which you use. Spending time familiarizing yourself with this, and deciding exactly what you want to code and how before you start, is not a luxury: your eventual analysis will only be as good as the transcription it is based on.

PART V
Coding and analysing the data

Once you have gone out to collect your data, what do you do with it? How do you get from a large dataset of individual results to a group comparison of attrition effects? Part V will go into the processes of presenting, representing, analysing and interpreting your data.

There are two extremely scary moments in the course of any research project. The first occurs when you have done all your fieldwork and return with a pile of questionnaires, tapes, tests and whatever else you have collected, and you realize that the time has come where you have to start turning this rather chaotic pile into a well-structured database. The second comes when you actually have that well-structured database, and have to begin finding out what the data mean – that is, when you have to begin your statistical analysis. At these watershed moments, you first have to decide how to code and organize your data, and then how to analyse it.

TIP

I strongly advise sticking to this order – coding first, analysis later! You will, of course, be tempted to run intermediate analyses once you have finished a third, half, or three quarters of your coding – but these analyses will be worthless and take up a great deal of your time. The worst-case scenario here is that you conduct an analysis on a subsample and present the findings at a conference somewhere – only to discover later on that the findings from the whole dataset contradict the conclusions you had confidently asserted before.

15 Transcribing and coding free speech: the CHILDES project

> There are many features which we may want to transcribe and code in free data, but what is the best system of transcription that will allow us to do so? This chapter will discuss a widely used system called CHAT.

In the previous chapter I addressed the problem of how to analyse free speech. I proposed that it is important to analyse naturalistic speech data from the point of view of complexity, accuracy and fluency. That is, each utterance should be coded for its lexical, morphological, morphosyntactic and syntactic complexity and accuracy, each disfluency and hesitation should be marked, and overall lexical diversity should be assessed.

You can imagine how quickly the wrong coding system can make an entirely unreadable mess of your data. However, do *not* do what I did when I wrote my Ph.D., which was to print out all of my data (comprising some 175,000 words) multiple times, and to go through them with different coloured text markers to code features such as singular and plural noun phrases, main clauses, subordinate clauses, different tenses, different genders of noun phrases, different cases, and so on, subsequently counting them all by hand. Instead, I recommend that you use the system of coding and transcriptions which has been developed by Brian MacWhinney in the CHILDES (Child Language Data Exchange System) project (http://childes.psy.cmu.edu; see also MacWhinney, 2000).

There are, of course, many other systems of coding and transcription (another well-known resource is PRAAT, which can be accessed at www.fon.hum.uva.nl/praat), and many universities or departments have developed their own tools which you may prefer to the CHILDES way. If there is substantial support available at your institution, that may be a very good reason to use what everyone else is working with. However, CHILDES does have some important advantages that you should be aware of – most importantly that a number of other ongoing and completed projects on language attrition are using it, not to mention many other studies of bilingualism in general.

The investigations which participate in the CHILDES project use a transcription system called CHAT which is extensively documented in the manuals available on the CHILDES website (and this information is regularly updated). The CHILDES internet resource also contains, among other things, a database of transcripts as well as audio and video files from a large number of language acquisition contexts, and a very useful program for the analysis of CHAT transcripts called CLAN. It also offers resources which can perform automatic morphological tagging, lexical identification and lemmatization for a number of languages. All of these resources are freely accessible. I shall therefore keep the discussion here to the bare bones and minimal requirements.

THE STRUCTURE OF CHAT FILES

CHAT files are in plain-text format (they have the extension .txt or one of the CLAN-specific extensions .cha or .cex), so if you work on them in a program such as Word or WordPerfect, you have to choose to save them as text only. Each CHAT file contains the transcript from one data collection session. Here is an example from a film retelling task, transcribed according to the CHAT conventions (the symbol → denotes a tabulator).

```
(59)
@Begin
@Languages:→eng, nld
@Participants:→ATR Marilyn_Monroe Subject, INT
Monika_S_Schmid Investigator
@ID:→eng|attrenginnl|ATR|||||Subject||
@Font: → Courier New
*ATR:→that it is not the same story.
*ATR:→it (i)s a ah@fp drastic whole other story.
*ATR:→well it seems to be directed towards Chaplin like
before.
*ATR:→it has to deal with that.
*ATR:→yeah[ x 2] ah@fp &laughs I don't know what sort of detail
you[ x 2] (a)re interested.
*INT:→just try to remember &every.
*ATR:→< I can be forgotten >[ *] a lot of it.
%err:→tense
```

```
*ATR: →anyway he ah@fp ah@fp he is applying for a job.
*ATR: →he has a letter of recommendation.
@End
```

The first thing you will probably notice about this text is that there are three different ways for a line to begin. These characterize three different types of paragraphs, or 'tiers', which are essential in CHAT:

- header tiers, which start with the symbol @, and where general information about the file is provided
- utterance tiers, which start with an asterisk * followed by a three-letter code identifying the speaker, and which contain the actual linguistic data which was produced during the session (and some additional coding)
- dependent tiers, which start with a % followed by a three-letter code (e.g. %spa for a dependent tier where speech act information is coded, or %err for a tier giving specific information about errors) and contain additional data which you wish to code and analyse, pertaining to the preceding utterance. Each utterance can have several dependent tiers associated with it (or none, as the case may be)

The speaker code at the beginning of the utterance, the obligatory header codes (except for @Begin and @End) and the dependent tier codes are all followed by a colon (:) and a tabulator (not a space).

Header tiers

Every CHAT file starts with a number of obligatory header tiers, identified by the symbol @.

- @Begin and @End
  CHAT files begin with a line which contains the expression '@Begin' and end with a line which contains the expression '@End'. No empty lines are allowed either before @Begin, after @End, or anywhere else in the file.
- @Languages
  Here you code which is the main language of the text. If there is more than one language you can specify this as well. A list of abbreviations for different languages can be found in the CHAT manual on the CHILDES website. In this particular case the text is in English, with Dutch as the second language, as the speakers in this corpus are attriters of English living in the Netherlands.

- @Participants
  In this line a three-letter code must be specified for each person who participates in the interaction transcribed in the file. This code will be used to identify the speakers for each utterance in the main body of the text. You may choose a code which identifies each individual speaker, e.g. the first three letters of the name, but I have found it useful to pick the same code for the same type of speaker across all the files in a particular corpus. This is helpful later on, when you want to run CLAN commands to analyse the utterances of the people you want to investigate (and exclude others, for example, the interviewer) for a whole set of files in one go. In this case, ATR was chosen for the attriters, and INV for the investigator.
  This three-letter code is (optionally) followed by the name or identification code of the person. I have used the name of a famous actress here as a placeholder, but you might also use identifiers such as Participant1. Note that no spaces or punctuation are allowed, so the name should be e.g. Monika_S_Schmid or MonikaSSchmid.
  The name is followed by the 'role' of this speaker, in the present case 'Subject'. The CHAT manual lists a number of possible roles (Child, Mother, Adult. . .). Note that roles are case-sensitive, so the role 'subject' with a lowercase s will lead to an error message when you check your files in CLAN.
- @ID
  The identification tier has a complex structure, specifying slots for the following information:
  @ID:→language|corpus|code|age|sex|group|SES|role|education|
  Not all of this information is obligatory, the slots which do have to be filled in are underlined here. In the example above all optional information has been omitted:
  @ID:→eng|attrenginnl|ATR|||||Subject||
  During the initial transcription, you may choose to omit this line, once you check your files in CLAN it will automatically be added, based on the information on the @Participants tier.
- @Font
  Under this header the font which is used in the file has to be specified. This will normally be Courier New.

In addition to these obligatory headers, there are optional headers, e.g.

- @Coder (to enter the name of the person who did the coding, useful if several people work on the same project)
- @Activities (to describe the situation which was recorded)
- @Comment

- @Date
- @Location

For a full list, and how to fill these in, see the CHAT manual.

Utterance tiers

On the main utterance tier, the actual linguistic material is transcribed. Lines which contain utterances have to start with an asterisk (*) followed by a three-letter code for the speaker, followed by a colon and a tabulator. Every utterance consists of one sentence, and has to end with an 'utterance delimiter' (a full stop, exclamation mark or question mark). None of these utterance delimiters may appear anywhere within the line except at the end. In other words, no utterance may contain more than one sentence.

```
(60)
*ATR:→ah@fp he has to look for [ x 2] pieces of wood of a
certain shape.
*ATR:→and ah@fp < he was > [ //] he is not very good at this.
*ATR:→eventually he sees ah@fp < a couple > [ /] a couple
of pieces of wood.
```

While more complex information that you wish to code for the analysis of your data is best placed in the dependent tiers in order to keep the actual text readable, utterances themselves contain a number of basic codes pertaining to errors, repetitions, retractions, pauses etc. Here are some of the basic nuts and bolts which you need to take into account:

Errors

Where an error occurs, it is followed by an asterisk enclosed between square brackets. If the error extends across more than one word, it is enclosed between angled brackets. Note that it is important to ensure that each opening bracket, < or [, has to have a closing bracket, > or] on the same utterance tier. Utterances containing an error may be followed by an 'error tier' (%err: →) where you can specify and classify the error type.

```
(61)
*ATR:→< I can be forgotten > [ *] a lot of it.
%err:→tense
```

Repetitions and retractions

Repetitions (speech material that is repeated in exactly the same way) and retractions (where the speaker repeats some material, but applies a change or correction) are coded similarly to errors. Repetitions are indicated by a single slash between square brackets, [/], and for retractions a double slash is used, [//]. Again, where the repetition or retraction extends across more than one word, the entire stretch of text which is repeated or corrected is enclosed between angled brackets.

It is important to code repetitions and retractions faithfully if you intend to analyse either fluency or lexical diversity, since linguistic material that has been coded as a repetition or a retraction will be ignored for CLAN analyses pertaining to type–token frequencies or other lexical diversity measures and will therefore not artificially inflate these variables.

(62)

```
*ATR:→and ah@fp < he was >[ //] he is not very good at this.
*ATR:→eventually he sees ah@fp < a couple >[ /] a couple
of pieces of wood.
```

Code-switches

Code-switches are indicated by the symbol @s suffixed to the word which is in the second language (see the CHAT manual on how to code switches affecting entire utterances and longer stretches of discourse).

(63)

```
*ATR:→and he has to find a wig@s.
```

Non-linguistic material

Non-linguistic actions, such as laughter, coughing etc. may be coded by preceding them with the symbol &=. Note that such codes must always be followed by a space, and cannot be directly followed by a punctuation mark (not '&=laugh.' but '&=laugh .').

Other codes

There are a number of other restrictions to orthographic transcription that have to be observed in CHAT coding:

- Since you may not use full stops anywhere except at the end of the utterance, you cannot use abbreviations such as *Mr.* or *Mrs.* and these words have to be spelled out (the CHAT manual suggests *Mister* and *Missus*)

- Uppercase letters within words are not allowed. Acronyms, such as *USA*, are represented as *U_S_A*
- Numbers have to be spelled out (not *4* but *four*)
- Hyphenation is not allowed, and hyphens have to be replaced by a plus sign (not *target-like* but *target+like*)

Dependent tiers

Each utterance can have several dependent tiers pertaining to it on which additional information may be coded for analysis. These are preceded by a % symbol, plus a three-letter code indicating what type of information they contain, such as the %err tier included in some of the examples above, where information about the errors contained in the previous utterances is specified. You might also have a %com tier, where you can enter comments (such as 'the telephone rings'), a %syn tier where you code syntactic structure, and so on. You may not have more than one tier of the same type per utterance, so if there is more than one error in the same utterance they all have to be coded in the same %err line.

The CHAT manual contains a list of pre-defined dependent tiers. Should these not be sufficient for your own coding needs, you can add new tiers of your own. In such cases, the three-letter code you are using should be preceded by the letter x, so a tier where you code sentence types might be labelled %xsen.

The option of creating dependent tiers to accompany each utterance is what makes the CHAT transcription system such a powerful and useful tool, as it allows the researcher to tag utterances for any number of characteristics and then relate these to each other. With the help of the CLAN program, frequency analyses can be extended or limited to any type of tier – the utterance tier, a particular set of dependent tiers, but also dependent tiers of a specific kind, such as a specific error code. A detailed description of coding and analysis with the help of CHAT/CLAN is provided in Schmid, Verspoor and MacWhinney (2011).

CHECKING YOUR FILES

Once you have prepared all of your transcriptions in text-only files according to these rules, you are ready to begin using the CLAN program. The first thing you need to do is to verify whether there are any problems or oversights left, by running them through the CHECK command in CLAN. At this stage you may get very discouraging results with huge numbers of mistakes. In order to keep these to a minimum, make sure you stick to the guidelines above and check your files regularly as you go along.

The most common errors in CHAT files are:

- utterance delimiters (punctuation marks such as ., ?, !) within the utterance
- no utterance delimiter mark at the end of utterance lines
- the obligatory headers are not all there, or not in the correct order
- uppercase letters within words
- numbers in the text (they have to be spelled out)
- two tiers of the same kind are associated with one utterance tier
- a comma is immediately followed by the next word (there has to be a space between the two)
- a code starting with & (e.g. &=laugh) is immediately followed by a punctuation mark (there has to be a space between the two)
- there is an empty line after the @End line
- there is an empty line before the @Begin line
- there are empty lines in the text

ANALYSING YOUR TEXTS WITH THE HELP OF THE CLAN PROGRAM

The CLAN program, which can be freely downloaded from the CHILDES website, can perform a number of analyses on files that have been transcribed and coded according to the CHAT guidelines. Three functions are particularly relevant here:

- analysis of lexical diversity (type–token frequencies or the measure referred to as D, see the CLAN manual for details)
- morphological analysis (for a number of languages morphological taggers are available in CLAN, see the CHILDES website for details)
- frequency analysis

The frequency analysis can provide you with details on the distribution of particular words or codes across a range of files. For example, if you have coded repetitions or errors in all of your files, a single command will provide you with a list of files and the number of these codes which each of the files contains. These frequency counts can then be related to either the total number of words a speaker has used or to the total number of obligatory contexts, and analysed statistically.

If you do decide to work with CHAT and CLAN you will have to spend some time familiarizing yourself with the coding conventions and the program commands. However, they are all well documented and easy to access and install, and you will almost certainly find that your learning curve will be steep and the eventual benefits in terms of ease of analysis will be well worth the effort.

16 Coding and reporting experimental data

> The results from experimental data come in various forms – reaction times, accuracy scores, judgments on a five-point scale, yes/no answers, and so on. This chapter will discuss how such different types of data can be coded, what information you need to give when you describe them, and how you may present this information in tables and graphs.

The transcription and tagging of free speech, as discussed in the previous section, is by far the most difficult and time-consuming way of coding linguistic data. Data elicited by controlled experiments or tests, on the other hand, can usually be coded relatively quickly once you have set up your database. During my own fieldwork I was usually able to enter all of the data (the sociolinguistic questionnaire, two Verbal Fluency Tasks, five C-Tests in each language, two Wug-tests and two Can-Do Scales) into my database while the next participant was completing the written tasks.

Before you start setting up this database, however, there are some important considerations and decisions to make. These mainly concern the following issues:

1. Types of data
2. Missing data
3. How to report and visualize your results

TYPES OF DATA

The first thing that you will be taught in any statistics course is that numbers are not always numbers: the mathematical and statistical operations you are allowed to perform crucially depend on how the numbers within the scale that you are applying relate to each other. Two questions are relevant here.

- Do the numbers imply any kind of progression?
- Are all the numbers on the scale equidistant from each other?

For example, you may choose to give each of your subjects a number for the sake of anonymity. This numbering could represent the order in which you contacted them or in which the testing sessions took place, it could be based on an alphabetical list of their last names, or be done totally randomly. This means that you might get a table, for example containing the scores of your C-Test, such as the one represented in Table 16.1.

Table 16.1 *A representation of a C-Test score by participants*

Subject	C-Test score
Subject 1	87
Subject 2	79
Subject 3	59
Subject 4	66
Subject 5	45
Subject 6	90

Of course, you could conceivably turn this table into a graph such as Figure 16.1, where your speakers are ordered by their subject number. Such a graphical representation is not very illuminating for your audience, since we tend to assume that there is some kind of progression implied in the way in which these data points are ordered. This is particularly the case for line charts such as the one used here (I shall discuss different types of graphical representations below). In this example, however, there is no such progression or development, as the individual data points on the *x*-axis (the subject numbers) merely represent data from different participants, without carrying any underlying mathematical value. Such numbers are referred to as *nominal data*. Numbers which do imply some kind of progression but which are not relatable to each other in the strict mathematical sense are called *ordinal*, while true numerical scales are referred to as *interval* (or *scale* in SPSS).

In order to illustrate these three different types of data, recall the discussion on the types of judgments invited by a grammaticality or acceptability task from chapter 15. Three types of ratings were discussed here:

1. binary (yes/no)
2. Likert Scale (from 'totally unacceptable' to 'totally acceptable' in e.g. five or seven steps)
3. Magnitude Estimation

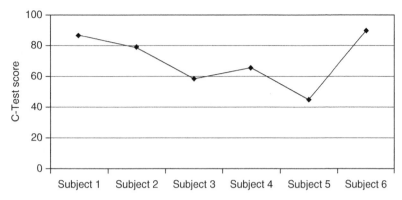

Figure 16.1 A line graph representing C-Test scores by six speakers

Yes/no questions elicit a *nominal* type of judgment. We refer to data as nominal when they merely represent a label – another example might be the classification of the sex of our participants, e.g. males as 1 and females as 2. You may encounter categories in your data which you have to differentiate, but which are not logically ordered in any way – the fact that the 'label' for the females has twice the numerical value of the label for the males here has no significance whatsoever, and you could equally well have switched them around, or called men 13 and women 91. So, nominal data are values which serve to identify and differentiate categories, but do not imply any ranking order.

Such data are therefore not in a numerical relationship to each other – a 'yes' on a grammaticality judgment cannot be taken to be twice as much, or five times as much, as a 'no'. In order to capture this relationship it is common practice to code one type of response as a 0 and the other as a 1. If you have a larger number of judgments you can then calculate how often the response was accurate, and thus convert such values to percentages. However, be very careful when you work with nominal data, as restrictions apply to the types of mathematical and statistical operations which you are allowed to carry out on them.

Likert Scale data can be even more deceptive. Recall the discussion above, where I suggested that some speakers may avoid the extreme ends of this scale, not so much because they do not feel that the sentences they heard are unambiguously (un)grammatical, but because they themselves have come to distrust their own intuitions. These considerations reflect the fact that on such scales, not all numbers may be perceived to be at exactly the same distance from each other. Furthermore, on a scale which has a 'neutral' middle point, the numbers may not have relations to each other which can be captured by mathematical operations. Consider a 7-point scale, where 1 stands for 'entirely unacceptable' and 7 implies 'entirely acceptable'. On such a scale, a sentence which receives a rating of 4 (which would stand for 'marginally acceptable') cannot necessarily be taken to be twice as 'good' as a sentence which has received a 2.

Data which imply some kind of progression (a higher rating on the scale reflects higher acceptability), but where it is not unambiguously known whether all numbers are the same distance from each other and can be related to each other by mathematical operations, are referred to as *ordinal data*.

NOTE

Another example of ordinal data are the grades which pupils receive in school, or students at university. Such grade point scales typically vary from country to country and are often extremely difficult to convert. For example, in Germany, a 1 is the best grade, a 4 is the lowest pass grade, and a 6 (the lowest possible mark) reflects no work submitted; in the Netherlands, grades are given on an ascending scale from 0 to 10, with 6 being the lowest pass grade. However, at German schools and universities, the highest grade (1) is relatively common, reflecting a very good performance. In the Dutch grade system, this would correspond to no more than an 8 or, at most, a 9, as the highest grade is only given in extremely rare cases: Kees de Bot once told me that, when he was at school, the pupils were told that a 9 would be for the teachers, while 10 was reserved for God.

While in each system, a 'better' grade reflects better performance, this progression cannot be captured by mathematical operations: a Dutch student who receives a 4 has produced very disappointing work, while one who receives an 8 has excelled. However, the numbers cannot be taken to imply that the latter student was twice as good, or invested twice as much work, as the former. Nor, of course, would you want to imply that God, who would receive a 10, was only twice as good as a moderately substandard student essay that had been given a 5.

Given these considerations, it becomes obvious that treating such data as 'normal' numbers, and performing mathematical operations on them such as the calculation of averages or the use of *parametric statistics* is highly problematic. Nevertheless, it has become common practice (in particular in the Social Sciences and Humanities) to ignore these restrictions: we cheerfully produce means, standard deviations, grade point averages etc. on Likert Scale data. Whether you feel that 'everybody does it' is a good enough rationale to justify your doing it as well depends on how much of a mathematical/statistical purist you are. If you do decide to proceed in the accepted (but admittedly sloppy) fashion, it is a good idea to include a disclaimer to the effect that you are aware of these problems, but have decided to accept them in line with common practice.

NOTE

Parametric statistics are statistical procedures which may only be applied to data that fulfil a set of criteria. One of these criteria is that the data have to be on an interval scale (see below). They also have to be *normally distributed* (see below) and independent of each other (the score of one participant may not influence the score of the other). If your data do not conform to these criteria, you should choose a non-parametric test. Parametric tests include well-known statistical procedures such as Analyses of Variance (ANOVAs), *t*-tests, and linear regressions. The most widely used non-parametric tests are probably the Chi-Square test and the Kruskal-Wallis test, a non-parametric equivalent to the ANOVA. These tests are explained in chapter 17 below.

The last type of measurement – 'honest', 'real' numbers – are referred to as *interval* data. Magnitude estimations are one type of such data. If you are not entirely certain whether data you have elicited are ordinal or interval, the easiest test is always to ask yourself whether a progression from one data point to the next can be expressed in mathematical terms: someone who is 60 years old is twice as old as someone who is 30, and someone who is two metres tall is twice as tall as someone whose height is only one metre, so age and height are interval data. A Dutch student who received a 6 on a test did not necessarily do twice as well as one who got a 3, but one who answered 60 per cent of the questions on a test correctly did do twice as well as one who only got 30 per cent right.

Converting one type of data to another

Depending on the type of analysis which you intend to do, it may be necessary to convert different types of data. On the one hand, you may have a test which elicits a large number of binary variables, such as a grammaticality judgment task or a C-Test. For each item on this task the answer can be classified as 'correct' (an ungrammatical structure has been correctly identified as deviant, an item on the C-Test has been filled in as expected) or 'incorrect'. If you give one point for each correct response, each participant will then achieve a certain score which reflects his or her overall performance, thereby converting a set of nominal variables to an interval one.[1]

On the other hand, you may sometimes want to convert interval to nominal or ordinal, in particular where your independent variables are concerned. For example, if you want to assess whether the age of migration plays a role in predicting the performance of your speakers, you may want to classify the age range 0–12 years as 'pre-puberty' and the age range above that as 'post-puberty'. Such operations are always arbitrary to a certain degree, as the researcher has to set the cutoff points between the groups. You may either choose a classification which results in subgroups that have an even number of participants (as far as possible), or base the range on previously existing literature.

NOTE

Recall my study of German L1 among German-Jewish migrants for which the two speakers Gertrud U. and Albert L., introduced at the very beginning of this text, were investigated. The overall study comprised data from thirty-five speakers. In order to assess to what degree individual experiences of anti-Semitic persecution had played a role for the attrition or maintenance of German as a first language, I divided the overall population into subgroups which were based on historical research and the time period during which they had emigrated. The literature on the Nazi era suggested very clearly defined phases, which were separated from each other by events such as the Nuremberg laws in September 1935 and the pogrom of 9 November 1938.

I therefore converted the continuous (or interval) variable 'time of emigration' to a grouping, or ordinal, variable with three values: migration between January 1933 and August 1935, between September 1935 and October 1938 and between November 1938 and August 1939. This classification then allowed me to compare the linguistic data from migrants who had experienced different degrees of persecution and abuse at the hands of the Nazis.

Types of data in the language attrition test battery

The experiments which I suggested in the above chapters elicit a range of different variables belonging to different types of data. The *dependent variables* or *outcome variables* (the data collected by means of the linguistic tests proposed above) are either measured on an interval scale (e.g. reaction times or number of items named on a Verbal Fluency Task) or can easily be converted to such a scale, e.g. by calculating the proportion of correct responses. I will therefore not go into the analysis of ordinal or nominal dependent variables here.

The situation is somewhat more complex with respect to the *independent* or *predictor variables*. The sociolinguistic questionnaire proposed here elicits data of all three types. There are a number of *nominal variables*, such as the sex of the speaker or the family situation (married, single, divorced etc.). As these variables cannot be averaged or computed in any other way, they have to be treated as individual factors where they are assumed to be of relevance.

The bulk of the sociolinguistic questionnaire (SQ) consists of ordinal/Likert Scale questions on language use and on language and cultural attitudes. Since the SQ contains a large number of these variables, it is desirable to reduce them to a smaller set of factors by calculating average values over a set of variables for each individual. For example, there are a large number of questions on how often each person uses their first language and it is desirable to boil down the responses to as few variables as possible. However, it is often not easy to see which variables should be grouped together to form such factors. There are three possibilities:

1. You may decide to calculate averages for those variables which you assume belong together on the basis of theoretical considerations. I applied such a classification in an analysis of the impact of L1 use on attrition (Schmid, 2007): based on the model of *language mode* proposed by François Grosjean (see chapter 7) I calculated three factors. Firstly, I averaged the reported use in those situations where I assumed that the language mode was *bilingual* (L1 use with other bilinguals in informal settings, e.g. within the family or with friends). I then also calculated averages for *intermediate* speech situations (L1 use in settings where other speakers may be bilingual but where code-switching is contextually inappropriate, e.g. in work-related settings such as the language classroom) and *monolingual* (L1 use with speakers who do not understand or regularly use the speakers' L2).

2. Instead of basing your analysis on such theoretical models or assumptions, you may prefer to establish which factors belong together in your own data on the basis of statistical procedures such as *data-mining* or *factor analysis*. Operations such as these allow you to detect unexpected patterns in your data – for example if the statistical analysis were to show that speakers who report a higher degree of homesickness also tend to watch more movies or read more books in their first language, you might want to include these variables together as a single factor.

3. If you are uncomfortable with option 1, but do not feel enough confidence in your own statistical skills to apply option 2, you could choose to base your factors on patterns which have previously been reported with respect to data elicited by the test battery proposed here. Such an analysis is provided in Schmid and Dusseldorp (2010). We conducted a factor analysis (a statistical procedure called a *principal component analysis*) on the data which I elicited from two large groups of attriters. The outcome of this analysis suggested that the sociolinguistic background variables may be classified into the following categories:

- bilingual mode L1 use (with partner, children and friends)
- intermediate mode L1 use (language for religious purposes, L1 use in language clubs)
- monolingual mode language use (for professional purposes, with speakers in country of origin)
- exposure to target-like L1 (non-interactive L1 use through TV or reading, communication with speakers in the home country or visits to that country)
- perceived importance of intergenerational maintenance
- linguistic and cultural affiliation (L1 use in inner speech, such as when dreaming or thinking, linguistic and cultural preferences)

We have since tested this model for the calculation of compound variables on data from a number of other investigations, and have found it to be valid in other settings. In other words, if you classify the data which you elicit by means of a sociolinguistic background questionnaire into these groups and calculate averages across the factors, you will probably achieve a valid set of predictors. You can test this by checking the internal reliability of the scale, through calculating what is known as the Cronbach Alpha.

On the website www.let.rug.nl/languageattrition/tools you can find more detailed, step-by-step descriptions of how to calculate and validate these factors.

TIP

When you code your data (i.e. when you enter them into your database), you should keep in mind the issue of *scales*. Some of the Likert Scale questions may have a range of three possible answers, others may have five or seven. If you do eventually decide to average some of these variables together, it is imperative that they all have the same possible range – that is, the same maximum and minimum – most usefully a minimum of 0 and a maximum of 1. This would mean that, for a 3-point scale, the lowest answer would be coded as 0, the intermediate answer as 0.5 and the highest as 1. On a 5-point scale, the values then become 0, 0.25, 0.5, 0.75 and 1 – and so on.

MISSING VALUES

When you are coding your data, you also need to keep in mind the problem of *missing values*. Inevitably, there will be some questions or some test results that you have not obtained for some of your participants. This can sometimes be due to equipment failure or to the fact that you needed to finish your data collection early for some reason, and so the participant was either unable to complete a task or you did not record it. On the other hand, the answers to certain questions may not be applicable in some cases: a speaker who is single will not be able to answer any questions about language use with their partner, and speakers who have no (grand)children cannot reply to an entire section of our questionnaire.

Such missing values should never be simply coded as zero. If there is no result for a certain type of test but a zero implies the lowest possible score, this would obviously distort the overall impression for this particular speaker. For example, the test battery I applied in my field-work contained two Verbal Fluency Tasks, and most people achieved somewhere between 15 and 30 responses on each of them. In a few cases, the recording device malfunctioned during one of these tasks. A certain speaker might therefore have scored a respectable 24 items on the 'fruit and vegetable' task, but I would have no score on the 'animals' task. If I coded this result as a zero, the average value for that speaker would then go down to $(24 + 0)/2 = 12$. Clearly, that would be an unfair representation of that person's performance.

Statistics software (for example SPSS) therefore allows you to pick a number that lies outside the possible range of a certain variable and define it as 'system missing'. You could pick a negative number, or something like 999 or 99999. The program will then exclude these values from any calculations. In the SPSS files which are accessible on the website accompanying this book (www.let.rug.nl/languageattrition/tools) as templates for the coding and analyses of your results I have used 999 as the pre-defined missing value (you can see this in the Variable Viewer).

Descriptive vs inferential statistics

NOTE

Once you have coded and classified all of your data, there are two distinct steps for your analysis: *descriptive* and *inferential* statistics. The descriptive analysis confines itself to exploring the findings within the context of your own investigation. That is, you present the results of your experiments, reporting central tendencies such as the *mean* or the *median*, the *standard deviation*, the *range* (maximum and minimum) and so forth. You may also want to visualize some of these measures in graphs and figures.

Inferential statistics explore *probabilities* concerning the results. When you investigate two or more groups of participants (say a group of thirty attriters and a group of thirty controls), there will always be differences between their performances. You might have the situation that the attriting group achieves a mean score on the C-Test of 87 and the controls have a mean score of 89. Descriptively, you can therefore say that the controls did 'better'. However, the difference is very small and there will be a number of attriters who achieved a higher score than some of the controls.

Inferential statistics are used to estimate how likely it is that the difference you found in your sample would also obtain in the population at large. In other words, the goal of a statistical procedure is to assess the probability that variability in performance between two groups is coincidental: if you were to make every single attriter and every single non-attriter in the world do your test, what is the probability that those two huge groups of speakers would be different from each other in a similar way to what you discovered in your small subsample?

DESCRIPTIVE STATISTICS AND VISUAL REPRESENTATION

Before you begin your statistical analysis, it is good practice to report your results descriptively by means of tables and/or graphs. Your descriptives should always include the mean and the standard deviation for each reported variable; in addition you may want to report matters such as the range or the median, or convert the numbers to a different format, such as percentages.

Table 16.2 *Unformatted SPSS output table*

	Group					
	GECA		GENL		GECG	
	Mean	Standard deviation	Mean	Standard deviation	Mean	Standard deviation
C-Test L1	77.075471 70	11.527307 14	78.509433 96	14.042001 06	83.433962 26	8.945367 16

Table 16.3 *Formatted SPSS output table*

		Group		
		GECA	GENL	GECG
C-Test L1	Mean	77.08	78.51	83.43
	St.Dev.	11.53	14.04	8.95

Statistics and spreadsheet software, such as SPSS or Microsoft Excel, allow you to easily produce tables containing all the relevant information. Do note, however, that the tables generated in this manner are often rather ugly and reader-unfriendly in the way that they distribute their columns, shade the borders of cells, outline the text in the cells, in the numbers of decimals they report, and so on. They will also usually be in a font that is different from your own text. It is therefore preferable not to simply copy-paste these tables but to reformat them in a way that is both aesthetic, easy to read (rounded to a sensible number of decimals), and consistent with the overall layout of your text. Compare the layout of Tables 16.2 and 16.3.

You can see that it is considerate to your audience to take some trouble over how you present your tables and results. If you are uncertain about how to present any findings, or for that matter how to structure your report, the style guide of the American Psychological Association (APA) is a very useful companion.

TYPES OF GRAPHS AND WHAT THEY CAN DO

In addition to reporting your findings in the form of numbers or tables, it can be extremely illuminating to visualize them in

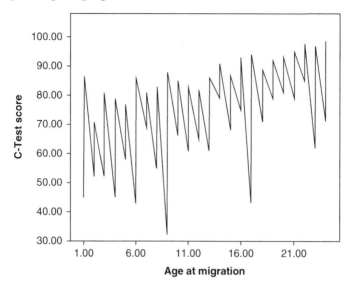

Figure 16.2 A line graph representing two interval variables

graphs which your statistics software can also provide. Again, you should bear in mind basic aesthetic considerations. For example the graphs produced by SPSS and Excel by default use a shaded background and colours to distinguish the different categories, both of which may not reproduce very well on the printed page, so you may want to remove the shading and distinguish categories by different tones of grey or different patterns.

Other important considerations concern the type of graph and the information it represents. In order to illustrate this, I have made up a set of data (you may download the data file, called 'CTest.sav' from www.let.rug.nl/languageattrition/tools, but do keep in mind that they originate entirely from my imagination). The file contains three variables. The first one is the age at migration, and you will see that there are 144 participants, six of whom were one year old, six 2 years old, and so on until 24 years at migration. The second column contains their C-Test score. In other words, the first two variables are both on an interval scale.

If we want to make a figure representing two interval variables, our choice of the type of graph is relatively limited. Choosing a representation such as a line or bar chart would produce a relatively uninformative nonsense graph, as you can see in Figure 16.2.

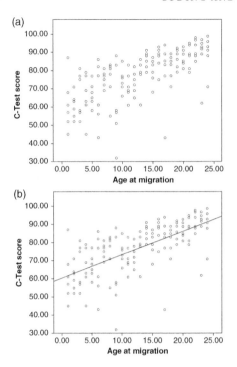

Figure 16.3 A scatterplot representing two interval variables (a) without and (b) with fit line

We could make this graph somewhat simpler by choosing not to have each individual data point represented but to average the C-Test results for each age level, but the result would still be far from ideal.

The only really viable option for a graphic representation of two interval variables is the so-called *scatterplot* (Figure 16.3). In Figure 16.3a, each individual result is displayed as a circle, and no attempt is made to connect all of the data points. You may choose to add a *fit line* to the graph (Figure 16.3b), in order to capture an overall trend (which here is the tendency for speakers with a higher age of migration to achieve a better score).

If you want to represent your data in ways that acknowledge the cumulative effect of a certain interval variable, you have to transform this variable into a grouping factor. For example, in the data I am using here we might want to see a comparison of the scores achieved by those participants who migrated before they were 12 years old (prepuberty) and those who were older than 12 (post-puberty). I have therefore created a third variable in the SPSS file, transforming the age range

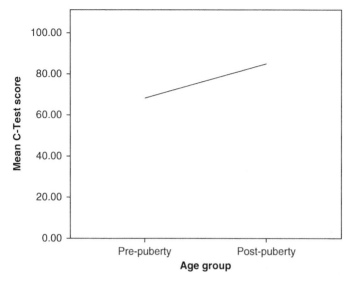

Figure 16.4 A line chart based on one interval and one ordinal variable

1–12 to one value (1, labelled 'pre-puberty'), and 13–24 to another (2, labelled 'post-puberty'). This variable is called 'agegroup'.

I might now want to try producing my line chart again, and the result would indeed give the strong visual impression that the C-Test scores which were achieved by my participants increase as a function of age at migration (see Figure 16.4). However, there is a problem here: the fact that the line chart implies a connection between the different categories strongly suggests that there is a *progression* in my actual data. This, of course, is not true: for each speaker I have only *one* measurement, so the progression is based solely on the interpretation of a set of single scores.

Line charts are therefore best used to represent those cases where there are *truly longitudinal data* which do show a genuine case of development over time, for example if I had tested a language learner at regular intervals and taught him or her between these testing sessions, so that the line would represent the actual improvement that had taken place between the two data points. In other cases, a different type of graph is more appropriate, such as a *bar chart* (see Figure 16.5). Such a chart can represent the average values for the different categories, but makes no attempt to imply a progression from one category to the next.

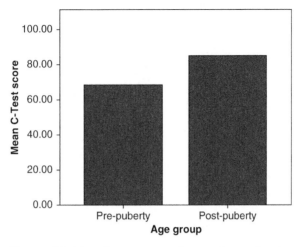

Figure 16.5 A bar chart representing one interval and one ordinal variable

You will sometimes see such chart representations reporting relatively minor differences between their categories, but 'cheating' in how they depict them. Recall my example above, where the experimental group achieved a mean score of 87, while the controls scored 89 on average. Figure 16.6 shows two possible ways of representing this difference. Above, you see the 'honest' representation, which depicts the full data range and thus reveals the group differences to be very small. The figure below, on the other hand, zooms in on the data range between 85 and 92, and therefore makes the differences look very pronounced indeed. At the risk of sounding judgmental: don't do that sort of thing. It is bad science.

If you really think that you need this kind of representation in order to highlight some small difference, say so clearly in the accompanying text.

Correctly used, bar charts can give a valuable impression of differences between categories. However, they can visualize only one measurement: the mean. I mentioned above that it is often very useful to include other measures in your descriptive statistics, such as the standard deviation or the median. These values, which tell us about the overall distribution of the data, can also be captured in the graphical representation if you choose the chart type known as a *boxplot*. Figure 16.7 gives such a representation of my hypothetical age-at-migration/C-Test data.

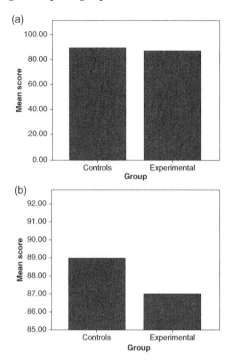

Figure 16.6 Reporting data in bar charts: (a) honest scale and (b) 'cheating'

In Figure 16.7 both categories are represented as a shaded area with 'whiskers'. The shaded area is the data range which contains half of all cases. This means that half of my hypothetical pre-puberty migrants have achieved a score between 60 and 77, while half of the post-puberty group has scored somewhere between 81 and 91. The whiskers then represent the top and bottom 25 per cent in each category. Within the shaded area, you can see a dark line. This line represents the score that divides the sample in two halves of equal size: the same number of participants achieved a score below and above it. That value is known as the *median*.

In addition to this, a number of data points are here represented below the actual boxplot. These refer to individual cases which are *outliers*: data points which fall so far outside the range of their category that it would be unwise to include them in statistical calculations, since they might distort the overall picture. The cases which are represented by circles are the ones that are further than one standard deviation away from the mean, while the asterisk marks a person who scored more than two standard deviations below it.

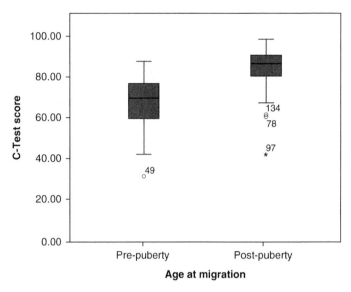

Figure 16.7 A boxplot chart representing one interval and one ordinal variable

TIP

Before you begin your inferential or statistical analysis, make sure that you have presented all of your results in detail in a clear, orderly and aesthetic manner. For each variable, reporting not only the mean but also the standard deviation is considered obligatory these days. In addition, you may find it valuable to provide measures such as the data range.

Used in the correct manner, graphical representations of your data can often be very helpful to your reader, summarizing results at one glance.[2] If you choose to do this, keep in mind practical restrictions: Will the colours you use in your charts translate properly to the black-and-white printed page? Will the charts and tables fit on the page, and will they be large enough to allow your middle-aged supervisor (who is reluctant to admit that she is now in need of reading glasses) to make out the details? Is the typeface used for the captions, titles and tables the same as the one you use in the text?

Most importantly, however, make sure that the type of graph you have chosen is appropriate for reporting the information that you want to convey!

17 Interpreting your data: inferential statistics

Investigations of attrition are all about *differences* between your experimental and your control population. However: *what* is different? At which point can you say that your attriters did worse on a certain task than your controls? This chapter introduces you to statistical procedures which can help you make this determination.

While descriptive statistics are concerned with, and limited to, the exploration of your own dataset, inferential statistics go a step further: they deal with *probabilities*. In other words, they address questions such as: how likely is it that a difference found between two groups in an experiment would obtain in the population at large? These probabilities or likelihoods are expressed by the ominous expression $p = x$, where p stands for 'probability' and x for a percentage, as assessed by some statistical procedure such as the ones I shall discuss below. When this value becomes smaller than 0.05, that is, when the probability that the group difference is a coincidence is smaller than 5 per cent, we speak of a *significant* difference. This means that we find the margin of error acceptable and therefore assume that the different performance of the two groups is the outcome of the variable we investigated, not of chance.

NOTE

A substantial proportion of the world's population suffers from a phobia of statistics, and this is particularly true among those of us who work in the Arts and Humanities. If you are engaged on a larger investigation, for example an M.A. or Ph.D. thesis, and you have this fear, it has the potential to dramatically impede your progress. You may find yourself procrastinating while pretending to yourself that you need to write up the theory part of your thesis, re-analyse and re-arrange your data, reconstruct your bathroom – anything but tackle the dreaded s-word.

If you do crank up the courage to follow a course in statistics, you may end up feeling even more frustrated than you were to begin with, and weighed down with the conviction that you will never, ever understand this. I myself had the experience that, although in both the courses I took I had absolutely excellent teachers (I'm still grateful to Martina Penke and Cor Koster), I was not yet at the point in my own research where I could really apply the tests we learned about (using examples such as the effects of placebos vs real medicine) to my own data. It all remained terribly abstract and just seemed to pass through my brain.

There is therefore really only one thing to do if you don't know how to tackle the statistics part of your analysis: get help. Getting good advice from people who know their stuff is important at any stage of your experiment, but probably most vital at this stage. It is also the kind of advice that is easiest to give. Once you have your data in a well-structured format, the actual analysis itself can usually be done very quickly. In the case of my own Ph.D., Kees de Bot put me in contact with his colleague Frans van der Slik, to whom I gave my data and who performed the statistics for me within a day.

Before you turn to a colleague or teacher for assistance, you may find it useful to take a recently published paper with data that are roughly comparable to yours in the manner in which they were elicited, and to simply follow the methods and analyses that are described there. That may already provide very illuminating results, and if you are uncertain how to interpret them, you can then ask your personal guru for advice.

If there is no one that you feel you can turn to, I highly recommend Andy Field's fantastic treatment, *Discovering Statistics Using SPSS* (2nd edition 2005). This is a comprehensive, clear, helpful and even entertaining guide, which takes you from the very first steps in your data collection through running the tests in SPSS to interpreting and reporting the outcomes. Since Field (and other statistics textbooks, such as Larson-Hall (2009) which focuses specifically on the use of statistics in research on bilingualism) give very detailed accounts on how to perform analyses, I will limit the discussion here to very brief descriptions of the actual tests that are relevant for the analysis of the experiments explained above.

For investigations of language attrition there are two types of general questions, which can be assessed by means of different statistical tasks:

- *group differences*: do the results which my participants achieved on the individual tasks differ across the groups (that is, between attriters and controls)?
- *variability*: can I explain the fact that some of the individual attriters have achieved higher scores than others on the basis of individual aspects, such as length of residence (LOR) or amount of use?

For any analysis you will first have to establish whether there are group differences between your experimental and your control population. If this is not the case – if the attriters perform as well as the controls – then it does not make sense to assess the individual differences among your attriters: if performance on a task is unaffected by the global factor of attrition, variance within the task cannot have been affected by sub-aspects of the attritional process (such as LOR or L1 use).

GROUP DIFFERENCES

When you want to test whether there is a difference between two or more groups regarding the scores they achieved on a certain task, you are dealing with two variables: the *independent* variable, that is, the factor (attriters vs controls) and the *dependent* one (the task result). Your independent variable is a nominal one: it has a certain limited number of values (for example 1 for attriters and 0 for controls) which are not in a numerical relationship with each other. The *dependent* variable could be any type of data, but it is vital that you are aware which type it is, since this will determine which statistical test you may use.

In order to perform a statistical analysis, your findings need to be organized in a database where one row contains all the data from one particular attriter or control participant (see Table 17.1).

On the website www.let.rug.nl/languageattrition/tools, you can download an SPSS file called 'sampledata.sav'. These data come from my own investigation of language attrition, although I modified them somewhat (so they should not be taken to be actual experimental results). Their layout is illustrated in Table 17.2.

The first column contains the participant identifier. The second column specifies the group (CA are German attriters in Canada, NL are German attriters in the Netherlands, and CG are the German controls). The column AttCon specifies whether a participant is an

Table 17.1 *An example of a database for statistical analysis*

Participant	Group	Age	LOR	C-Test
Marilyn Monroe	1	56	31	87
James Dean	1	61	27	67
Paul Newman	0	81	999	81
Sophia Loren	0	73	999	94
. . .				

Table 17.2 *The database sampledata.sav (downloadable from www.let.rug.nl/languageattrition/tools)*

Participant	Group	AttCon	Sex	Age	AaO	LOR	Edu	L1 use	GJT	C-Test	VFT
CA1	CA	Attriter	F	65	37	28	4	0.25	1.00	95	22.5
CA2	CA	Attriter	F	59	32	27	2	0.23	0.92	77	24.5

attriter or a control. The columns Sex, Age, AaO (age at onset) and LOR (length of residence) should be self-explanatory. Edu contains a four-level ordinal variable specifying the participant's educational level, and L1 use is an average of all questions in the sociolinguistic questionnaire pertaining to the frequency of interactive use of German.

SPSS offers two perspectives on any dataset: the 'Data View' and the 'Variable View'. Under the latter, you can see the properties of each variable. If you click on this tab, you can see how I have coded the values for the nominal variables Group, AttCon and Sex and the ordinal variable Edu. You will also see that I have selected the number 999 as 'missing data' for all variables. If you go back to the 'Data View' and de-activate the option 'Value Labels' in the menu 'View', you will see the original numbers that represent each level, instead of the labels that I have assigned.

The next three columns contain three dependent variables: the proportion of correctly identified ungrammaticalities in a GJT, the score on a C-Test and the average score of two Verbal Fluency Tasks (VFTs).

NOTE

For many of the attrition-specific factors, such as length of residence, you will not have any values for your controls: they have never emigrated, so there can be no meaningful value here. Such cases then have to be coded as *missing values* (see above), and I have chosen the value 999 to represent this here.

Comparing two groups: the *t*-test

I mentioned above the difference between *parametric* and *non-parametric* statistics, and told you that in order to apply parametric statistics, your data have to conform to certain criteria. The most important ones of these are that your data have to be measured on an interval scale (see above) and that they have to be *normally distributed*. Normal distribution is one of the basic concepts in statistical analyses, it is based on the observation that, in a population that is either large enough or representative of a larger group, most people will perform neither exceptionally well nor exceptionally badly on any given task. In other words, the majority of your participants should achieve a score more or less in the middle of the total range: if you have a test with a minimum score of 50 and a maximum score of 100, the result that will be achieved most often in the normal distribution will be 75. Only a very small number of people will get a 50 or a 100. If you plot the number of people who received each individual score in a so-called *histogram*, the normal distribution results in the famous bell-shaped curve represented in every statistics textbook.

If your data are normally distributed, the histogram should therefore look approximately like this curve: it should be symmetrical (if the slope on one side is steeper than on the other, it is said to be *skewed*) and neither too flat nor too steep (this factor is known as *kurtosis*). An exploration of the data which I have provided shows that only the VFT scores follow a normal distribution, the scores on the GJT and the C-Test are *negatively skewed* (see Figure 17.1).

In his chapter on *Exploring Data*, Field (2005) gives a detailed description on how to test this, and what to do if your data are not normally distributed – sometimes a transformation to logarithmic scores helps, and so does using not the actual scores but their square root. For the purpose of this demonstration, I shall ignore the violations of the assumption of normal distribution.

If your data are measured on an interval scale (remember, we generally include Likert Scale data under this heading, although this practice may be a bit dodgy), as the dependent variables in the file sampledata.sav are, and normally distributed (which they are not, but we shall ignore this for now), you may test whether attriters and controls differ by means of a statistical procedure known as a *t*-test. A *t*-test compares the scores of

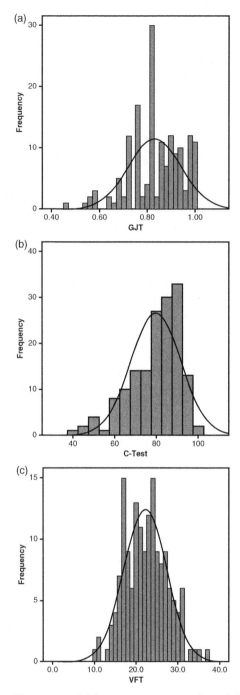

Figure 17.1 A histogram representation of the scores on the (a) GJT, (b) C-Test and (c) VFT, revealing GJT and C-Test to be *negatively skewed* (i.e. not normally distributed.)

two data samples, and estimates how likely it is that the two sample means were drawn from the same population. In our case, the test to choose is the *independent samples* test, because each result came from a different person (if I had tested them before migration and then again ten years later, I would have chosen a *dependent* or a *paired samples* test).

The output from this test is represented in Table 17.3. Firstly, you can see that the output per dependent variable is divided into two lines according to whether or not equal variances are assumed. The first two data columns report the outcome from a test which is called 'Levene's Test for Equality of Variances'. What this procedure does is assess to what degree the data are *homogeneous*: is there the same amount of variability at each level of the independent variable? In other words, is there the same spread of results among the attriters and the controls? You can see in Table 17.3 that, in our case, Levene's Test is not significant for the GJT and the VFT (the value in the column 'Sig.' is larger than 0.05 in both cases), but it is significant for the C-Test. This means that the variability is not equal across the two levels (which is only to be expected in this case, as the data were not normally distributed). You can see this by creating a scatterplot for these variables (see Figure 17.2): the circles for attriters and controls cover roughly the same data span for the GJT (Figure 17.2a) and the VFT (Figure 17.2c), but are spread out over a larger range for the C-Test (Figure 17.2b). We should therefore report the *t*-test outcome from the lower row (where equal variances are not assumed) for this variable.

The next three columns contain the values which we should report: the test outcome (*t*), the degrees of freedom (this value is based on how many cases there were in our analysis) and, most importantly, the significance. This is the first value you look for in your output, and we can see here that the test result is not significant for the GJT, but highly significant for the C-Test and the VFT.

You could therefore report the outcomes from this test as follows: 'There was no significant difference between attriters and controls on the scores for the GJT ($t(157) = -1.053$, $p = 0.294$). The differences achieved on the C-Test by the two groups were significant ($t(140.238) = -3.227$, $p < 0.01$). The differences achieved on the VFT by the two groups were highly significant ($t(157) = -5.782$, $p < 0.001$).'

TIP

For the VFT, p is reported in the output to be 0.000. Recall that p stands for probability. The finding that $p = 0.000$ therefore means

Table 17.3 SPSS output from a t-test on three dependent variables (GJT, C-Test and VFT) between the attriting and the control population

		Levene's Test for equality of variances		t-test for equality of means					95% Confidence interval of the difference	
		F	Sig.	t	df	Sig. (2-tailed)	Mean Difference	Std. Error Difference	Upper	Lower
GJT	Equal variances assumed	0.023	0.879	−1.053	157	0.294	−0.01953	0.01855	−0.05616	0.01711
	Equal variances not assumed			−1.060	106.124	0.291	−0.01953	0.01841	−0.05604	0.01698
C-Test	Equal variances assumed	6.985	0.009	−2.874	157	0.005	−5.642	1.963	−9.519	−1.764
	Equal variances not assumed			−3.227	140.238	0.002	−5.642	1.748	−9.098	−2.185
VFT	Equal variances assumed	0.017	0.898	−5.782	157	0.000	−4.5236	0.7823	−6.0688	−2.9783
	Equal variances not assumed			−5.768	103.436	0.000	−4.5236	0.7843	−6.0789	−2.9683

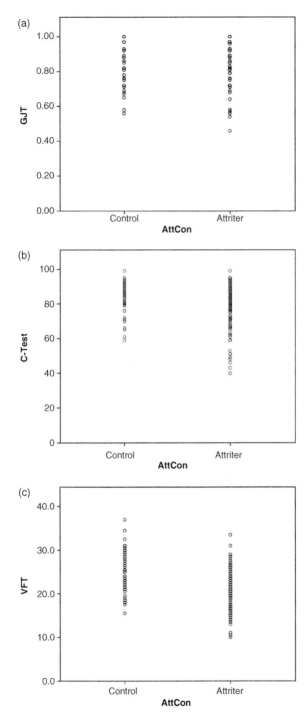

Figure 17.2 A scatterplot of the results from the (a) GJT, (b) C-Test and (c) VFT, showing the C-Test results not to be *homogeneous*

that it is *impossible* that the two group means came from the same population (the likelihood that this is so is 0.00 per cent). In practice, you should *never* report that $p = 0.000$, as this is only a rounding effect in SPSS, and instead put $p < 0.001$. In other words, it is not impossible that the two group means originate from the same population, but it is highly unlikely (less than 0.1 per cent likely).

It is a common misconception that a higher level of significance (i.e. a smaller *p*-value) means a *larger* difference. This is not the case: small but consistent differences will lead to highly significant findings, so the level of significance in itself tells us nothing about the *effect size*. It is therefore becoming more and more common to not only report the level of significance, but also the *explained variance*. This factor, commonly referred to as r, represents the amount of variability in your dependent variable that can be explained by the impact of the independent variable. Field (2005: 294) provides the following formula for the calculation of this value in the *t*-test:

$$r = \sqrt{\frac{t^2}{t^2 + d}}$$

For the C-Test results given above, the effect size is therefore calculated in the following way:

$$r = \sqrt{\frac{(-3.227)^2}{(-3.227)^2 + 140.238}} = \sqrt{\frac{10.414}{150.652}} = \sqrt{0.0691} = 0.263$$

As you can see, the effect size here is 0.263, which means that 26.3 per cent of the variability in this particular dataset are explained by the group division. The same calculation yields an effect size of 0.176 for the VFT. If the group comparison is not significant, as in the case of the GJT here, we do not calculate or report the effect size. We speak of a small effect with an r of around 0.1 (as in the case of the VFT), a medium effect when it is around 0.3 (as in the case of the C-Test) and a large effect for anything over 0.5 (Field, 2005: 32).

More than two groups: one-way ANOVA

The *t*-test can compare a normally distributed interval variable across two samples, and tell you whether these two samples are likely to have originated from the same population. But what if you have more than two samples? Say you want to compare a group of attriters, a

Interpreting your data   235

Table 17.4 *ANOVA output from a comparison of three dependent variables*

		Sum of squares	df	Mean square	F	Sig.
GJT	Between groups	0.016	2	0.008	0.661	0.518
	Within groups	1.896	156	0.012		
	Total	1.912	158			
C-Test	Between groups	1360.113	2	680.057	5.025	0.008
	Within groups	21111.736	156	135.332		
	Total	22471.849	158			
VFT	Between groups	734.909	2	367.454	16.943	0.000
	Within groups	3383.358	156	21.688		
	Total	4118.267	158			

group of L2 learners, and a group of controls, or – as in our example –
two groups of attriters living in different countries, against one
control group?

In such cases, where you want to compare the scores achieved by
more than two groups, you can choose a procedure called analysis of
variance, or ANOVA. In its simplest form, this test is quite similar to
the *t*-test. The dataset in the SPSS file sampledata.sav contains data
from a control group of German speakers in Germany (CG), a group of
German attriters in Canada (CA) and a group of German attriters in the
Netherlands (NL). Table 17.4 contains the SPSS output from running an
ANOVA on the three dependent variables contained in this sample.

The last column in this output contains the significance, and you
can see that there were no group differences on the GJT, but that
the groups performed differently on the C-Test and the VFT. When
we report these results, we should mention the degrees of freedom,
the *F*-value and the significance in the following way: 'No differences
between the groups were found on the GJT ($F(2, 156) = 0.661, p = 0.518$)'
and so on.

Where you do have a significant finding, for example in the case of
the C-Test above, you can calculate the effect size by dividing the value
given in the column 'Sum of Squares' for 'Between Groups' by the
'Total', and then calculating the square root. In our case, this yields
the following equation:

$$\eta^2 = \sqrt{\frac{1360.113}{22471.849}} = \sqrt{0.060525} = 0.246019$$

The effect size, which for an ANOVA is usually called η^2 (eta squared), is therefore 0.246 (24.6 per cent of the variance in the data are accounted for by the group to which an individual belonged). Again, this constitutes a medium effect, similar to the one we found above between attriters and controls. We can therefore report that 'The results of the C-Test were significantly different between the populations, with a medium effect size ($F(2, 156) = 5.025$, $p < 0.01$, $\eta^2 = 0.246$).'

The ANOVA test only tells you whether there was an *overall* difference between your groups, not which individual groups were different from each other. If you want to know this, you can establish it either by means of a *planned contrast* or a *post hoc* test, which will compare the individual subgroups. Which contrast or test you choose depends on your sample (for example, it is important whether or not your group sizes are the same, and whether variance is equal across populations), and you can find all the criteria in Field (2005). In the present case, the *Gabriel* post hoc procedure tells me that, on the C-Test, there is only a significant difference between the control group and the attriters in Canada ($p < 0.01$), but not between controls and attriters in the Netherlands ($p = 0.083$) or between the two attriting groups ($p = 0.773$). On the Verbal Fluency Task, both attriting groups are different from the controls ($p < 0.001$), but not from each other ($p = 0.842$) (see Table 17.5).

NOTE

In itself, a significant result does not tell you in which way the results were different. It could, in theory, equally well be the case that the attriters have performed *better* than the controls. That is why it is so important to explore your data descriptively, reporting group means etc., before you proceed to the statistical analysis.

The impact of other factors: analysis of covariance (ANCOVA)

Analyses which compare group means can tell you whether there is a difference in scores between two or more populations. However, as we know, there are a number of factors other than group membership which may impact on the score a participant achieves for a certain task. For example, we know that more highly educated participants will probably perform better on the C-Test, and that younger speakers will usually get a higher score on a VFT. If populations are not equally matched on these factors, the findings can be

Table 17.5 *Output from the ANOVA post hoc test (Gabriel)*

Dependent variable	(I) group	(J) group	Mean difference (I–J)	Std. error	Sig.	95% Confidence Interval Upper bound	Lower bound
C-Test	CG	CA	6.94340(*)	2.25984	0.007	1.4910	12.3958
		NL	5.00000	2.25984	0.083	−0.4524	10.4524
	CA	CG	−6.94340(*)	2.25984	0.007	−12.3958	−1.4910
		NL	−1.94340	2.25984	0.773	−7.3958	3.5090
	NL	CG	−5.00000	2.25984	0.083	−10.4524	0.4524
		CA	1.94340	2.25984	0.773	−3.5090	7.3958
VFT	CG	CA	4.85849(*)	0.90467	0.000	2.6758	7.0412
		NL	4.18868(*)	0.90467	0.000	2.0060	6.3714
	CA	CG	−4.85849(*)	0.90467	0.000	−7.0412	−2.6758
		NL	−0.66981	0.90467	0.842	−2.8525	1.5129
	NL	CG	−4.18868(*)	0.90467	0.000	−6.3714	−2.0060
		CA	0.66981	0.90467	0.842	−1.5129	2.8525

* The mean difference is significant at the 0.05 level.

distorted: we might get a significant result which is not, in fact, due to attrition but to the fact that the attriters are older, or less highly educated, than the controls.

Education and age are factors which we can measure across our entire population (unlike, for example, length of residence and age at emigration, which pertain only to the attriters but not to the controls). Such factors can be included in the ANOVA design as *covariates*, and then the analysis is referred to as an *analysis of covariance* (or ANCOVA). Running an ANCOVA, with group (CG, CA, NL) as the main factor and education and age as covariates, on the results from my C-Test and my Verbal Fluency Task, produces the results shown in Tables 17.6 and 17.7.

These two tables tell you that, for the C-Test, education does indeed have a significant effect ($F = 46.631$, $p < 0.001$), while the impact of age is not significant for this task ($F = 0.985$, $p = 0.322$). The picture is reversed for the VFT, where age is significant ($F = 5.896$, $p < 0.05$) but education is not ($F = 1.379$, $p = 0.242$). Most importantly, however, the factor group (attriters vs controls) remains significant for both tasks, even when the impact of the covariates is partialed out.

Table 17.6 *SPSS output from an ANCOVA for the C-Test*

Source	Type III sum of squares	df	Mean square	F	Sig.
Corrected model	7060.958	4	1765.239	17.604	0.000
Intercept	14870.479	1	14870.479	148.300	0.000
Education	4675.800	1	4675.800	46.631	0.000
Age	98.813	1	98.813	0.985	0.322
group	1412.880	2	706.440	7.045	0.001
Error	15442.036	154	100.273		
Total	1031800.000	159			
Corrected total	22502.994	158			

Table 17.7 *SPSS output from an ANCOVA for the VFT*

Source	Type III sum of squares	df	Mean square	F	Sig.
Corrected model	947.487	4	236.872	11.504	0.000
Intercept	2027.976	1	2027.976	98.496	0.000
Education	28.399	1	28.399	1.379	0.242
Age	121.386	1	121.386	5.896	0.016
group	673.878	2	336.939	16.365	0.000
Error	3170.781	154	20.589		
Total	81,625.250	159			
Corrected total	4118.267	158			

Parametric tests and covariates

NOTE

As the above examples illustrate, covariates are often a very important consideration in research on language attrition. Recall that, when we initially tested the normal distribution of our three dependent variables, we found that two of them (the GJT and the C-Test) violated the assumptions of normality, as the histogram revealed a *skewed* distribution. In principle, this means that we should not have used a *t*-test or an ANOVA, but their non-parametric counterparts, a Mann-Whitney test (for two populations) or a Kruskal-Wallis test (for more than two groups). These tests, however, do not allow for the inclusion of covariates or more than one factor. If you perform these analyses on the data provided in the sample file, you will find that their findings are very similar to the ones reported above.

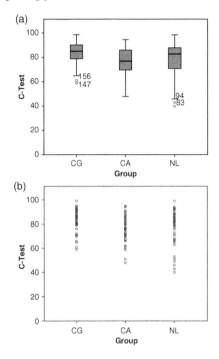

Figure 17.3 Group differences on the C-Test: (a) boxplot and (b) scatterplot

WITHIN-GROUP VARIATION: THE IMPACT OF INDEPENDENT INTERVAL VARIABLES

In the section entitled 'Group differences' above, I introduced various test methods to determine whether or not there is a difference between two or more groups with respect to the score which they have achieved on a particular task. Based on the tests we ran, we can therefore say that the attriting populations which we have investigated were outperformed on the C-Test and on the VFT by the controls. This attrition effect is clearly visible in the boxplot of the C-Test represented in Figure 17.3(a). However, the scatterplot for the same data, represented Figure 17.3(b), also shows that there is considerable within-group variation: some attriters do much better than others, and even better than some controls.

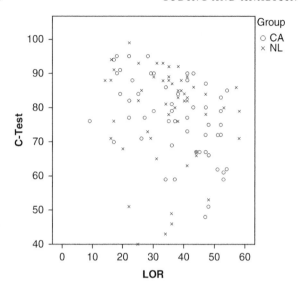

Figure 17.4 A scatterplot representing the relationship between length of residence and C-Test scores

In order to get a clearer picture of attrition effects, we want to know what factors are responsible for these individual differences: what is it that makes one attriter achieve a C-Test score of 95, while someone else was able to get only 48? We have already seen that general factors, such as education or age, can be important; but when it comes to attrition, the truly interesting questions pertain to variables that are specific to the migrant situation. Attriters are different from controls in that they live in an L2 setting, but they can vary from other attriters with respect to how often they speak the L1, how long they have lived there, how old they were when they migrated, and so on.

The relationship between two interval variables: the Pearson Correlation

The factors I just named are all *interval* variables, and as such, we could visualize them in a scatterplot. For example, it would appear reasonable to expect that attriters with a longer emigration span will do worse than those who migrated more recently. In order to check this assumption, we can produce a scatterplot with LOR on the *x*-axis and the C-Test score on the *y*-axis. Such a graph is represented in Figure 17.4.

You can indeed see that the scores are grouped in a general area that slopes downwards, indicating a tendency for lower scores for speakers with a longer LOR.

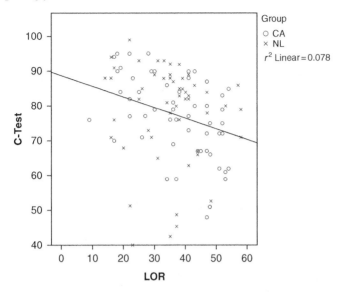

Figure 17.5 A scatterplot with a fit line representing the trend of the relationship between length of residence and C-Test scores

If we were to draw a line at random across this graph, we could calculate the vertical distance of each of the dots from that line, and then add all of these distances up. We could then draw another line, do the same, and compare the sum of the distances, and so on. The best representation of the trend that is present in the data is the line for which the sum of the distances is the smallest.[1]

Statistics software can find the one line among all potential ones for which this fit best represents the data. In Figure 17.5 you can see very clearly how the line slopes; and the program also tells you how much of the variance present in the data this line can account for: $r^2 = 0.078$ – a medium effect with around 8 per cent of the variance explained. But, as we now know, the question is not so much whether the effect is small or large, but whether it is *significant*. We can test this by running a *Pearson Correlation* with the output shown in Table 17.8.

For each correlation, this output tells you the r-value (multiplying $(-0.280) \times (-0.280)$ gives you the r^2 of 0.078 that we saw above), the significance, and the number of cases that the calculation is based on.

The impact of other factors: partial correlations

At first glance, the test we did in the section entitled 'Within-group variation' appears to imply that the relationship between LOR and the

Table 17.8 *SPSS output from a bivariate correlation between LOR and C-Test score*

		LOR	C-Test
LOR	Pearson correlation	1	−0.280(**)
	Sig. (2-tailed)		0.004
	N	106	106
C-Test	Pearson correlation	−0.280(**)	1
	Sig. (2-tailed)	0.004	
	N	106	106

**Correlation is significant at the 0.01 level (2-tailed).

C-Test scores is beyond doubt. However, beware: in a very complex dataset we have only looked at two variables, and not taken into account that they might both be influenced by or related to something else.

Such a factor might lie, for example, in historical differences concerning the migration context: shortly after World War II, in the 1950s, many people migrated from Germany to Canada and the Netherlands. These migrants mostly had a relatively low level of formal education, but were skilled labourers and artisans. In later periods, the migrants were often more highly educated. This means that there may be a difference in the average LOR for the different levels of education represented in this dataset. And indeed, if we calculate the mean LOR for each of the four educational levels, we find that for levels 1 and 2 (the lower levels) this is around forty years, whereas levels 3 and 4 have only thirty years' migration time on average. Now, as we saw above (and as stands to reason), the C-Test is a task where educational level plays an important role.

Fortunately, there is a way of controlling for the impact of other independent variables. All we need to do is choose to calculate not a bivariate, but a partial correlation, with LOR and C-Test as the variables, and education as the factor to be controlled for (see Table 17.9).

As you can see, once the effect of education is partialed out, the correlation between C-Test and LOR is no longer significant ($r = -0.094$, $p = 0.342$). You should therefore always be extremely careful when you interpret the results from correlations (or any other statistical procedure): if you find that two variables are in some way related to each other at the statistically significant level, this does *not* automatically mean that one has caused the other. There is always the possibility that both were independently affected by some third factor.

Table 17.9 *SPSS output from a partial correlation between LOR and C-Test score, controlling for education*

Control variables			C-Test	LOR
Edu	C-Test	Correlation	1.000	−0.094
		Significance (2-tailed)	.	0.342
		df	0	103
	LOR	Correlation	−0.094	1.000
		Significance (2-tailed)	0.342	.
		df	103	0

NOTE

Storks and babies
In the first ever statistics class I attended, the teacher Martina Penke gave us a very memorable example of the fact that a correlation between two variables does not necessarily imply causality. Apparently someone had investigated the number of births per head of population during a year, and the number of storks which were nesting in the surrounding area. The two variables correlated at a very high level. Martina asked us whether we thought that this significant finding would allow us to deduce that the traditional account that it was the storks who were bringing the babies was, in fact, correct – or whether it might not be more convincing to assume that both had something to do with life in more rural surroundings?

The interaction of several independent variables

The partial correlation which I discussed above allows you to investigate the impact of one independent interval variable on a dependent one, while controlling for the impact of other factors. However, there is also the possibility of an interaction effect between several predictors, so that their impact will only become visible once you try to account for them all in a single model.

NOTE

Use and time
Kees de Bot, Paul Gommans and Carola Rossing published an article in 1991 (in the Seliger and Vago volume *First Language Attrition*) on the L1 attrition of Dutch in an L2 French setting. In this article, the impact of *amount of use* and *length of residence* on performance was assessed. De Bot *et al.* come to the conclusion that

there is only a linear relation between 'time' and attrition when
there are few contacts with the first language . . . 'time elapsed
since emigration' and 'amount of contact' should not be used as
independent measures: 'time' only becomes relevant when there is
not much contact with the language (de Bot *et al.*, 1991: 94).

If you want to investigate the impact which several independent variables have *together* on your outcome variable, you can do so by creating
an *interaction variable*. In the case of the sample data I provided, you
can see that there is one variable called *LOR*, which gives the emigration span in years, and one called *L1use*. In this variable, I have averaged
the answers on all items in the sociolinguistic questionnaire which
pertain to *interactive* L1 use – that is, anything that is not either
passive exposure (reading, watching TV) or communication with self
(thinking, praying, swearing etc.). The highest possible value here is 1,
which would represent anyone who used the L1 on a daily basis in *all* of
these contexts, while a 0 is someone who *never* uses the L1 for *any* of
these things.

In order to see whether there is an interaction effect between contact and time, I should first create a new variable, where for each
participant the value for *LOR* is multiplied by the value for *L1use*, and
I could call this variable *contacttime*. Once I have created this variable,
I can run another partial correlation, again controlling for the impact
of variation – and doing this tells me that, while *contacttime* is still not a
significant factor, it now does approach significance ($r = 0.168$, $p =
0.086$).

The individual contribution of several factors: multiple regression

Correlations can tell you about the impact which a *single* independent
variable has on an outcome variable. However, we may also be interested in the power which several factors have, taken *together*, to predict
the result for the dependent variable. For example, I might want to
know how much of the variance in my C-Test scores is explained by
educational level, sex, length of residence, L1 use and our *contacttime*
interaction variable together. This can be established by means of an
analysis called *multiple linear regression*.

In order to demonstrate how such an analysis could be carried out
and what it could tell us, I conducted a linear regression for the C-Test
scores for the attriters in the file sampledata.sav. I entered the predictor variables in different blocks. Firstly, I chose the variable

Interpreting your data 245

Table 17.10 *SPSS Output 'Model Summary' for a multiple linear regression for C-Test scores*

Model	r	r^2	Adjusted r^2	Std. error of the estimate
1	0.535[a]	0.286	0.279	10.872
2	0.548[b]	0.301	0.287	10.811
3	0.573[c]	0.328	0.301	10.703
4	0.582[d]	0.338	0.305	10.672

[a] Predictors: (Constant), Edu
[b] Predictors: (Constant), Edu, Sex
[c] Predictors: (Constant), Edu, Sex, L1use, LOR
[d] Predictors: (Constant), Edu, Sex, L1use, LOR, contacttime

education, since this has been shown to have an impact on the C-Test, not only for these data but also in previous research. Secondly, I entered 'sex', another general variable which is often associated with differences in achievement among bilingual populations. In the next block, I entered the two attrition specific variables *LOR* and *L1use*, and lastly, I added the interaction variable *contacttime*.

The first part of the SPSS output is the *Model Summary*, shown in Table 17.10. Here, we can see for each block how much of the explained variance (r^2) increases when the predictor variables are added. In the first block, the regression analysis establishes that the factor education alone accounts for 28.6% of the variance – a very strong predictor. Adding *sex* as another predictor allows the model to account for no more than another 1.5%, so men and women were apparently not much different from each other. Taken together, *L1use* and *LOR* do not fare that much better: the model which includes them can account for 32.8% of the variance, and the interaction between the two factors adds another 1%.

The next part of the output is an ANOVA table, telling me whether each of the models can make a significant contribution towards explaining the overall variance. Table 17.11, labelled 'Coefficients', tells you what the contribution of each individual factor is.

You can see here that, in all four models, education makes a significant contribution ($p < 0.001$) and that none of the other variables contributes significantly to the outcome. The column 'Beta' tells you how strong the contribution of each predictor is.

Regressions are quite a complex procedure, and if you are interested in conducting such an analysis, I recommend that you thoroughly familiarize yourself with the underlying assumptions, the different ways of entering the variables, and the options for interpreting the

Table 17.11 *SPSS output 'Coefficients' for a multiple linear regression for C-Test scores*

Model		B	Std. error	Beta	B	Std. error
		Unstandardized coefficients		Standardized coefficients	*t*	Sig.
1	(Constant)	62.659	2.572		24.366	0.000
	Edu	6.146	0.952	0.535	6.454	0.000
2	(Constant)	60.907	2.819		21.604	0.000
	Edu	5.993	0.953	0.521	6.291	0.000
	Sex	3.269	2.216	0.122	1.475	0.143
3	(Constant)	59.504	6.087		9.776	0.000
	Edu	5.661	1.021	0.493	5.542	0.000
	Sex	3.290	2.194	0.123	1.500	0.137
	LOR	−0.036	0.101	−0.033	−0.359	0.720
	L1use	9.210	5.149	0.154	1.789	0.077
4	(Constant)	66.586	8.286		8.036	0.000
	Edu	5.802	1.025	0.505	5.662	0.000
	Sex	3.328	2.188	0.124	1.521	0.131
	LOR	−0.244	0.193	−0.224	−1.260	0.211
	L1use	−8.854	15.277	−0.148	−0.580	0.564
	contacttime	0.534	0.425	0.320	1.255	0.212

[a] Dependent variable: C-Test

output before you attempt to carry them out yourselves (again, the chapters on regression in Field (2005) are invaluable). An example of a set of linear regression analyses and their findings on a large set of language attrition data is given in Schmid and Dusseldorp (2010), and that may also be helpful to you.

CONCLUSION

I have no doubt that for many readers, this chapter was the most difficult of the whole book to get through. However, congratulations and rejoice: you made it!

Should you be among those people who have the nasty tendency to skip tedious bits of text and fast-forward to the conclusion in the hope that this will tell them all they need to know, you have my sympathy and I'll therefore provide you here with a short checklist of how to approach your data. I know that I shouldn't encourage your bad habits, but I think the list may be equally useful to those faithful readers who have plodded through this chapter – if not more so.

A step-by-step guide to data analysis in language attrition

Step 1: Provide descriptive statistics for all your dependent variables. These should minimally include averages and standard deviations per population, but can include more information.

Example:

		CG	CA	NL
GJT	mean	0.84	0.82	0.83
	St.Dev.	0.11	0.12	0.10
	median	0.86	0.81	0.81
	max	1.00	1.00	1.00
	min	0.56	0.54	0.46
C-Test	mean	83.43	77.08	78.51
	St.Dev.	8.95	11.53	14.04
	median	85.00	77.00	83.00
	max	99.00	95.00	99.00
	min	59.00	48.00	40.00
VFT	mean	25.09	20.24	20.91
	St.Dev.	4.67	4.62	4.68
	median	25.00	20.00	20.50
	max	37.00	33.50	31.00
	min	15.50	10.50	10.00

Step 2: Where they are illuminating, provide graphs to illustrate and visualize these descriptives (see Figure 17.6).

Step 3: Establish whether your data are *normally distributed* (see Figure 17.7).

Step 4: Establish whether there are group differences between the attriters and the controls by means of a *t*-test (two groups) or an *ANOVA* (more than two groups).

Step 5: Assess the impact of other possible covariates, such as age or education, by means of an *ANCOVA*.

Step 6: For those dependent variables in which you have found group differences between attriters and controls, assess the impact of attrition-specific independent variables, such as LOR, age at onset, amount of use, attitudes etc., by means of *bivariate* and/or *partial correlations*. Keep in mind that some factors may interact with others!

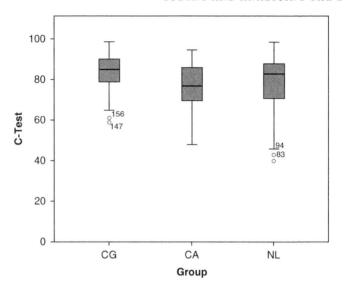

Figure 17.6 A boxplot of the C-Test scores

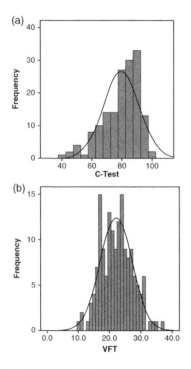

Figure 17.7 A histogram representation of the scores of (a) the C-Test (not normally distributed) and (b) the VFT (normally distributed)

Step 7: For those dependent variables on which you have found group differences between attriters and controls, assess the impact which several independent variables have taken together by means of a *multiple linear regression*.

Step 8: Interpret and discuss!

Step 9: Publish!

18   Conclusion

I pointed out above that the intuitive appeal of the phenomenon of language attrition can be both a blessing and a curse for those of us who are doing research in this area. A blessing because it is usually easy to find speakers who are interested enough to invest their time in participating in our research. Furthermore, ours is one of the few areas of science that others – linguists and non-linguists alike – tend to find fascinating. Most of our colleague scientists will generally reap anything from politely feigned interest to outright boredom when they attempt to tell others about their research passion (remember poor Ross the palaeontologist, from the TV series *Friends*?). However, few people will not be intrigued and moved by stories such as those of Gertrud U. or Albert L.

The potential curse, as I also pointed out above, lies in the fact that for many of our interlocutors the fascination of the subject is rooted in some resonance in their own experience. For example, few Dutch people do not have an Uncle Wim or an Aunt Agada who moved to Canada, Australia or New Zealand in the 1950s and, these days, has *such* a strong English accent or simply *cannot* use articles properly any more. Like Mma Ramotswe in the quotation at the very start of this book, those who have experienced this (either in themselves or by proxy) often feel puzzled, unsettled, saddened or shocked. As experts on the phenomenon of language loss, we are expected not only to provide an explanation but also to alleviate such feelings. This is fine if the conversation occurs at a dinner party, but less so in the five-minute discussion period after a conference talk. In such situations, we should always be prepared to gently cut off questions or comments that become too personal and/or too lengthy, and offer to talk about it over coffee later on.

However, the real danger lies not in the fascination which others feel for our subject, but in what we feel ourselves. The mere fact that a research topic is valid, meaningful and important does not make the research itself good, and emotional investment is not a get-out-of-jail-free card which allows you to ignore the standards of scientific rigour. Since I have been working on language attrition, I have often been asked to read and evaluate others' research, for example as external reader of theses or anonymous reviewer for journals. It pains me to say that, probably more so than is the case with research I have seen on other topics, I have often felt that the work I read was not up to scratch.

The purpose of the present book has therefore been to try and lay out those principles which, in my own view, should guide attrition research, and the yardsticks against which it should be measured. Of course we have to recognize and accept certain limitations. If I want to investigate second-year students of English, all I have to do is walk into one of my own classrooms in order to find a beautifully balanced population, comprising several dozen speakers largely matched for age, education, language background and length of exposure (though not normally for gender). If I want to study attriters, there is no such easy recourse. Populations in attrition studies therefore always have been and always will be smaller *and* less homogeneous than those investigated in studies of acquisition. That cannot be helped – but it has to be acknowledged. It also means that what attrition studies cannot accomplish by quantity, they have to compensate for in terms of quality.

In order to achieve this, before you can even begin to start thinking about designing your study and gathering your results, you crucially need to thoroughly familiarize yourself with what you are investigating. This means firstly to study and understand the language which you propose to look at. Being a native or near-native speaker is probably a prerequisite for investigating the attrition of any one language, but it is not enough. Your investigation has to be conceived, set up and conducted in terms of linguistic, psycholinguistic or neurolinguistic model(s) of the grammatical phenomenon or phenomena that you want to investigate.

Secondly, you have to be aware of the existing body of literature on attrition, in particular of the recent publications. This, I am afraid, is one of the most frequent shortcomings of attrition studies. The late 1990s saw a hiatus of several years during which there were extremely few publications on this topic (particularly on L1 attrition), and many current studies only base themselves on the work which had appeared before then. Unfortunately, there is nothing that makes a piece of scientific writing look more parochial than an outdated bibliography. As a general rule of thumb, if you quote anything that is older than ten years you should consider carefully if you should not substitute or add a reference to a more recent publication. Attrition studies have been extremely prolific over the first decade of the twenty-first century, and any piece of work which you attempt should show that you are aware of this. In this age of electronic databases, online journals and internet search engines, there really is no excuse for not doing so.[1]

Lastly, it is of paramount importance in language attrition research that you know your speakers. I have tried to illustrate this through the frequent (I hope not too frequent) references I made throughout this book to the cases of Gertrud U. and Albert L. When I first collected the corpus that contained the interviews with these and thirty-three other speakers who had left Germany under similar circumstances, I had been hoping to find predictor variables, such as age at migration or amount of use of German, which would allow me to explain the variance in L1 proficiency that these speakers retained. However, after considering everything that I could think of, I found myself at a loss – none of these factors appeared to make sense of my data.

When you reach such a dead end, it often helps to select a few speakers who are paragon examples of a certain development – as Albert L. represents the near-perfect maintainer and Gertrud U. is an extremely good attriter – and to try to understand what it is that makes them different from each other. This was what I did, looking in great detail at Albert L. and two other maintainers, and three excellent attriters, one of whom was Gertrud U. What struck me almost immediately was that all three of the latter narratives contained the experience of the pogrom of 9 November 1938, while the three maintainers had all left Germany relatively soon after the Nazi seizure of power in 1933.

I confess that, not being a historian, I had not originally expected there to be such a marked difference according to the time of migration, but once the picture had emerged, I found it corroborated in the historical literature. It also immediately became clear to me that a classification of the narrators into certain historical phases on the basis of the time at which they had left Germany allowed me to account for the differences in L1 proficiency far better than any other variable I had been able to think of. Moreover, I have since encountered numerous other cases of Jewish refugees for which the same was true. For example, Judy Kroll of Penn State University told me that she had been fascinated by my explanation, since it fitted the case of her husband's parents perfectly: the father-in-law had left Germany in 1935 and was still a very competent speaker of German, while the mother-in-law, having fled after the pogrom, hardly retained any knowledge of her native tongue.

Fortunately, most investigations of language attrition will deal with less traumatic events and with less clear-cut situations. All the more, this means that we can leave no stone unturned and have to immerse ourselves in speakers' experiences, in order to arrive at an understanding of what makes some of them strong maintainers and others strong attriters.

That said, it is now time to take our leave from Gertrud U. and Albert L., and from each other. It may be that our different journeys take both you and me towards new investigations of attrition, towards new populations, new results and new insights. If so, maybe we will sit down together one day at some conference or other and compare notes.

I should like that.

Glossary

Activation Threshold Hypothesis: Developed by Michel Paradis, the Activation Threshold Hypothesis proposes that all items of knowledge that we store in memory have a certain activation level, which determines the amount of effort required to retrieve them. This status is partly determined by previous activations: the more frequently and recently the item has been called upon, the easier it is to activate again. The second process which impacts on this status is inhibition: every time a related item, such as an equivalent in another language, is called upon, the item has to be inhibited in order to prevent its being activated by mistake. Inhibition raises an item's activation level, making it more difficult to retrieve from memory the next time. This implies that, if a bilingual speaker uses one language predominantly and consequently routinely inhibits the other; it gradually becomes more and more effortful to reactivate again. Activation requires less effort if it is triggered by an external stimulus, which means that it is easier to recognize a word that the speaker is exposed to in spoken or written input than it is for the speaker to produce the word.

Calque: A calque is a loan-translation where every item of a particular expression is literally borrowed into another language. Calquing often produces words which then become part of the lexicon, such as the English *skyscraper* which has been calqued into French as *gratte-ciel* and, in a slightly modified version, into German as *Wolkenkratzer* (literally, *cloud-scraper*), and is used in all three languages to refer to a very tall building. Calquing can also occur ad hoc, sometimes without the speaker being aware of this, and then lead to expressions that are difficult to understand if the interlocutor happens not to be familiar with the donor language or with that particular item. The quote from Albert L. in the introduction to this book contains the English word *preparatory school*, which he calques to produce German *Vorbereitungsschule*. In the German educational system, this calque does not make much sense, since there is no equivalent to that phase of education (an independent, fee-paying institution for pupils up to around age 13, preparing them for entry to a *public school*).

Categorical: A categorical variable or measure is one with two or more discrete and distinct levels or values, such as a yes/no question or an exam with only a pass/fail grade. In categorical data, no gradient distinction is made within these levels – all pass grades are considered equal, regardless of the fact that some students may have performed very well while others just barely scraped a pass mark. This makes categorical data different from *ordinal* or *interval* data, where different values or levels imply some kind of progression.

Ceiling effect: If a test or experiment is administered which is too easy for the target population, all participants may do extremely well, so that the variance that is obtained in the results is too low to allow for analysis. The absence of significant differences between populations in such a case is known as a *ceiling effect*, indicating not necessarily that the populations are all equally proficient or skilled, but that the level of difficulty was set too low. For example, we might want to adapt one of the experiments which Pallier *et al.* (2003) were using with their Korean adoptees to post-puberty migrants. This experiment involves asking participants to identify from a larger set of languages in which they hear the numbers *one* to *ten* which of these languages is their L1. It is highly unlikely that any of these migrants, regardless of how far they had attrited, would find it difficult to identify the number sequence in their native language, and so the results would not be indicative of their level of L1 maintenance or attrition.

Closed-class system: All languages contain two types of lexical items: *lexical* or *content words* and *grammatical* or *function words*. The latter category is often referred to as *closed-class*, because it is rare for languages to add new function words, while the content repertoire expands and changes constantly and is therefore called an *open-class* system. Content words refer to items, concepts or other entities that exist outside the discourse, such as nouns which can denote concrete or abstract 'things' or verbs which can refer to activities. Conversely, function words such as pronouns or prepositions acquire their meaning based on the discourse itself and its context: I may use the word *you* a hundred times on any given day but mean a different person each time, or point at a different location every time I say *there*. Similarly, conjunctions such as *and* or *because* only serve to make specific kinds of connections (in this case, additive or causal) between different parts of the text, and do not carry this kind of meaning in themselves.

Cognate: Cognates are words in two languages which are derived from a common etymological origin, such as English *father*, Dutch *vader*, French *père* and Italian *padre*, many of which trace back to Latin *pater* (and probably beyond). You can already see from this example that identifying cognates is not a straightforward process: some of the items listed above appear much more similar to each other and to their origin than others. Cognates play different roles in different branches of linguistic investigation: for diachronic linguistics, for example, it is of great importance to trace back items from different languages to their common roots in order to identify regularities in change (e.g. the sound shift that led to the Germanic languages using /f/ for the sound that was originally /p/ in Latin *pater*). In psycholinguistics, cognates are of interest particularly where the word shape is similar, since the mental representation of such items may partly overlap for speakers who are proficient in both languages. A Dutch–English speaker, for example, would probably be faster recognizing the word *father* than a word of similar frequency and length which did not have a cognate equivalent in his or her other language. To what extent near-cognates, such as *father* and *père*, influence speed in retrieval or recognition is doubtful, and for the purpose of experiments, one should either choose items that are full and undisputed cognates, or equally undisputed non-cognates.

Corpus: A corpus is a dataset, typically comprising a number of texts from different interlocutors. We distinguish between large *corpora*, collections of texts from different genres and authors or speakers, which may be used for text analysis in order to infer grammatical rules, distributional patterns or processes of language change on the one hand, and the kinds of smaller corpora typically used in applied linguistic research on the other. For investigations of language attrition, for example, no pre-existing, multimillion-word corpora are available, so researchers have to collect their own datasets.

Creolization: Creolization is a particularly productive process of language change under conditions of very extensive language contact. Creole languages are contact languages which retain some properties of all of the original donor languages. In some cases, the grammar of the new language is largely based on one of the original contact languages (substrate) while the lexicon comes mainly from the others (superstrate), but often all languages contribute to some degree. Many creole languages developed as a result of the slave trade of the sixteenth to nineteenth centuries, in particular since slave merchants often made great efforts to keep together captives from different linguistic origins, in order to make it more difficult for them to revolt. However, creoles have also arisen in other situations – there is even a view (albeit much contested) which holds Middle English to be a creole.

Disfluency markers: Natural speech is characterized by phenomena such as hesitations (empty pauses), repetitions of single words, clauses or entire stretches of text, self-corrections and filled pauses such as *uh, ahm*. These *disfluency markers* are highly frequent, particular in informal, unplanned discourse, and do not normally impede conversation – we are usually not even aware either of using them ourselves or of others' being disfluent. However, second language learners and language attriters can become noticeably disfluent, when such phenomena either occur with a much higher frequency (due to problems of lexical access) than in natives, or take on characteristics of hesitation patterns in the speaker's other language. For example, the typical filled pause in American English is a relatively open front vowel, /æ/ or /a/, while in German it tends to be somewhat more closed, /ɛ/ and in French it is more to the back, /ə/. Cross-linguistic influence in such relatively subtle differences in hesitation patterns can make a speaker appear far less native-like than if she or he were to conform to the native pattern.

Distracters: In linguistic experiments, it is often of paramount importance that the participants are unaware of the grammatical or lexical phenomenon which is being tested, in order to prevent them from applying explicit knowledge to their answers. In order to muddy the waters, it is therefore important to include items which contain different grammatical features or are in other ways unrelated to the objective of the experiment. There should be at least as many distracters as there are targets.

Distributed normally: see Normal distribution.

Grammatical morphemes: Usually, the term 'grammatical morphemes' is used to refer to so-called *bound morphemes*, parts of words which cannot stand alone, such as the English inflectional affix -s which signals the plural on nouns, or case inflections. However, *free morphemes*, which are words in their own right, can also be grammatical, as opposed to lexical, morphemes, as is the case with pronouns, prepositions or conjunctions (see closed-class system).

Grammaticalization: see Semantic bleaching.

Inhibition: see Activation Threshold Hypothesis.

Mean: The mean, or average, of any dataset is the value that is calculated by adding all individual values and then dividing this sum by the total number of observations.

Median: The median is a measure of a central tendency in a dataset, similar to the mean. It is the value which splits the dataset in half, so that the same number of observations fall above and below it. The median is calculated instead of the mean in order to prevent individual values which fall far outside the range of the other observations ('outliers') from distorting the overall picture. In datasets which are *normally distributed*, the mean and the median are identical. Since many parametric statistical procedures, such as the *t*-test or the ANOVA, are based on the mean, non-normally distributed data are best analysed by non-parametric procedures such as the Mann-Whitney test, which are based on the median instead.

Multicompetence: The concept of multicompetence was developed by Vivian Cook, partly as a response to what he considered overly modular models of multilingual knowledge. The multicompetence view considers all language systems which co-exist in the same mind to be linked and merged to some degree, so that, they all affect each other in the process of language production, processing and development (acquisition and attrition).

Normal distribution: The normal distribution is a crucial concept in statistics. It is based on the assumption that, in a random sample, most observations will fall close to the middle of the range, and only very few will be at the upper or lower extremes. This means that in any population which is large enough and not distorted by any sampling bias, a plot of the total scores will be in the form of a symmetrical bell-shaped curve which is neither too flat nor too narrow, and the *mean* and the *median* will be identical (i.e. exactly half the population will score above and below the average). Data which are normally distributed may be analysed by means of *parametric statistical procedures* such as *t*-tests or ANOVAs, whereas if they are not normally distributed, then *non-parametric* tests, such as the Mann-Whitney test, have to be used.

Open-class system: see Closed class system.

Parametric statistics: Parametric statistics are tests which are based on central tendencies of a dataset, such as the mean and the standard deviation. They can therefore only be applied to data which fulfil the assumptions of the *normal distribution*.

Semantic bleaching: Semantic bleaching is a consequence of the diachronic process of *grammaticalization* which is considered to be one of the universals of language change. In this process, as linguistic development unfolds, some lexical items can lose their fully lexical properties and turn into *grammatical* morphemes, for example, full verbs which change into modal auxiliaries. In this process, the original lexical meaning of the word erodes and it takes on a more textual-based meaning. The processes of grammaticalization and semantic bleaching have been extensively explored and described in the work of e.g. Paul Hopper and Elisabeth Closs Traugott.

Social Network Theory: Social Network Theory is a model developed by Lesley and James Milroy to capture the complexity of relationships which human beings have with others as well as the impact of these relationships on language development and change. The model hinges on the observation that we interact with each other in various capacities – as friends, relatives, colleagues, neighbours and so on. Furthermore, networks can be of various density: if all participants in a network know each other, it is said to be dense, but if each person knows only one or two of the others and otherwise has their own, unconnected network, this is a loosely-knit network. These properties affect the speed of language change among populations.

Standard deviation: The standard deviation of a dataset is calculated as the square root of its variance. It indicates how well the mean represents the sample: if the standard deviation is small, this means that all observations occur close to the mean (that is, the distribution curve is very steep), if it is large, the data are more widely distributed (and the curve is flat). In a normally distributed sample, 34.1 per cent of all cases fall within one standard deviation above and below the mean, respectively.

Notes

Notes on Preface
1 Grant number 275-70-005.

Notes on Chapter 1
1 This extract from *The Full Cupboard of Life* by Alexander McCall Smith is reproduced by permission of Polygon, an imprint of Birlinn Ltd.
2 Subordinate clauses in German are fairly complicated, since they involve a word order which is quite different from that which applies in main clauses. They are discussed in some more detail in the section 'Shift' in chapter 3 below, and yet more detail can be found in Schmid (2002).
3 The use of 'zerstreut', *scattered*, instead of 'zerstört', *destroyed*, is discussed on page 33.
4 *Language attrition* is sufficiently established as a technical term by now that its derivatives *to attrite, an attriting language, an attriter* (i.e. a person who is experiencing attrition) are also acceptable and commonly used.

Notes on Chapter 2
1 It has, for example, been established that bilingual speakers are faster at naming pictures of objects in their L1 if the word is similar ('cognate') in their L2 than if it is not (van Hell and Dijkstra, 2002), and that syntactic processing (Hernandez, Bates and Avila, 1994) and phonetic properties (Cutler, Mehler, Norris and Segui, 1989; Flege, 1987) of the first language are influenced by the second.
2 Note that the discussion in Seliger and Vago is somewhat complicated by speculations on how the development is determined not only by cross-linguistic influence but also by the potential influence from Universal Grammar (UG) at the different stages, a factor which will not be discussed here.

Notes on Chapter 3
1 Estimating the size of the average vocabulary of a speaker is a highly complex matter. It has been shown that, even for native speakers of a similar educational background (high school students or undergraduates), these estimates can vary wildly from study to study. However, converging evidence seems to suggest that native speakers of that education level have an active vocabulary of some 15,000 items, on average (Zechmeister, d'Anna, Hall, Paus and Smith, 1993).
2 The processes of cross-linguistic interference can be, and usually are, bidirectional for bilinguals – that is, the L2 can influence the L1, and vice versa. Since the focus of the current book is L1 attrition, the discussion below will focus on traffic from L2 to L1. This does not preclude the possibility of similar phenomena going the other way.

3 This particular instance of borrowing may have been supported by the fact that a similar sounding word, *graulen* 'to dread', exists in German. This will be further discussed under *convergence* below.

Notes on Chapter 4

1 For this calculation, words that are different forms of the same lexical item or lemma, such as *war* ('was') and *waren* ('were') are counted as the same word.

2 *D* is based on recurrent sampling of different stretches of fifty items each from the text in question. A full discussion on how it is calculated is beyond the scope of this text. *D* can be calculated with the help of the CLAN program developed by Brian Mac-Whinney (2000) or the website of the CHILDES project (http://childes.psy.cmu.edu).

3 At the time of this analysis, there were no tools available to calculate this, so the analysis had to be done by hand. For some languages, such tools have more recently become available, e.g. through the CELEX database (see http://celex.mpi.nl).

4 Schmid and Beers Fägersten also conduct an analysis of the word classes of the elements following the disfluency marker. Their findings show that an overuse of such markers by attriters is most prominent preceding lexical items (nouns and verbs), and they argue that hesitation patterns can indeed be an indication of problems of lexical accessibility.

Notes on Chapter 5

1 I am grateful to Tal Caspi for helping me with these examples.

2 In chapter 15, I will discuss a widely used system of coding spoken data called CHAT, and demonstrate how this can be applied to coding and analysing spoken data such as these.

3 One of the readers of this text, also a native speaker of Italian, argues that this claim is inaccurate and that both sentences are ambiguous between the old lady and the girl. I subsequently asked two other Italians their interpretation, and they agreed with the criticism. Since I do not speak Italian, I cannot judge who is correct and am accepting the interpretation provided by Tsimpli, Sorace, Heycock and Filiaci (2004).

4 This sentence is slightly awkward, as a native speaker would probably prefer the periphrastic past tense *gelesen habe* 'have read'. Since the presence of the auxiliary further complicates the word order issue, I have chosen to preserve the simple past tense.

Notes on Chapter 7

1 Interestingly, while most subjects reported using both languages to some degree for thinking and dreaming, almost 95 per cent had a clear preference for one or the other language in all mathematical functions (Vaid and Menon, 2000: 331).

Notes on Chapter 8

1 Information on these so-called *Kindertransporte* can be found at www.kindertransport. org/history.htm or in Göpfert, 1999.

Notes on Chapter 9

1 I shall refer to the population of potential attriters (migrants) in investigations of attrition as the 'experimental group', while the population of subjects in the country of origin, used as a baseline for comparison, is called the 'control group'.

Notes on Chapter 10

1 In neurolinguistics, the terms *declarative* and *procedural* knowledge are often used to refer to *explicit* and *implicit* knowledge, respectively. These terms make

assumptions about the representation of knowledge in the brain and the under-lying neural mechanisms which subserve its use. I shall not be discussing the declarative/procedural distinction here; for an excellent and in-depth treatment see Paradis, 2008.

Notes on Chapter 12

1 It is sometimes pointed out that terms such as *grammaticality*, *acceptability* and *acceptability judgment* refer to different underlying concepts: while *grammaticality* is a characteristic of a certain sentence, *acceptability* refers to how this sentence is perceived by a participant, and the *acceptability judgment* is then a reflection of this perception (Bard, Robertson and Sorace, 1996). However, I shall adopt the label 'grammaticality judgment task' here, since that appears still to be the one that is most commonly used.

Notes on Chapter 13

1 The example sentences and pictures relating to the experiments on Turkish pronouns are taken from Gürel, 2002 and 2004, and used with her kind permission.
2 This explanation is slightly simplified, if you are interested in a full discussion, you can find it in Köpcke, 1998. Note also that what I say here only applies to the spoken form. In written English, things can become a bit more tricky – just think of cases such as *thief* – *thieves* or *potato* – *potatoes* (the word which so famously troubled the then candidate for the US vice-presidency Dan Quayle when he insisted, on live national television, that the spelling of the singular form of *potato* included an -e at the end).
3 Verbs which form their past tense through vowel mutation, like *sing* – *sang* – *sung*, are also often called *irregular*. I prefer to reserve this term for verbs which have truly unpredictable declensions, such as *to be*.

Notes on Chapter 14

1 The excerpt which is generally used contains the following scenes: (1) Charlie Chaplin (CC), newly released from jail, arrives at a shipyard with a letter of recommendation, is given work, commits a major blunder, and leaves again. (2) A hungry girl steals a loaf of bread and encounters CC, who takes the blame for the theft and is taken away by the police, but a bystander reveals that the true thief was the girl, and so CC is released again. (3) CC goes into a restaurant and eats a large meal, but cannot pay for it, so he is taken into custody again. Meanwhile, the girl is apprehended. (4) The policeman calls for a car to take CC to jail. While his attention is diverted, CC takes a cigar from a stall and gives some chocolate to two boys, but cannot pay for this, either. (5) CC is loaded into the truck with some other miscreants, and after a few moments, the girl is put on the truck as well. They reacquaint themselves. (6) There is an accident, and both can escape. (7) They walk along a street and sit in front of a house where they witness a blissfully domestic scene. (8) CC has a little dream about how it would be if he and the girl were to share similar domestic bliss. (9) They awake from the daydream and CC resolves to make this happen, even if it means he has to get work. (10). A policeman appears behind them, and they walk off together.
2 A variant of this task is called the 'film commentary' task. Here, you show the film twice and invite the participant to describe what she or he is seeing while watching it for the second time.
3 You should, of course, make sure that the actual text does not give any clues as to the speaker's status, in particular if it was taken from an autobiographical

interview. It is also important that no actual lexical or grammatical errors or code-switches occur anywhere in the segments you use.

Notes on Chapter 16

1 Note that even this strategy is problematic to some extent, since it assumes that all items in the test are equally difficult, which is almost certainly not the case.

2 In papers for scientific journals, graphs are generally used only for those variables for which there are significant findings.

Notes on Chapter 17

1 A technical problem here is that, for some of the dots, the distance is positive (they are above the line), while for others it is negative (they are below the line), so in the addition, they will cancel each other out. We can circumvent this by the old trick of squaring every number, and so turning the negative values into positive ones.

Notes on Chapter 18

1 A good way of getting an overview of a field is to start with the most recent publications and anything which is quoted in their bibliographies. Some recent collections which may serve as a starting point are the special issues of the *Journal of Neurolinguistics* (2004, Vol. 17(1)), the *International Journal of Bilingualism* (2004, Vol. 8(3)) and *Bilingualism: Language and Cognition* (2010, Vol. 13(1)), as well as the edited volumes of Köpke *et al.* (2007) and Schmid *et al.* (2004). At the time of writing, further special issues on language attrition are under preparation for the *International Journal of Bilingualism* and the journal *Language, Interaction and Acquisition*.

References

Abrahamsson, Niclas and Hyltenstam, Kenneth (2008). The robustness of aptitude effects in near-native second language acquisition. *Studies in Second Language Acquisition* 30: 481–509.

Aitchison, Jean (1991). *Language Change: Progress or Decay?* Cambridge University Press.

Altenberg, Evelyn P. (1991). Assessing first language vulnerability to attrition. In *First Language Attrition*, ed. Herbert W. Seliger and Robert M. Vago. Cambridge University Press. 189–206.

Altenberg, Evelyn P. and Vago, Robert M. (2004). The role of grammaticality judgments in investigating first language attrition: a cross-disciplinary perspective. In *First Language Attrition: Interdisciplinary Perspectives on Methodological Issues*, ed. Monika S. Schmid, Barbara Köpke, Merel Keijzer and Lina Weilemar. Amsterdam/Philadelphia: John Benjamins. 105–29.

Ammerlaan, Tom (1996). 'You get a bit wobbly...' – Exploring bilingual lexical retrieval processes in the context of first language attrition. Ph.D. thesis, Katholieke Universiteit Nijmegen.

Andersen, Roger W. (1982). Determining the linguistic attributes of language attrition. In *The loss of language skills*, ed. Richard D. Lambert and Barbara F. Freed. Rowley, MA: Newbury House. 83–118.

Audring, Jenny (2009). Reinventing pronoun gender. Ph.D. thesis, Vrije Universiteit Amsterdam.

Baker, Colin (1992). *Attitudes and Language*. Clevedon: Multilingual Matters.

Bard, Ellen Gurman, Robertson, Dan and Sorace, Antonella (1996). Magnitude estimation of linguistic acceptability. *Language* 72(1): 32–68.

Bardovi-Harlig, Kathleen and Stringer, David (2010). Variables in second language attrition: advancing the state of the art. *Studies in Second Language Acquisition* 32: 1–45.

Bates, Elizabeth, D'Amico, Simona, Jacobsen, Thomas, *et al.* (2003). Timed picture naming in seven languages. *Psychonomic Bulletin & Review* 10(2): 344–80.

Beganović, Jasminka (2006). First language attrition and syntactic subjects: a study of Serbian, Croatian, and Bosnian intermediate and advanced speakers in Dutch. M.A. thesis, University of Edinburgh.

Ben-Rafael, Miriam (2004). Language contact and attrition. The spoken French of Israeli francophones. In *First Language Attrition: Interdisciplinary Perspectives on Methodological Issues*, ed. Monika S. Schmid, Barbara Köpke, Merel Keijzer and Lina Weilemar. Amsterdam/Philadelphia: John Benjamins. 164–87.

Berko, Jean (1958). The child's learning of English morphology. *Word* **14**: 150–77.

Birdsong, David (2006). Age and second language acquisition and processing: a selective overview. *Language Learning* **56**(S1): 9–49.

Breakwell, Glynis M. (1986). *Coping with Threatened Identities*. London/New York: Methuen.

Brown, Janis C. (2001). L1 attrition among native speakers of English residents abroad: a sociolinguistic case study from Foggia, Italy. M.A. thesis, University of Surrey.

Bylund Spångberg, Emanuel (2008). Age differences in first language. Ph.D. thesis, Stockholm University.

(2009). Maturational constraints and first language attrition. *Language Learning* **59**(3): 687–715.

Carroll, Susanne E. (2001). *Input and Evidence. The Raw Material of Second Language Acquisition*. Amsterdam/Philadelphia: John Benjamins.

Caskey-Sirmons, Leigh A. and Hickerson, Nancy P. (1977). Semantic shift and bilingualism: variation in the color terms of five languages. *Anthropological Linguistics* **19**(8): 358–67.

Cherciov, Mirela (2010). Between attrition and acquisition: the dynamics between two languages in adult immigrants. Ph.D. dissertation, University of Toronto.

Cook, Vivian J. (1991). The poverty-of-the-stimulus argument and multi-competence. *Second Language Research* **7**(2): 103–17.

(1998). Internal and external uses of a second language. *Essex Research Reports in Linguistics*. 100–10.

(2003). Introduction: The changing L1 in the L2 user's mind. In *Effects of the Second Language on the First*, ed. Vivian Cook. Clevedon: Multilingual Matters. 1–18.

(2005). The changing L1 in the L2 user's mind. Plenary lecture presented at the 2nd International Conference on First Language Attrition, Amsterdam, August.

Cook, Vivian, Iarossi, Elisabet, Stellakis, Nektarios and Tokumaru, Yuki (2003). Effects of the L2 on the syntactic processing of the L1. In *Effects of the Second Language on the First*, ed. Vivian Cook. Clevedon: Multilingual Matters. 193–213.

Crezee, Ineke H.M. (2008). I understand it well, but I cannot say it proper back: language use among older Dutch migrants in New Zealand. Ph.D. thesis, University of Auckland.

Crystal, David (1980). *A Dictionary of Linguistics and Phonetics*. Oxford: Blackwell.

Cummins, James (1979). Linguistic interdependence and the educational development of bilingual children. *Review of Educational Research* **49**(2): 222–51.

Cutler, Anne, Mehler, Jacques, Norris, Dennis and Segui, Juan (1989). Limits on bilingualism. *Nature* **340**: 229–30.

Davis, Kathryn A. and Lazaraton, Anne (eds.) (1995). Qualitative Research in ESOL. Special issue of *TESOL Quarterly* **29**(3).

de Bode, Stella (1996). First language attrition: productive morphology disintegration and neurobiological support. A case study. M.A. thesis, California State Polytechnic University.

de Bot, Kees and Clyne, Michael (1989). Language reversion revisited. *Studies in Second Language Acquisition* **11**(2): 167–77.

(1994). A 16-year longitudinal study of language attrition in Dutch immigrants in Australia. *Journal of Multilingual and Multicultural Development* **15**(1): 17–28.

de Bot, Kees and Stoessel, Saskia (2000). In search of yesterday's words: reactivating a long-forgotten language. *Applied Linguistics* **21**(3): 333–53.

de Bot, Kees, Gommans, Paul and Rossing, Carola (1991). L1 loss in an L2 environment: Dutch immigrants in France. In *First Language Attrition*, ed. Herbert W. Seliger and Robert M. Vago. Cambridge University Press. 87–98.

de Leeuw, Esther (2004). An instrumental and auditory phonetic comparison of hesitation markers in English, German and Dutch. M.A. thesis, University of Trier.

(2007). Hesitation markers in English, German, and Dutch. *Journal of Germanic Linguistics* **19**(2): 85–114.

(2008). When your native language sounds foreign: a phonetic investigation into first language attrition. Ph.D. thesis, Queen Margaret University, Edinburgh.

de Leeuw, Esther, Schmid, Monika S. and Mennen, Ineke (2010). The effects of contact on native language pronunciation in an L2 migrant setting. *Bilingualism: Language and Cognition* **13**(1): 33–40.

Dewaele, Jean-Marc (2004a). Blistering barnacles! What language do multilinguals swear in?! *Estudios de Sociolingüística* **5**(1): 83–105.

(2004b). Perceived language dominance and language preference for emotional speech: the implications for attrition research. In *First Language Attrition: Interdisciplinary Perspectives on Methodological Issues*, ed. Monika S. Schmid, Barbara Köpke, Merel Keijzer and Lina Weilemar. Amsterdam/Philadelphia: John Benjamins. 81–104.

(2006). Learning to express love in a foreign language. Paper presented at EUROSLA 16, Antalya, September.

Dewaele, Jean-Marc and Pavlenko, Aneta (2003). Productivity and lexical diversity in native and non-native speech: a study of cross-cultural effects. In *Effects of the Second Language on the First*, ed. Vivian Cook. Clevedon: Multilingual Matters. 120–41.

Dostert, Susan (2009). Multilingualism, L1 attrition and the concept of 'native speaker'. Ph.D. thesis, Heinrich-Heine Universität, Düsseldorf.

Dussias, Paola E. (2004). Parsing a first language like a second: the erosion of L1 parsing strategies in Spanish–English bilinguals. *International Journal of Bilingualism* **8**(3): 355–71.

(2010). Uses of eye-tracking data in second language sentence processing research. *Annual Review of Applied Linguistics* **30**: 149–66.

Dussias, Paola E. and Sagarra, Nuria (2007). The effect of exposure on syntactic parsing in Spanish–English bilinguals. *Bilingualism: Language and Cognition* **10**(1): 101–16.

Ellis, Rod (1994). *The Study of Second Language Acquisition*. Oxford University Press.

(1999). *Learning a Second Language through Interaction*. Amsterdam/ Philadelphia: John Benjamins.

Ferreira, Fernanda and Henderson, John M. (1990). Use of verb information in syntactic parsing: evidence from eye movements and word-by-word self-paced reading. *Journal of Experimental Psychology: Learning, Memory, and Cognition* **16**(4): 555–68.

Field, Andy (2005). *Discovering Statistics using SPSS*. London: Sage.

Flege, James Emil (1984). The detection of French accent by American listeners. *Journal of the Acoustical Society of America* **76**(3): 692–707.

(1987). The production of 'new' and 'similar' phones in a foreign language: evidence for the effect of equivalence classification. *Journal of Phonetics* **15**: 47–65.

Fronditha Care Inc. (2005). Senate community affairs references committee inquiry into aged care. Submission from Fronditha Care Inc. and Dutchcare Ltd., January 2005. www.aph.gov.au/senate/committee/ clac_ctte/aged_care04/submissions/sub224.pdf.

Gardner, Robert C. and Lambert, Wallace E. (1972). *Attitudes and Motivation in Second-Language Learning*. Rowley, MA: Newbury House.

Gass, Susan (1997). *Input, Interaction and the Second Language Learner*. Mahwah, NJ: Lawrence Erlbaum.

Giles, Howard, Bourhis, Richard Y. and Taylor, Donald M. (1977). Towards a theory of language in ethnic group relations. In *Language, Ethnicity and Intergroup Relations*, ed. Howard Giles. London: Academic Press. 307–48.

Goodglass, Harold and Kaplan, Edith (1983). *The Assessment of Aphasia and Related Disorders*. Philadelphia, PA: Lea & Febiger.

Göpfert, Rebekka (1999). *Der jüdische Kindertransport von Deutschland nach England 1938/39*. Frankfurt a. M./New York: Almqvist and Wiksell.

Green, David W. (1986). Control, activation and resource: a framework and a model for the control of speech in bilinguals. *Brain and Language* **27**(2): 210–23.

Grosjean, François (1982). *Life with Two Languages: An Introduction to Bilingualism*. Cambridge, MA: Harvard University Press.

(1989). Neurolinguists, beware! The bilingual is not two monolinguals in one person. *Brain and Language* 36(1): 3–15.

(2001). The bilingual's language modes. In *One Mind, Two Languages. Bilingual Language Processing*, ed. Janet L. Nicol. Oxford: Blackwell. 1–22.

Grosjean, François and Py, Bernard (1991). La restructuration d'une première langue: l'intégration de variantes de contact dans la compétence de migrants bilingues [The restructuring of a first language: the integration of contact variants into the competence of bilingual migrants]. *La Linguistique* 27(2): 35–60.

Gross, Steven (2004). A modest proposal: explaining language attrition in the context of contact linguistics. In *First Language Attrition: Interdisciplinary Perspectives on Methodological Issues*, ed. Monika S. Schmid, Barbara Köpke, Merel Keijzer and Lina Weilemar, Amsterdam/Philadelphia: John Benjamins. 281–97.

Grotjahn, Rüdiger (2010). *The C-Test: Contributions from Current Research (2010)*. Frankfurt: Peter Lang.

Gürel, Ayşe (2002). Linguistic characteristics of second language acquisition and first language attrition: Turkish overt versus null pronouns. Ph.D. thesis, McGill University Montreal.

(2004). Attrition in L1 competence: the case of Turkish. In *First Language Attrition: Interdisciplinary Perspectives on Methodological Issues*, ed. Monika S. Schmid, Barbara Köpke, Merel Keijzer and Lina Weilemar. Amsterdam/Philadelphia: John Benjamins. 225–42.

(2008). Review article: Research on first language attrition of morphosyntax in adult bilinguals. *Second Language Research* 24(3): 431–49.

Haegeman, Liliane (1991). *An Introduction to Government and Binding Theory*. Oxford: Blackwell.

Hagoort, Peter and Brown, Colin M. (2000). ERP effects of listening to speech compared to reading: the P600/SPS to syntactic violations in spoken sentences and rapid serial visual presentation. *Neuropsychologica* 38(11): 1531–49.

Haines, Timothy K. (1999). *STTARS & refugee resettlement in South Australia*. www.international.metropolis.net/events/washington/Haines.doc.

Herdina, Philip and Jessner, Ulrike (2002). *A Dynamic Model of Multilingualism: Perspectives of Change in Psycholinguistics*. Clevedon: Multilingual Matters.

Hermans, Daan (2000). Word production in a foreign language. Ph.D. thesis, University of Nijmegen.

Hernandez, Arturo E., Bates, Elizabeth A. and Avila, Luis X. (1994). On-line sentence interpretation in Spanish–English bilinguals: what does it mean to be 'in between'? *Applied Psycholinguistics* 15(4): 417–46.

Hilton, Heather (2008). The link between vocabulary knowledge and spoken L2 fluency. *Language Learning Journal* 36(2): 153–66.

Hopp, Holger and Schmid, Monika S. (forthcoming). Perceived foreign accent in L1 attrition and L2 acquisition: the impact of age of acquisition and bilingualism. *Applied Psycholinguistics*.

Hopper, Paul and Traugott, Elisabeth Closs (1993). *Grammaticalization*. Cambridge University Press.

Housen, Alex and Kuiken, Folkert (2009). Complexity, accuracy, and fluency in second language acquisition. *Applied Linguistics* 30(4): 461–73.

Huls, Erica and van der Mond, Anneke (1992). Some aspects of language attrition in Turkish families in the Netherlands. In *Maintenance and Loss of Minority Languages* ed. Willem Fase, Koen Jaspaert and Sjaak Kroon. Amsterdam/Philadelphia: John Benjamins. 99–115.

Hulsen, Madeleine (2000). Language loss and language processing. Three generations of Dutch migrants in New Zealand. Ph.D. thesis, Katholieke Universiteit Nijmegen.

Hulsen, Madeleine, de Bot, Kees and Weltens, Bert (2002). 'Between two worlds.' Social networks, language shift and language processing in three generations of Dutch migrants in New Zealand. *International Journal of the Sociology of Language* 153: 27–52.

Hutz, Matthias (2004). Is there a natural process of decay? A longitudinal study of language attrition. In *First Language Attrition: Interdisciplinary Perspectives on Methodological Issues*, ed. Monika S. Schmid, Barbara Köpke, Merel Keijzer and Lina Weilemar. Amsterdam/Philadelphia: John Benjamins. 189–206.

Isurin, Ludmila (2000). Deserted islands or, a child's first language forgetting. *Bilingualism: Language and Cognition* 3(2): 151–66.

Isurin, Ludmila, Winford, Donald and de Bot, Kees (2009). *Multidisciplinary Approaches to Code Switching*. Amsterdam/Philadelphia: John Benjamins.

Jarvis, Scott (2006). Examining the properties of lexical diversity through quantitative and qualitative means. Paper presented at the 16th Sociolinguistics Symposium, Limerick, Ireland, 7 July, 2006.

Jaspaert, Koen and Kroon, Sjaak (1989). Social determinants of language loss. *Review of Applied Linguistics (I.T.L.)* 83–84: 75–98.

(1992). From the typewriter of A.L.: a case study in language loss. In *Maintenance and Loss of Minority Languages*, ed. Willem Fase, Koen Jaspaert and Sjaak Kroon. Amsterdam/Philadelphia: John Benjamins. 137–47.

Johnson, Carla J., Paivio, Allan and Clark, James M. (1996). Cognitive components of picture naming. *Psychological Bulletin* 120(1): 113–39.

Keijzer, Merel (2007). Last in first out? An investigation of the regression hypothesis in Dutch emigrants in anglophone Canada. Ph.D. thesis, Vrije Universiteit Amsterdam.

Keller, Rudi (1995). The epistemic *weil*. In *Subjectivity and subjectivisation*, ed. Dieter Stein and Susan Wright. Cambridge University Press. 16–30.

Klein-Braley, Christine (1985). A cloze-up on the C-Test: a study in the construct validation of authentic tests. *Language Testing* 2(1): 76–104.

Köpcke, Klaus-Michael (1988). Schemas in German plural formation. *Lingua* 74: 303–55.

(1998). The acquisition of plural marking in English and German revisited: schemata versus rules. *Journal of Child Language* 25(2): 293–319.

Köpke, Barbara (1999). L'attrition de la première language chez le bilingue tardif: implications pour l'étude psycholinguistique du bilinguisme. Ph.D. thesis, Université de Toulouse-Le Mirail.

(2002). Activation thresholds and non-pathological L1 attrition. In *Advances in the Neurolinguistics of Bilingualism. Essays in Honor of Michel Paradis*, ed. Franco Fabbro. Udine: Forum. 119–42.

Köpke, Barbara and Schmid, Monika S. (2004). Language attrition: the next phase. In *First Language Attrition: Interdisciplinary Perspectives on Methodological Issues*, ed. Monika S. Schmid, Barbara Köpke, Merel Keijzer and Lina Weilemar. Amsterdam/Philadelphia: John Benjamins. 1–43.

Köpke, Barbara, Schmid, Monika S., Keijzer, Merel and Dostert, Susan (eds.) (2007). *Language Attrition: Theoretical Perspectives*. Amsterdam/Philadelphia: John Benjamins.

Krashen, Stephen D. (1985). *The Input Hypothesis: Issues and Implications*. London: Longman.

Kroll, Judith F. (2005). [title to be confirmed]. Plenary lecture at the 5th International Symposium on Bilingualism, Barcelona, March.

Larsen-Freeman, Diane and Long, Michael H. (1991). *An Introduction to Second Language Acquisition Research*. London: Longman.

Larson-Hall, Jenifer (2009). *A Guide to doing Statistics in Second Language Research using SPSS*. Mahwah, NJ: Lawrence Erlbaum.

Leppänen, Nana (2004). What happened to Finnish? First language attrition in a second language environment – Case assignment in the Finnish spoken in the USA. M.A. thesis, University of Oulu.

Luck, Steven J. (2005). *An Introduction to the Event-Related Potential Technique*. Cambridge, MA: MIT Press.

MacWhinney, Brian (2000). *The CHILDES project: Tools for Analyzing Talk*. Third edition. Mahwah, NJ: Lawrence Erlbaum Associates.

Mägiste, Edith (1979). The competing language systems of the multilingual: a developmental study of decoding and encoding processes. *Journal of Verbal Learning and Verbal Behavior* 18(1): 79–89.

Major, Roy C. (1992). Losing English as a first language. *The Modern Language Journal* 76(2): 190–208.

(2007). Identifying a foreign accent in an unfamiliar language. *Studies in Second Language Acquisition* 29(4): 539–56.

Malvern, David D. and Richards, Brian J. (2002). Investigating accommodation in language proficiency interviews using a new measure of lexical diversity. *Language Testing* 19(1): 85–104.

Masson, Michael E. J. (1983). Conceptual processing of text during skimming and rapid sequential reading. *Memory & Cognition* 11(3): 262–74.

Meier, Helmut (1967). *Deutsche Sprachstatistik, Vol. I.* Hildesheim: Olms.

Mennen, Ineke (2004). Bi-directional interference in the intonation of Dutch speakers of Greek. *Journal of Phonetics* 32(4): 543–63.

Milroy, Lesley (1987). *Language and Social Networks.* Oxford: Basil Blackwell.

Mithun, Marianne (1998). The sequencing of grammaticization effects. In *Historical Linguistics 1997*, ed. Monika S. Schmid, Jennifer R. Austin and Dieter Stein. Amsterdam/Philadelphia: John Benjamins. 291–314.

Montrul, S. (2004). Convergent outcomes in L2 acquisition and L1 loss. In *First Language Attrition: Interdisciplinary Perspectives on Methodological Issues*, ed. Monika S. Schmid, Barbara Köpke, Merel Keijzer and Lina Weilemar. Amsterdam/Philadelphia: John Benjamins. 259–79.

Murphy, Brian (2007). A study of notions of participation and discourse in argument structure realisation. Ph.D. thesis, Trinity College, Dublin.

Neuman, Susan B. and Koskinen, Patricia (1992). Captioned television as comprehensible input: effects of incidental word learning from context for language minority students. *Reading Research Quarterly* 27(1): 94–106.

Ni, Weijia, Fodor, Janet Dean, Crain, Stephen and Shankweiler, Donald (1998). Anomaly detection: eye movement patterns. *Journal of Psycholinguistic Research* 27(5): 515–39.

Otheguy, Ricardo and García, Ofelia (1988). Diffusion of lexical innovations in the Spanish of Cuban Americans. In *Research Issues and Problems in U.S. Spanish: Latin American and Southwestern Varieties*, ed. Jacob L. Ornstein-Galicia, George K. Green and Dennis J. Bixler-Márquez. Brownsville: University of Texas. 203–42.

Pallier, Christophe (2007). Critical periods in language acquisition and language attrition. In *Language Attrition: Theoretical Perspectives*, ed. Barbara Köpke, Monika S. Schmid, Merel Keijzer and Susan Dostert. Amsterdam/Philadelphia: John Benjamins. 155–68.

Pallier, Christophe, Dehaene, Stanislas, Poline, Jean-Baptiste, *et al.* (2003). Brain imaging of language plasticity in adopted adults: can a second language replace the first? *Cerebral Cortex* 13(2): 155–61.

Paradis, Michel (2007). L1 attrition features predicted by a neurolinguistic theory of bilingualism. In *Language Attrition: Theoretical Perspectives*, ed. Barbara Köpke, Monika S. Schmid, Merel Keijzer and Susan Dostert. Amsterdam/Philadelphia: John Benjamins. 121–33.

(2008). *Declarative and Procedural Determinants of Second Languages.* Amsterdam/Philadelphia: John Benjamins.

Pavlenko, Aneta (2002). Bilingualism and emotions. *Multilingua* 21(1): 45–78.

(2003). 'I feel clumsy speaking Russian': L2 influence on L1 in narratives of Russian L2 users of English. In *Effects of the Second Language on the First*, ed. Vivian Cook. Clevedon: Multilingual Matters. 32–61.

(2004). L2 influence and L1 attrition in adult bilingualism. In *First Language Attrition: Interdisciplinary Perspectives on Methodological Issues*, ed. Monika S. Schmid, Barbara Köpke, Merel Keijzer and Lina Weilemar. Amsterdam/Philadelphia: John Benjamins. 47–59.

(2005). *Emotions and Multilingualism*. Cambridge University Press.

(2011). Kitchen Russian: cross-linguistic differences and first-language object naming by Russian-English bilinguals. *Bilingualism: Language and Cognition* **14**(S1): 19–45.

Pelc, Linda A. (2001). L1 lexical, morphological and morphosyntactic attrition in Greek–English bilinguals. Ph.D. thesis, City University of New York.

Perdue, Clive (1993). *Adult Language Acquisition: Cross-Linguistic Perspectives*. Cambridge University Press.

Phillipson, Robert (2003). *English-only Europe? Challenging Language Policy*. London/New York: Routledge.

Polinsky, Maria (1994). Structural dimensions of first language loss. *Chicago Linguistic Society* **30**: 257–76.

Roberts, Patricia M. and Le Dorze, Guylaine (1998). Bilingual aphasia: semantic organization, strategy use, and productivity in semantic verbal fluency. *Brain and Language* **65**(2): 287–312.

Ross, Lisa B. (2002). The role of word class in the attrition of school-learned French: are nouns or verbs more likely to be lost? www.hofstra.edu/ Pdf/lib_undergrad_res_award_2003.pdf.

Ruoff, Arno (1985). *Häufigkeitswörterbuch gesprochener Sprache*. Tübingen: Niemeyer.

Schmid, Monika S. (2002). *First Language Attrition, Use and Maintenance: The Case of German Jews in Anglophone Countries*. Amsterdam/Philadelphia: John Benjamins.

(2007). The role of L1 use for L1 attrition. In *Language Attrition: Theoretical Perspectives*, ed. Barbara Köpke, Monika S. Schmid, Merel Keijzer and Susan Dostert. Amsterdam/Philadelphia: John Benjamins. 135–53.

Schmid, Monika S. and Beers Fägersten, Kristy (2010). Disfluency markers in L1 attrition. *Language Learning* **60**(4): 753–91.

Schmid, Monika S. and Dusseldorp, Elise (2010). Quantitative analyses in a multivariate study of language attrition. *Second Language Research* **26**(1): 125–60.

Schmid, Monika S. and Köpke, Barbara (2007). Bilingualism and attrition. In *Language Attrition: Theoretical Perspectives*, ed. Barbara Köpke, Monika S. Schmid, Merel Keijzer and Susan Dostert. Amsterdam/Philadelphia: John Benjamins. 1–8.

Schmid, Monika S., Köpke, Barbara, Keijzer, Merel and Weilemar, Lina (eds.) (2004). *First Language Attrition: Interdisciplinary Perspectives on Methodological Issues*. Amsterdam/Philadelphia: John Benjamins.

Schmid, Monika S., Verspoor, Marjolijn H. and MacWhinney, Brian (2011). Coding and extracting data. In *A Dynamic Approach to Second Language Development: Methods and Techniques*, ed. Marjolijn Verspoor, Kees de Bot and Wander Lowie. Amsterdam/Philadelphia: John Benjamins. 39–54.

Schmitt, Elena G. (2001). Beneath the surface: signs of language attrition in immigrant children from Russia. Ph.D. thesis, University of South Carolina.

Schütze, Carson T. (1996). *The Empirical Base of Linguistics: Grammaticality Judgments and Linguistic Methodology*. University of Chicago Press.

Seliger, Herbert W. (1991). Language attrition, reduced redundancy, and creativity. In *First Language Attrition*, ed. Herbert W. Seliger and Robert M. Vago. Cambridge University Press. 227–40.

Seliger, Herbert W. and Vago, Robert M. (1991). The study of first language attrition: an overview. In *First Language Attrition*, ed. Herbert W. Seliger and Robert M. Vago. Cambridge University Press. 3–15.

Senft, Gunter (1996). *Classificatory Particles in Kilivila*. Oxford University Press.

Sharwood Smith, Mike (1983). On first language loss in the second language acquirer. In *Language Transfer in Language Learning*, ed. Susan M. Gass and Larry Selinker. Rowley, MA: Newbury House. 222–31.

Sharwood Smith, Mike and van Buren, Paul (1991). First language attrition and the parameter setting model. In *First Language Attrition*, ed. Herbert W. Seliger and Robert M. Vago. Cambridge University Press. 17–30.

Snodgrass, Joan Gay and Vanderwart, Mary (1980). A standardized set of 260 pictures: norms for name agreement, image agreement, familiarity, and visual complexity. *Journal of Experimental Psychology: Human Learning and Memory* 6(2): 174–215.

Soesman, Aviva (1997). An experimental study on native language attrition in Dutch adult immigrants in Israel. In *Dutch Overseas: Studies in Maintenance and Loss of Dutch as an Immigrant Language*, ed. Jetske Klatter-Folmer and Sjaak Kroon. Tilburg University Press. 181–94.

Sorace, Antonella (2005). Selective optionality in language development. In *Syntax and Variation. Reconciling the Biological and the Social*, ed. Leonie Cornips and Karen P. Corrigan. Amsterdam/Philadelphia: John Benjamins. 55–80.

(2006). Near-nativeness. In *The Handbook of Second Language Acquisition*, ed. Catherine G. Doughty and Michael H. Long. Oxford: Blackwell. 130–51.

Tagliamonte, Sali A. (2006). *Analysing Sociolinguistic Variation*. Cambridge University Press.

Tajfel, Henri (1981). *Human Groups and Social Categories*. Cambridge University Press.

(1982). Social psychology of intergroup relations. *Annual Review of Psychology* **33**: 1–39.

Traugott, Elizabeth C. and Dasher, Richard B. (2002). *Regularity in Semantic Change.* Cambridge University Press.

Tsimpli, Ianthi, Sorace, Antonella, Heycock, Caroline and Filiaci, Francesca (2004). First language attrition and syntactic subjects: a study of Greek and Italian near-native speakers of English. *International Journal of Bilingualism* **8**(3): 257–77.

Tyler, Lorraine K. (1992). The distinction between implicit and explicit language function: evidence from aphasia. In *Neuropsychology of Consciousness,* ed. Michael D. Rugg and Anthony D. Milner. New York: Academic Press. 159–78.

Vaid, Jyotsna and Menon, Ramdas (2000). Correlates of bilinguals' preferred language for mental computations. *Spanish Applied Linguistics* **4**(2): 325–42.

Van Daele, Siska, Housen, Alex, Kuiken, Folkert, Pierrard, Michel, and Vedder, Ineke (eds.) (2007). *Complexity, Accuracy and Fluency in Second Language Use, Learning and Teaching.* Brussels: Koninklijke Vlaamse Academie van België voor Wetenschappen en Kunsten.

van Hell, Janet G. and Dijkstra, Ton (2002). Foreign language knowledge can influence native language performance in exclusively native contexts. *Psychonomic Bulletin & Review* **9**(4): 780–89.

van Hell, Janet G. and Tokowicz, Natasha (2010). Event-related brain potentials and second language learning: syntactic processing in late L2 learners at different L2 proficiency levels. *Second Language Research* **26**(1): 43–74.

Ventureyra, Valérie and Pallier, Christophe (2004). In search of the lost language: the case of adopted Koreans in France. In *First Language Attrition: Interdisciplinary Perspectives on Methodological Issues,* ed. Monika S. Schmid, Barbara Köpke, Merel Keijzer and Lina Weilemar. Amsterdam/Philadelphia: John Benjamins. 207–21.

Vermeer, Anne (2000). Coming to grips with lexical richness in spontaneous speech data. *Language Testing* **17**(1): 65–83.

Waas, Margit (1996). *Language Attrition Downunder.* Frankfurt: Peter Lang.

Walk, Joseph (ed.) (1981). *Das Sonderrecht für die Juden im NS-Staat. Eine Sammlung der gesetzlichen Maßnahmen und Richtlinien – Inhalt und Bedeutung.* Heidelberg/Karlsruhe: C.F.Müller.

Weinreich, Uriel (1953). *Languages in Contact: Findings and Problems.* New York: Linguistic Circle of New York.

Weskott, Thomas and Fanselow, Gisbert (2008). Variance and informativity in different measures of linguistic acceptability. In *Proceedings of the 27th West Coast Conference on Formal Linguistics,* ed. Natasha Abner and Jason Bishop. Somerville, MA: Cascadilla Proceedings Project. 431–9.

Wierzbicka, Anna (1992). *Semantics, Culture, and Cognition: Universal Human Concepts in Culture-specific Configurations*. Oxford University Press.

Yağmur, Kutlay (1997). *First Language Attrition among Turkish speakers in Sydney*. Tilburg University Press.

Yılmaz, Gülsen (in prep.) The development of bilingual proficiency among Turkish speakers in the Netherlands. Ph.D. dissertation, University of Groningen.

Yukawa, Emiko (1997). L1 Japanese attrition and regaining. Three case studies of two early bilingual children. Ph.D. thesis, Centre for Research on Bilingualism, Stockholm University.

Zechmeister, Eugene B., d'Anna, Catherine A., Hall, James W., Paus, Cynthia H., and Smith, Julie A. (1993). Metacognitive and other knowledge about the mental lexicon: do we know how many words we know? *Applied Linguistics* **14**(2): 188–206.

Index

Printed in Great Britain
by Amazon